OFF WHITEHALL

OFF WHITEHALL

A view from
Downing Street
by Tony Blair's adviser

Derek Scott

I.B. TAURIS

LONDON · NEW YORK

Published in 2004 by I.B.Tauris & Co Ltd
6 Salem Road, London W2 4BU
175 Fifth Avenue, New York NY 10010
www.ibtauris.com

In the United States of America and in Canada distributed by
Palgrave Macmillan, a division of St Martin's Press
175 Fifth Avenue, New York NY 10010

ISBN 1 85043 677 0
EAN 978 1 85043 677 5

A full CIP record for this book is available from the British Library
A full CIP record for this book is available from the Library of Congress

Library of Congress catalog card: available

Typeset in Palatino Linotype by Steve Tribe, Andover
Printed and bound in Great Britain by TJ International Ltd, Padstow, Cornwall

Contents

vi   Off Whitehall

Acknowledgements

I would like to thank the friends, former colleagues and many acquaintances who have assisted in the writing of this book, but who bear no responsibility for any errors.

I have never attempted to write a book before and at the beginning David and Debbie Owen provided not only encouragement, but also practical advice on how to go about and complete the enterprise. One of their most fortunate recommendations was to get in touch with their friend Susan Watt, and without her many hours of freely provided professional advice and support I should have been lost.

Many people have influenced my economic views over the years and few more than my old colleagues at Barclays de Zoete Wedd (BZW), David Bowers, Mark Brett, David Hillier, Michael Hughes and Simon Knapp (who was particularly helpful in reading and commenting on an early draft). My thanks are also due to Hanako Birks and Iradj Bagherzade at I.B.Tauris.

However, my biggest debt is to Bernard Connolly, whose personal and intellectual integrity is second to none, and from whom I have learnt more economics over the years than from any other single individual.

Finally, and not entirely frivolously, I would like to thank the Cabinet Office for attempting to censor this book, and Gordon Brown and the Treasury spokesman for their intemperate response to it before even reading the text. Their joint efforts have helped transform a work on the politics and economics of Europe into a publicist's gift.

Acronyms

CAP	Common Agricultural Policy
CFHR	Charter of Fundamental Human Rights
CFSP	Common Foreign and Security Policy
EC	European Community
ECB	European Central Bank
Ecofin	Council of Economic and Finance Ministers
ECU	European Currency Unit
ECSC	European Coal and Steel Community
EEC	European Economic Community
EDC	European Defence Community
EDF	European Defence Force
EFTA	European Free Trade Area
EMF	European Monetary Fund
EMS	European Monetary System
EMU	Economic and Monetary Union
EPC	European Political Community
ERM	Exchange Rate Mechanism
EU	European Union
EURATOM	European Atomic Energy Community
FDI	Foreign Direct Investment
GDP	Gross Domestic Product
IGC	Inter-Governmental Conference
IMF	International Monetary Fund
JHA	Justice and Home Affairs
MPC	Monetary Policy Committee
NAFTA	North American Free Trade Area
NATO	North Atlantic Treaty Organisation
QMV	Qualified Majority Voting
SEA	Single European Act
SGP	Stability and Growth Pact

Introduction

Notwithstanding the attempts to censor this book and the charges levelled at me just before its publication about my motives for writing it, this is a work about the economics and politics of Europe, or rather 'Europe': the institutional framework now known as the European Union (EU) and previously as the European Community (EC), and before that as the European Economic Community (EEC).

This remains important, even though much of the world, including much of Europe, has had its eyes on Iraq, the 'war on terrorism' and the dangers of even more instability in the Middle East, or is shifting its gaze to the emergence of new economic powers such as China or India and the implications for the world economy. These latest events have merely served to highlight that Europe has lost its way and until it finds it again it will not be able to meet the challenges of the twenty-first century, or help resolve them.

At the end of the Second World War, few people could have anticipated the shared prosperity and peaceful relations between the countries of Europe that would be achieved fifty years later. The draft EU constitution of 2003 could be seen as consolidating the political and economic model that began in the rubble of war, but this model had become dated and was already showing signs of strain. The failure, in December 2003, to agree on the text of the constitution provided a breathing space to think again about where the EU should be heading, but the opportunity was missed. There were a few months of quiescence but, after the terrorist attack on Madrid railway station in March 2004 and the subsequent change of government in Spain, a renewed commitment was made to agree on a constitution by June 2004. After the breakdown of the talks in 2003, Tony Blair argued that there was plenty of time to reach a conclusion, but by March 2004 he had changed his mind, becoming an enthusiast for a speedy decision: the opportunity for reflection was missed. This increased the chance that the EU could face a bigger threat to its existence than at any time in its history – in the next decade and possibly sooner.

Economics and politics are almost invariably entwined, and nowhere more so than in Europe. It may appear improbable that Britain will soon seek entry to Economic and Monetary Union (EMU), and the Blair Government has promised that the British people will ultimately decide in a referendum whether to keep the pound sterling or adopt the euro. However, in 2003, Tony Blair said that the draft constitution would 'define the relationship between Britain and the rest of Europe, the prospects for the euro and last for a generation'.[1]

In practice, if Britain had signed up to the proposed EU constitution in 2003, it would have become more difficult for it to stay out of EMU while remaining in the EU; given the interconnection between any constitutional settlement and membership of the single currency, in the wake of the renewed commitment to seek agreement, it is important that as well as understanding the implications of any constitutional proposals put before it, the British people are clear about the political and economic impact of the single currency.

I entered Downing Street as economic adviser to the Prime Minister immediately after the election in May 1997 and was there for over six years. It was a privilege to work in such a position, and I would like to think I gave good service to Tony Blair with honest and coherent advice on a range of economic issues, including EMU. In most fields I supported fully what Tony Blair tried to do as Prime Minister; indeed I might have been described as 'more Blairite than Blair' since I thought he should have pressed on more vigorously with some of the bolder proposals for reform. Compromise is an essential part of politics, but sometimes it merely diluted the potential benefits of reforms without significantly reducing the political problems they usually aroused, not least in the more traditional parts of the Labour Party. On occasions the Government ended up with the worst of all worlds: less potential gain from reform, but no less political pain from the attempt. Examples included proposals to give hospitals more independence to run their affairs ('foundation hospitals') and the controversial attempt to put university funding on a sound footing. Nonetheless, on most fronts, Tony Blair took the country in the right direction and as far as economic policy was concerned he instinctively recognised the importance of properly functioning markets if Britain was to be prosperous and fully employed. If I had a criticism in this regard it was only that he was not prepared to follow through his instincts with some of his Cabinet colleagues, including Gordon Brown. I was at one with his decision to take Britain to war with Iraq and thought the case for intervention was justified, even without weapons of mass destruction (WMD), and I share passionately his commitment to the American Alliance. However, I did have important differences with Tony Blair on Europe.

Whether or not to join the single currency is a decision with permanent implications for Britain and not one to be taken on the wrong grounds, but the nature of the debate on the euro and the EU constitution has become distorted. On EMU, Tony Blair cannot really make the case he and its proponents want to make. They have convinced themselves of a political case for entering, but they cannot make it because of their fear that the British electorate would reject its implications and so they hope to make an economic case to achieve what are essentially political objectives. However, the issues at the heart of any economic decision on joining the single currency have been muddled. In 1997 the Government set out five economic tests for membership, but these only addressed what were essentially second-order questions. The degree of economic convergence that is necessary to make the single currency work (for existing members as well as Britain), the costs that arise if this is not attained and the political implications if it is have been passed over and were barely considered in the mass of background papers that accompanied the Government's own assessment of the tests in 2003.

Tony Blair has stressed the importance of ratifying the proposed EU constitution for the future of the EU and Britain's position and influence within it. But there was confusion about its real nature and significance. On the one hand, the people were told it ranked in importance with the Treaty of Rome, and that is what many on the continent were saying too. On the other hand, in Britain the Government argued that very little was changing at all or that it was just tidying things up. Both stances couldn't be right and the British people need to be clear about the implications before this country signs up to any new constitutional settlement. That is why, despite my time in Downing Street and my privileged and valued association with the Prime Minister, I decided at this time to write this particular book.

The book is divided into four sections. The first part sets the scene, and two men dominate it: Tony Blair and Gordon Brown. The relationship between Prime Minister and Chancellor is important for most governments, but that between Tony Blair and Gordon Brown has been unique and between them they will set the tone and determine the case put to Parliament and the electorate for entering Economic and Monetary Union or signing any constitutional settlement for Europe. Before the British people make up their minds about these important decisions, it is important that they have as much understanding as possible about the views and motives of Tony Blair and Gordon Brown and how the two men reached their decisions. In view of this, in order to shed some light on how it may affect Britain's policy towards Europe, Chapter 1 describes how the Blair-Brown relationship looked to me. Chapter 2 summarises the challenges facing all British politicians in their dealings with Europe and sets the scene for the economic and political issues to be addressed in the rest of the book.

The second section of the book is made up of three short chapters to help put some contemporary controversies about the EU into perspective. Parts of this may be familiar to some readers who may just want to peruse the contents, but for others this section may help reawaken hazy historical memories and many younger readers may be totally unaware of some of the important events and trends that help explain the present relationship between Britain and the rest of Europe. Chapter 3 briefly describes the political evolution of Europe and Chapter 4 outlines various proposals for monetary integration that preceded the adoption of the euro, and both chapters include items omitted in some recent assessments of the period.[2] Chapter 5 sets out some of the reasons for Britain's ambivalence towards Europe and how this has played out in the shifting positions within and between the Labour and Conservative parties.

The third section of the book concentrates on the economics of Europe and its single currency, the euro. The case for EMU made by proponents of Britain's membership is outlined in Chapter 6, and the economics at the heart of EMU are set out in Chapter 7. The world economy is very different from that which existed when 'the Six' signed the Treaty of Rome in 1957 and during the following thirty years. The international economy is now characterised by large flows of private-sector capital, and this has huge implications for the economics of EMU, but is rarely referred to in political speeches, the press or even in academic literature.

Despite my best efforts, readers who are not economists may still find Chapter 7 quite difficult; some may choose to skim or return to it after reading subsequent chapters that illustrate its themes. However, the chapter is central to an understanding of the economic implications of EMU, not just for Britain but also for its existing members. It deals with issues that get scant attention in most economic commentary, including the two thousand pages of background papers that accompanied the Government's review in 2003 of the five economic tests; it gets no attention at all in the two hundred pages of the Government's own assessment.

Chapter 8 examines how EMU has affected the countries that have already joined and explores the prospects for economic reform in Europe, suggesting that while EMU is bringing about some convergence in Euroland it is rather different from that envisaged at the start. Chapter 9 explores the impact of EMU on the wider international economy and how the euro will affect and be affected by the adjustment of the economic imbalances that developed in the USA during the long upswing of the 1990s, drawing out the implications for Britain. There then follow two chapters devoted specifically to Britain. Chapter 10 identifies what lessons, if any, can be drawn from Britain's brief experience in the Exchange Rate Mechanism (ERM) and Chapter 11 brings together and expands on the previous economic chapters to assess the merits of Britain entering EMU sometime in the future.

The final section of the book is as much about the politics of Europe as about the economics, if not more so. Chapter 12 examines some examples of previous monetary unions to shed light on the economic and political implications of EMU. This includes an assessment of the Gold Standard, sometimes put forward as an example of a multinational currency union that did not involve political union; and a brief examination of the lessons for Europe from the USA: a continent that clearly has benefited from having a single currency. Chapter 13 clarifies some of the political trends in the EU and how these might be reinforced by the economics of EMU, including the pressures on the Stability and Growth Pact (SGP). Chapter 14 explains some of the recurring themes in Britain's attitude towards Europe, from Macmillan to Blair, and the implications of these at a time when many in the EU seek to emulate, in some respects at least, the international role of the USA. Chapter 15 sets out Tony Blair's attitude to EMU and his perception of Britain's position in Europe, and explores the way in which he has sought to persuade a sceptical electorate about the merits of his case. The chapter outlines the interaction between Blair and Gordon Brown between 1997 and 2003 and its implications for the future. The final chapter, Chapter 16, brings together the earlier political and economic arguments. The significance of the draft EU constitution, proposed in 2003 and revived in 2004, and the connection of any constitutional settlement with a decision by Britain on EMU are assessed, and conclusions drawn as to how Britain can best exert its influence within Europe and the wider world.

Just as this book was going to press, I was accused of 'the deliberate peddling of lies and distortions' by people who should have known better, including the Chancellor Gordon Brown's official spokesman and his Chief Economic Adviser. I leave it to readers to make their own judgement about these accusations and the case I set out.

PART ONE

Setting the Scene

CHAPTER ONE

Neighbours in Downing Street

Blair and Brown

Gordon Brown declared that, 'Tony and I will put the patriotic case for British engagement with Europe. We propose to take on the anti-European prejudices and anti-European myths'.[1]

It is difficult to think of any relationship between two politicians quite like that between Tony Blair and Gordon Brown. Whether the partnership holds together in one way or another or ends in tears has implications for Britain's role in Europe and beyond, including the very future of the Government. However, the impact of this unique relationship on the Government's policy towards the European Union and its single currency, the euro, will continue to be profound, and for this reason alone it is worth giving a flavour of the relationship between Blair and Brown. From my perspective, the most striking feature was the readiness of Tony Blair to cede an unprecedented amount of control over economic policy to his Chancellor. This became apparent very early on and set the pattern for the whole of my time in Downing Street, but it created its own tensions between No. 10 and No. 11 that in turn affected the behaviour of the two men towards each other.

Many reasons have been put forward to explain all this, but all must surely take into account the fact that Gordon Brown did not contest the leadership of the Labour Party after John Smith's death in May 1994. This decision was announced soon after Tony and Gordon had dined at the Granita restaurant in Islington, and this led to all sorts of speculation (and a television drama in the autumn of 2003) about the existence and nature of any deal between them. The former Labour leader Neil Kinnock has said that the two men had an understanding, dating back to the July 1992 leadership election not to stand against each other and 'if John Smith had died a year before, Tony would have said "yes" to Gordon.'[2] It is almost certainly true that, had there been a contest between the two of them at any time prior to 1994, Brown would have won comfortably and to that extent he was unlucky in the timing. The tide had turned. Brown was suffering from being the shadow chancellor and the man who had to say 'no' to his colleagues in the shadow cabinet in the cause of winning the election and he had been damaged in some sections of the Labour Party by his support for membership of the Exchange Rate Mechanism (ERM). Gordon Brown was a realist and even if there had been no agreement he must have known he would not have beaten Tony in any contest in 1994. If there was an agreement it may be that both men initially assumed that Brown was most likely to be the front runner, but that reflected their relative strength within the Labour Party at the time and this might change. Any agreement was to avoid running against each other, not that Brown would be the candidate whatever the circumstances. In 1994, Blair was stronger among Labour supporters and had the most appeal in the country at large. In these circumstances, Tony was justifiably determined to run and, with or without an agreement between the two of them, Brown was actually in a very weak position. Blair had no need to make significant concessions to Gordon about the powers the latter would have in any government. If he did so, and as will be seen later there is cause to think he did, it probably reflected Tony's instincts, seen in other contexts too, to smooth over differences and avoid confrontation. However, this characteristic tends to store up difficulties later, and Blair's handling of Brown in 1994 was a foretaste of things to come and made it more difficult to exercise an appropriate degree of prime ministerial authority over the Chancellor in government. Both men must take responsibility for the way the relationship developed, but one effect was to make it much more difficult for the Prime Minister to assert himself over the one area of economic policy that he was not prepared to cede because of its wider political implications: entry to EMU.

My first contact with the Blair-Brown partnership had been with the latter. This took place in the early summer of 1993 while John Smith was leader of the Labour Party, when Gordon Brown, the shadow chancellor, held a seminar with the rest of his economic team in the shadow cabinet room in the House of Commons. It was attended by a variety of economists: some were from the City, but most came from 'think tanks' or were academics. I arrived a bit late but rapidly became impatient at the tone of advice being offered by most of those present, including John (now Lord) Eatwell, a friendly Cambridge academic who had advised Neil Kinnock. The gist of the message being delivered was that if Labour got into government, it would be perfectly sensible to borrow large amounts of extra money. After a while, I apologised for 'sounding like a representative of the IMF', but explained why I believed such advice was bunk. This apparently came as some relief to the politicians as Nick Brown,[3] one of the team and still close to Gordon Brown, made clear to me afterwards. I kept in touch with Nick and met Gordon on several occasions subsequently, but there were no substantive economic discussions with either.

Tony Blair apparently thought he needed several full-time economic advisers when he became leader of the Labour Party, but he was persuaded correctly that this would be rather too much of a good thing and that in opposition one decent adviser working part time was probably enough. The person most responsible for this sensible steer was Gavyn Davies, whom I had known well since his days at No. 10 as Jim Callaghan's economic adviser when I had been in a similar role for Denis Healey at the Treasury, when Labour had last been in government in the late 1970s. He subsequently had a very successful career at Goldman Sachs and a brief time as Chairman of the BBC Board of Governors before returning to the City. In 1994, Tony Blair did not want an academic economist, but someone with practical experience and an understanding of financial markets. After twelve years in the City of London and the oil industry, I apparently fitted the bill. Peter Mandelson,[4] whom I had known for many years, phoned me at my office in the City on a Friday evening in the summer of 1994. We met the following week, when he asked whether I would be interested in becoming Tony's economic adviser. Since I had spent several years in the SDP[5] before rejoining the Labour Party, this offer was very unexpected and showed a generosity of spirit in Tony. I was very keen to take on the post as I thought under Blair's leadership the Labour Party was at last on the right track and a few days later I went to see him in his office in the House of Commons. At the time, apart from his friendliness and charm, what struck me most was the contrast with other politicians with whom I had worked closely, Denis Healey, Jim Callaghan and David Owen. Under Tony's direction, most of our conversation centred on 'what was it like in government?' The rise of Tony Blair had been meteoric, from candidate to leader in just over a decade, with no experience of government, but blessed with political good fortune and perhaps a sense of his own destiny. Early on, someone who had known him for a very long time told me, 'Tony is much better at taking than giving.' This was an interesting observation, and a very perceptive one as I learnt later. He was certainly very focused on the next step to No. 10 and quite self-absorbed, but wanting to be liked and a natural actor. He had not been preoccupied with politics as a young man and thus was not a traditional politician in the way that Gordon Brown has always been. Brown has built up a political network of contacts in a similar manner to Jim Callaghan, and has cultivated and expanded it assiduously. The contrast between the two men was brought home to me later. In November 1997, there was a by-election in Paisley South and Gordon pulled out all the stops to help Douglas Alexander, a bright young lawyer who had been a researcher in his office for a time. However, Pat McFadden, who was working in No. 10 and had been at Tony's side in opposition, was also interested in the seat. He had good local connections with the constituency and would have made a first-rate MP, a convincing supporter of modernisation but a serious political operator in his own right too and a man of independent mind. Pat sounded Tony out but received little encouragement, and faced with someone actively supported by Gordon Brown, Pat took his name out of the hat. Gordon helped his people, Tony didn't.

By the time I joined Blair in the autumn of 1994, juggling the post with my job in the City, the British economy was recovering from recession and the shambles surrounding the exit of the pound from the ERM in September 1992. In the early part of 1995, Gordon Brown and Ed Balls, his economic adviser, presented a fairly downbeat assessment of the economic outlook to shadow ministers in the shadow cabinet room in the House of Commons. Tony asked for my views and I said that I expected that the next general election, thought most likely in 1997, would be fought against the background of strong economic growth, low inflation and falling unemployment and this turned out to be broadly right. However, some of those attending refused to believe it, with Michael Meacher[6] particularly incredulous, but Tony Blair was very happy for me to challenge some of the conventional ideas about the state of the economy without the need for politically tinted glasses.

I had had even fewer contacts with Tony than with Gordon when I joined his team. However, things soon changed: when in opposition with a small staff, everyone mucked in with whatever was the most urgent task at the time and there was a very friendly and supportive spirit within the team and between its members and the boss. This was probably assisted by the working conditions too, since we were all squashed into a few rooms close to the shadow cabinet room in the House of Commons, with mine shared with several others, next to Tony's, the entrance to which was ruled from a small outer office by Anji Hunter.[7] We were all committed to Tony and getting Labour elected and rather surprisingly for such a political group there was no backbiting within the team and any large egos remained under wraps. Which was more than could be said of the politicians on occasion, with Gordon Brown and Robin Cook[8] seemingly particularly aware of their status. Every week, there was a meeting in Tony's office of the so-called 'Big Guns' – Tony, John Prescott,[9] Gordon and Robin. Needless to say, it was always difficult for Anji to juggle diaries and the meetings rarely started on time, but Gordon and Robin would vie with each other to arrive last and on occasions both of them would turn up, see the other had not arrived and leave to make their entrance later.

Inevitably, a number of my new colleagues had known and worked with Tony Blair for very much longer than I had. Several had been part of his campaign team for the leadership, including Anji and Pat McFadden, as well as Sally Morgan[10] and Peter Hyman,[11] with whom I shared an office, and a number of others too. All were committed to the New Labour 'project' and to Tony Blair personally with an intensity that I could not match. Such fierce loyalty is part and parcel of politics, but it was hard for me to repeat the deep affection and admiration I had for Denis Healey. To that extent I make no claims to be part of Tony's 'inner circle' and might have been better described as an 'outsider on the inside'; this was true in opposition and it remained so in government. Despite, or perhaps because of, this lack of partisanship, I felt I could play a useful role as provider of detached advice.

Any leader of the opposition is very busy, so advice needs to be succinct and clearly presented. For no good reason, much economic commentary is made unintelligible to the layman and all too often economists simply conceal their own lack of clarity with obfuscation and jargon. This is not much use to a busy and intelligent politician, who needs to feel reasonably confident about an important subject but who may be unfamiliar with its language and concepts. My task was to make economics accessible.

Part of the job of the economic adviser in opposition or during an election campaign is mundane enough, providing briefing for interviews and ammunition for attack and defence and drafting articles and speeches. In early 1995, Professor Geoffrey Wood asked me whether Tony Blair or Gordon Brown would be prepared to give the annual Mais Lecture at the City University later in the year.[12] This was an excellent opportunity for a substantial speech free of some of the turgid mantras that characterised too many addresses on Labour's economic policy. Tony's Mais Lecture in May 1995 was the most comprehensive statement of New Labour's economic policy made in opposition and has stood the test of time pretty well.

When I was drafting the speech and discussing its contents with Tony, I suggested that it include a commitment to make the Bank of England independent, something I had been urging on him from the very start. However, Tony was not persuaded about this, largely I think on the sensible judgement that there was little to be gained politically and the costs attached to an early announcement were perhaps too great, but also because Gordon had not made his own mind up. Ed Balls, his economic adviser, was certainly in favour of Bank of England independence and worked hard on the design of the framework for setting it up. Gordon Brown discussed the issue with a number of people between 1994 and 1997: Alan Greenspan, Chairman of the US Federal Reserve (the Fed) seems to have been particularly influential with the future chancellor, but at the time Gordon's own position was unclear to me. According to Geoffrey Robinson, a member of Gordon Brown's inner circle, and Paymaster General, 1997–1998, Gordon only came to a firm decision a few days before polling day.[13]

The Mais Lecture itself got a good reception among financial and economic commentators, including an excellent leader in the *Financial Times*: this itself caused some irritation in the shadow chancellor's office as their man had been temporarily upstaged on an economic platform. Gordon Brown was particularly critical of a very brief passage in the speech that was an ill-disguised swipe at Will Hutton,[14] whose views on 'stakeholding' and the 'European social model' were fashionable at the time. Gordon's concern was not about the substance of the passage, with which he agreed fully; it was just that he wanted to avoid upsetting one of Labour's natural supporters in the press.

As well as preparing speeches or looking ahead to policies that might be implemented after the election, I saw one of my tasks as being to make Tony Blair more at ease with some broader economic issues. No doubt I was more successful in some areas than others and no system is foolproof, as became apparent, even in government. During a trip to Brazil and Argentina in August 2001, Tony Blair failed to read either the Treasury's or my own economic brief and it showed in some of his comments while abroad. So much so that during his return trip a well-meaning official asked the Prime Minister whether he would like some economic textbooks to be included in his reading material for the forthcoming summer holiday. The normally genial Premier didn't think this suggestion very funny, but generally any failings were less glaring and informal discussions as well as more formal meetings on specific issues could be put to good effect.

It is obviously a privilege to work in Downing Street and very different from most places of work. It is a house as well as an office and in some respects feels more like working at home: pictures line the walls and when you arrive in the morning the carpets are still being vacuumed. No. 10 is much larger than it looks from the outside, but the building is not well designed for an office at the centre of government and it was poorly equipped at the start. Information technology was virtually unheard of when the new Government arrived in 1997 and when I asked for a screen to provide me with financial information in my little office over the front door I might have been asking for the moon. 'Funny, I think someone in the previous Government wanted one of those' was the response I received. In fact the only change I could see from when Jim Callaghan had occupied the place was the removal from the walls outside the room occupied by the Prime Minister's private secretaries of the bells that had at one time summoned servants. Inside No. 10, Tony liked to do most of his work from his 'den', rather than sitting at the Cabinet table as had John Major or from the large first-floor office favoured by Mrs Thatcher. The first den was a room looking out on St James's Park that I had sat in on many occasions when Tom McNally[15] was Jim Callaghan's political adviser. However, in those days rather more alcohol lubricated the political wheels in No. 10 and No. 11 than under New Labour – in Tony Blair's office it was all fruit and fizzy water. This room had a door linking it with one end of the Cabinet room itself and another opening onto the hall outside, where ministers gather every Thursday before Cabinet. The problem about this arrangement was that it was impossible to monitor those who went in or out, so anyone could pop in to see the Prime Minister who might himself wander off without his staff knowing where he was. Because of this, the den was transferred to a room at the other end of the Cabinet room, linked to an outer office through which anyone seeking access to the Prime Minister had to pass. Jonathan Powell, the Chief of Staff, sat in this office along with the Prime Minister's diary secretary and his principal private secretaries from the civil service. In both dens, the style and method of work were similar. Meetings were generally informal rather than businesslike with the principal participants scattered on one of the couches or comfortable wing chairs, with others making do with harder chairs surrounding a small round table or brought in from outside. The Prime Minister would sometimes sit behind his desk, topped with family pictures, but often leaning back with his feet resting on top.

For New Labour, keeping on the front foot with the media was a preoccupation in government as it had been in opposition. This was reinforced by the fact that most of the individuals closest to the Prime Minister, such as Alastair Campbell (the Prime Minister's Director of Communications), were often less interested in the content or practicality of policies than their part in a media strategy, pegs for a photo opportunity or an 'event', though they were still often included in policy discussions. On one occasion, in the middle of February 2002, there was a meeting in the Cabinet room chaired by the Prime Minister to discuss the next spending round with members of the Policy Directorate, the political office and communications people from No. 10. Not for the first time, I had been urging considerably more caution about the scale of additional public spending than most of my colleagues, but the discussion had been amicable enough and the Prime Minister certainly took no exception to my warnings and, in the end, not much notice either! Nonetheless, one of Tony Blair's communications strategists and most enthusiastic acolytes did. As the meeting was about to break up, he darted across from the other side of the Cabinet table, poked his finger in my chest, and accused me of not 'believing' in public investment and much else besides, and anyway my job was 'to implement the manifesto and do what Tony wants'. I didn't think I was employed to 'believe' in anything, but to give frank economic advice, and that is what I would continue to do. Afterwards, I went into the den with the Prime Minister, who laughed the little incident off, and certainly Tony expected straightforward advice from me and all the other policy advisers. And the overall quality and objectivity of the advice he received from them was first rate. They were on top of their subjects, generally managing to combine expertise with political savviness and all were very loyal to the Prime Minister without losing their sense of proportion about the New

Labour 'project'. But, in general, Tony Blair paid them too little attention and too much to the occasional outsider or those members of his inner circle who had no grasp or real interest in policy, but who were nonetheless keen 'believers' in launching policy 'initiatives', often without discussing them with those who had. Fortunately, some ill-thought-out proposals never saw the light of day and on one occasion the Prime Minister stopped an initiative making parents liable for their drunken teenage offspring just forty-eight hours before one of his own was found inebriated in Leicester Square in the summer of 2000. However, a lot of ill-thought-out proposals did get through and often with the Prime Minister's encouragement. Clearly, there is a problem for governments faced seven days a week with many-channelled, twenty-four hour news. But the notion that this requires a media strategy to dominate the headlines, every day for months or even years on end has only to be stated to be seen as an impossible and absurd objective. For a politician with an established reputation, silence is a powerful political weapon. Governments are ultimately judged by results and an excessive emphasis on presentation reflected an inability to change gear from opposition to government that was obvious even at the time to some of us and later to many more.

The relationship between the Prime Minister and his advisers obviously varies. The most distinguished and influential economic adviser at No. 10 was probably Sir Alan Walters, who was appointed in 1981 by Mrs Thatcher. He was very close personally to his boss, who herself had some very strong opinions on economics and made them felt throughout Whitehall. Walters had a significant impact on the groundbreaking 1981 budget that caused 364 economists to write to *The Times* in protest, and he remained a very powerful figure until he left in 1984, thinking that the policy of the Government was on the right track. Problems only arose when Alan returned in 1989 and he was openly critical of the Chancellor, Nigel Lawson. The economics behind this dispute had implications for EMU and will be considered in Chapter 10, but the political repercussions for the Conservative Government and Mrs Thatcher of this very public dispute were considerable. My relationship with Tony was not remotely comparable to that of Walters with Thatcher, but was more similar to the one I had seen between Callaghan and Gavyn Davies, although Blair certainly did not involve himself in economic policy as much as Callaghan, let alone Thatcher. And the unique relationship between Tony and Gordon reinforced my determination in the light of Alan Walters' experience, to keep private any disagreements I might have with the Chancellor. The job of economic adviser to Tony Blair had to be a low-profile one in the hope my advice and judgement would assist the Prime Minister to punch his own weight in economic decisions.

Inevitably, as Prime Minister, Tony Blair had even more on his plate than in opposition, so the most effective method to engage him on economic topics was very often through short notes written in clear English that he could respond to in his own time. In addition to routine office meetings and papers on matters preoccupying the Government at any particular time, the weekend 'red boxes' were good opportunities for brief papers on subjects that were important, but of less immediate concern. During the week, Tony Blair was not an assiduous reader of his red boxes. However, at weekends he did usually get through most of the papers that went to Chequers and very often responded with comments or questions that might be taken up face to face later or in further notes. During my six years in Downing Street, there was an extensive, if intermittent, exchange of views about a range of issues, a significant number of which were about EMU.

Yet it would be misleading to pretend that in opposition or government Tony Blair ever felt much inclination to engage in economics more than was necessary to get by; he could easily be distracted. During the peak of the dot-com boom in the late 1990s, some commentators were carried away by the significance of the 'new economy', implying not only that the new information and communications technology had huge potential significance, which it obviously did, but that it made all the old tenets of economics redundant. The idea that profits didn't matter as long as sales and revenues were booming was one fashionable notion that was soon shown to be nonsense. Of course, this view of the new economy had its attractions since it dispensed with the hard work of getting to grips with the old disciplines of economics. At the beginning of December 1999, Charlie Leadbetter, a writer and academic, was invited to a policy unit away day at Chequers to give a brief presentation on the 'new economics' and, knowing his views, I sent Tony a brief note a few days before expressing scepticism about some of them, but he was quite taken with some of this stuff.

For Tony Blair, any engagement with economic policy was, as much as anything, to serve his wider political strategy and this was preoccupied with 'positioning'. In opposition this served him very well, although the repositioning of the Labour Party was about dumping a lot of policies and reassuring the electorate about what a Labour government was not going to do (no 'tax and spend'), more than about detailed alternatives. Political positioning was sometimes discussed among political strategists in the jargon of 'triangulation', which seems an unnecessarily complicated way of describing how a politician decides where he or she wants to be perceived on any particular issue and then paints the purported alternatives, with caricature if necessary, into two 'extremes'. Tony was very keen on this – so 'New' Labour was contrasted with 'Old' Labour ('state planning and central control') and the Tories ('laissez-faire'), even though Labour had always favoured a mixed economy and the Conservatives had never been laissez-faire. And Tony was always ready to employ this technique over the single currency and Europe more generally, presenting his 'sensible and principled' approach to the 'federalist zealots' on the one hand and 'those who want to leave Europe' on the other, even though the real choices were (and remain) much less simplistic. However, political positioning itself does not require any command over the substance. It is about people's perception of policies and as such it is better suited to opposition than to government. In government, proposals have to be thought through more carefully and need to work: they are the real policies, not the 'virtual' ones of opposition. Inevitably, after the election of 1997, the prime responsibility for putting some meat on the new Government's economic policy rested with Gordon Brown, but from the start Tony Blair was disinclined to engage his Chancellor in decisions the way that most prime ministers have felt necessary.

The relationship between prime minister and chancellor is central to any government and it has been the making and breaking of some administrations and, in the case of Thatcher and Lawson, perhaps both making and breaking the Government. There is absolutely no need for any prime minister to be immersed in all the details of economic policy, and attempts to run it from No. 10 through a weak chancellor, in the way that Edward Heath tried to do when Anthony Barber was at No. 11, is a recipe for disaster. However, there has to be a balance and getting that right is not easy, but any prime minister should be involved fully in the key decisions at appropriate stages. Harold Wilson used Harold Lever, a delightful man, an MP who later went to the House of Lords, and also an extremely successful, rich and independent-minded businessman with an acute understanding of financial markets, as his eyes and ears within the Treasury. This worked pretty well because Lever and Denis Healey rather liked each other, but on occasions even Healey said it felt like having the fingers of No. 10 at the back his collar. Jim Callaghan was marked by his own experience of devaluation when Chancellor and when he got to No. 10 he never really trusted the Treasury. However, Callaghan and Healey generally got along with each other and, as the latter's special adviser, my relationship with my opposite number at No. 10 was one of genuine mutual trust and openness without in any way diluting our respective obligations to our political bosses, the Chancellor and Prime Minister. Tony Blair had no one in the Cabinet who could play the Harold Lever role and he didn't see the need for such a person anyway, while relations between Ed Balls, Gordon Brown's economic adviser and political confidant, and No. 10 were frosty from the start. Ed was clearly very bright and probably had more power than anyone else holding his position, but it was not tempered by much experience. This limited the constructive role he might otherwise have played in government as a whole and in the end he merely reinforced Gordon's own prejudices. They just egged each other on.

Gordon Brown and his closest team probably did get a firmer grip on the Treasury than any previous chancellor in living memory, but in the early days they were uncomfortable with some senior officials, who were themselves ill at ease with the new team, including the incumbent permanent secretary, Sir

Terry (now Lord) Burns. Terry later moved out of Whitehall to be replaced by Sir Andrew Turnbull and over time the circle of civil servants that Gordon was comfortable with did widen a bit. However, it required Sir Andrew's promotion to Cabinet Secretary, in effect top man in Whitehall, before Gordon got the permanent secretary he wanted in the form of Gus O'Donnell. Most officials in the Treasury soon learnt that advice needed to be tailored to get past the Chancellor's inner circle, dominated by Ed Balls, but it is a moot point whether the overall effect of this control was good either for the Treasury as an institution or for its impact on economic policy. However, the mutual dependency of Gordon and his closest advisers did sometimes have its comical side. On one occasion at the end of 1999, an irate Chancellor phoned the Treasury in the middle of the night from his hotel in Washington demanding to be put in touch immediately with Ed Balls and Tom Scholar, his principal private secretary. The startled duty-clerk in London pointed out that both were just down the corridor in the same hotel, only yards from where Gordon was phoning.

In government, the relationship between Tony and Gordon was still hugely influenced by the pattern set in opposition. They had shared a room together and as rising MPs they were both early 'modernisers', but for a long time Gordon Brown was the senior partner, the more seasoned politician and the potential leader. Tony Blair had had various economic posts in opposition before making his name as shadow home secretary, but his briefs had not required him to get stuck into the central questions of economic policy, and under Neil Kinnock's leadership that was left to Roy Hattersley and John Smith. Gordon Brown was different. As shadow trade secretary and then, when John Smith became leader, as shadow chancellor and chairman of the Labour Party's Economic Commission, Gordon was at the centre of policy across a broad front. And nothing much changed when Tony was elected leader of the Labour Party. His priority was reform of the party and positioning ahead of the election, it was Gordon Brown who kept a grip on their potentially spendthrift colleagues, doing the dirty work and making himself unpopular in the party. And in the run-up to the election in 1997 the two men ran a very tightly controlled operation that suited them both. Once in government, Gordon Brown still wanted to run everything on the domestic front.

It is a puzzle to me why the Prime Minister went along with this. It certainly had nothing to do with intellect. Tony Blair has just as good a brain as Gordon Brown and is more able to deal with several issues at a time, which of course he has been forced to do as Prime Minister. Maybe it was just a lack of genuine interest in the minutiae of domestic policies but the Prime Minister spent hours on the details of public-sector reform. Whether that was a sensible use of his time is another matter, the fact is he did it because he regarded it as important. Perhaps the reluctance to rein in Gordon was just a matter of personal inclination: whatever the irritations, letting Gordon get on with things ultimately delivered the goods. Or maybe it was just a personal style that generally liked to smooth away animosities if at all possible. Perhaps there was actually some sort of understanding made in the Granita restaurant that conceded special powers to Gordon in return for Tony's free run for the leadership of the Labour Party. I've no idea what was said or agreed there. But a copy of the background notes published in *The Guardian* nine years later[16] supports the notion that Blair agreed to make Brown a very powerful chancellor, with a remit to cover not only the economy but also large areas of welfare policy. Furthermore, it is important to recognise that Tony Blair is a very astute political strategist who focuses on the big picture, and in pursuit of his longer-term goals he may be less fastidious than some with narrower preoccupations, in turning a blind eye to certain things that he knows or suspects should not be supported, but are tolerable concessions in a longer game. That is a prerogative of being the Prime Minister. Whatever the reasons, far from being a control freak, as is sometimes suggested, Tony Blair delegated an unprecedented amount of prime-ministerial authority to the Chancellor that went well beyond the normal and inevitably central position played by the Treasury in all administrations.

Tony's readiness to allow Gordon a pretty free hand over economic policy was matched by his own personalised view of foreign policy and in particular his determination to bring European policy within No. 10. Problems inevitably arose between the two men where their two areas of responsibility clashed, as they did over EMU. The overall effect of ceding so much to Gordon was to add to the messy and confusing disorder that characterises all governments. Tony Blair's reluctance or disinclination to exercise proper authority over his Chancellor meant that other Cabinet ministers and Whitehall received confusing signals about the ultimate source of power in the Government. It unnecessarily increased the normal tensions that exist in most administrations between No. 10 and No. 11, irrespective of the particular occupants, and these were undoubtedly accentuated further by Gordon Brown's method of working.

Within months of the 1997 election Gordon declared that, 'the days of managing economic policy secretly behind closed doors and of unaccountable decision making are coming to an end.'[17] And he frequently expressed a preference for openness and transparency in policy-making. However, 'transparent' and 'open' were not the words that always sprung to the lips of Cabinet colleagues catching Gordon trying to settle matters affecting their departments behind their back, but he was only able to do this because the Prime Minister had allowed his own authority to be diluted. This started early in the first term, and continued: anyone who saw Alan Milburn's[18] anger as he stormed out of the Prime Minister's den at 9.10 a.m. on 9 April 2003 would not have been totally surprised at his later resignation, albeit explained for unrelated reasons. It became clear that, with the budget Cabinet due at 9.30, the Chancellor had just told Milburn and the Prime Minister that the budget would include the setting up of a further investigation into the efficiency of the NHS, although the ink on the previous one was barely dry. Alan was unaware of this and was opposed to it as he thought that the NHS needed a bit of time to digest the changes that were already underway. At the subsequent Cabinet meeting, Milburn expressed his anger forcefully and was apparently supported by Ian McCartney,[19] and in the end the proposals were watered down. This was only a small incident perhaps, but was indicative of the Chancellor's treatment of some of his colleagues and any reputation Gordon may have had for openness is pretty selective. Of course, because of its impact on financial markets, the decision to make the Bank of England independent had to be made in secret and the process of setting interest rates was certainly made more transparent as a result, but Gordon was subsequently a bit short on openness. For example, the initial membership of the Monetary Policy Committee (MPC) would have been difficult to better and both No. 10 and the Bank of England were adequately involved in choosing it. But later appointments sometimes appeared to be picked from Gordon Brown's back pocket with scant and often no consultation with No. 10. On one occasion this became absurd when the Chancellor's private office denied any intention of filling a vacancy that I knew from the Bank of England to be imminent. However, late in the evening a couple of days later, No. 10 was informed that the appointment of Richard Lambert[20] would be announced the following day. Most of those chosen for the MPC have been excellent, but the method of selection was unsatisfactory, certainly not open or transparent, and in my view the process probably did lead to a reduction in its overall quality.

Gordon Brown is a highly intelligent man and an astute politician with a strong moral code, as befits the son of a Church of Scotland Minister; he is driven by a genuine desire to improve the lot of the deprived and disadvantaged and he would have merited a place in any Labour cabinet of the past. He also seems to share some characteristics with Edward Heath, who it appears, was relaxed, self-deprecating and very funny amongst close friends with whom he was at ease, but outside that narrow circle displayed a different character. There is some evidence that the normally cheerful and extrovert Brown underwent a sea-change in 1994, perhaps due to the death of John Smith, but one commentator has said that Gordon made 'a conscious decision to become more serious and to view the burden of the shadow chancellorship more heavily'.[21] More was seen of the brooding, gloomy Brown and much less of the charming, funny and self-deprecating one. All this may be true; it is possible that, if he were to become Prime Minister, Brown would be less anxious, and flashes of the old Gordon did periodically break out, but I can only describe what I saw at the time, even if it is a partial picture. What I found odd about Gordon Brown for a man of powerful intellect and interested in ideas was the way he chose to put it and them to the test. He was very reluctant to discuss policy beyond a very narrow circle of people until he had made up his mind on something, and that came usually very late in the day, at which stage he was very difficult to shift. Some claim that this showed great inner strength and self-reliance and this may be the case, but it is very different to the way in which most of us come to decisions. This in stark contrast with Denis Healey, a man of undoubted intellect and unbounded self-confidence, who in government used vigorous and sometimes heated discussions with officials and outside advisers to clarify his own views. Others taking part in the process might get bruised but they never (or rarely) felt other than part of the process and there was never any personal antagonism should they take a contrary view to the Chancellor. This is not Gordon Brown's method and contrary opinions, particularly if forcefully expressed, were not welcomed.

The first difference I had with the new Chancellor came immediately after the election in 1997. Prior to the election, the previous Chancellor, Ken Clarke, had refrained from raising interest rates for political reasons. Inflation was heading for four per cent unless action of some sort was taken to head off the rise. The immediate issue for the new Government was whether to raise interest rates by a quarter or half per cent when it also announced independence for the Bank of England. Gordon Brown wanted a half per cent rise. This would be the last decision on interest rates made by politicians and a quarter or a half per cent didn't in itself make a huge difference. However, I thought it was likely that sterling would strengthen in the wake of the announcement on Bank independence, and a rise in the currency would amount to a further tightening of monetary policy on top of any rise in interest rates that was agreed. More importantly, I preferred to let the newly independent Bank of England establish its own credibility by raising rates if it thought appropriate when the MPC met. It was not a huge issue either way, but on balance I simply favoured the smaller rise and that's what the Prime Minister supported. Interest rates were increased by a quarter per cent. According to Geoffrey Robinson, who was and is very close to Gordon Brown, this irritated the Chancellor: 'the problem was No. 10 and Derek Scott.'[22] This was a ridiculous over-reaction since the difference was insignificant, but an early sign that Gordon Brown's Treasury would try to deny any role for No. 10 in the conduct of economic policy.

Even in opposition, Gordon Brown was not in favour of Tony Blair taking on an economic adviser. I don't think there was anything personal in this, just a reflection of his determination to keep economics firmly within his own team. This didn't change after the election and it affected his attitude to other appointments too. The Prime Minister normally has two key private secretaries, one from the Treasury and another from the Foreign Office. In late 1997, the Prime Minister wanted to appoint a new principal private secretary from the Treasury, as the incumbent, Moira Wallace, who had served through the transition from the Major Government, was due to leave for another post, and the Prime Minister wanted Jeremy Heywood as the replacement. He had worked for Norman Lamont when he was Chancellor – Lamont had described Jeremy as 'the best private secretary ever' – and had served at the International Monetary Fund in Washington. Gordon had another candidate in mind. It was a straightforward choice but it took several weeks of negotiation before Jeremy's appointment was confirmed and took a wholly disproportionate amount of prime-ministerial and others' time. Most prime ministers would have simply told their chancellor, 'I hear what you say, but I'm the Prime Minister and I'll appoint whom I choose thank you very much,' and the matter would have been swiftly settled. Tony didn't do this.

Gordon Brown's attitude towards any involvement in economic policy from No. 10 became clear soon after the election in 1997. I learnt from some old friends in the Treasury that the Chancellor's office had instructed all officials within the department that any contact they had with me had to be reported, together with the subject discussed. Needless to say a lot of officials ignored this ridiculous and somewhat Orwellian instruction, particularly the older and more self-confident ones. However, others did feel inhibited and Gordon Brown's overall attitude to No. 10 and its advisers was probably summed up in a gruff comment he made to me in November 2001 after a rather contentious meeting: 'You provide the questions, I'll provide the answers'! The problem, all too often, was that when No. 10 did ask the questions, there were no answers.

The speed and efficiency with which Bank of England independence was implemented has led to something of a myth that Labour arrived in office after the 1997 election with fully fledged policies that simply required implementation from a dutiful Civil Service. This was far from true, even for the 'windfall tax' which had been a prominent plank in Labour's platform in the run-up to the election. This was a tax in which the 'excess profits' of the privatised utilities would be clawed back by the Government. A lot of effort had gone into this in opposition on the part of the Brown team, but it required a great deal of hard work by officials after the election to get the proposals into a workable shape. In other areas, even less preparatory work had been carried out: for instance the proposal for introducing Individual Savings Accounts (ISA). This was little more than a phrase in the manifesto aimed at extending the saving schemes introduced by the Conservatives, such as Personal Equity Plans (PEPs) and Tax Exempt Special Savings Accounts (Tessas) to those on more modest incomes. A good idea, but no more than an idea and Gordon's initial plans would have killed off the whole market by putting a £50,000 cap on the total that any one individual could hold in ISAs. This is a lot of money, but a large number of people, admittedly the better off, had already exceeded that amount and if they were forced to sell some of their holdings or prevented from accumulating more, it would alter the economics for those providing the products. They in turn would then be unable or unwilling to provide products for people with more modest incomes who could only afford to save smaller amounts, so the whole purpose of the policy might be wrecked by the cap. No. 10 worked hard to get this changed and eventually Gordon was forced into a u-turn and removed the cap, but only after an unnecessary row in public with the savings industry.

Getting information about the contents of Gordon Brown's budgets was like drawing teeth. And the first one set the tone for all subsequent budgets and other set-piece occasions such as the November pre-budget reports (PBR) or 'mini-budgets', as well as the Comprehensive Spending Reviews (CSR) that set out public spending programmes for three years ahead, and much else besides. The process of getting alongside each other over the budget would start a couple of months or so before budget day, with No. 10 suggesting an early meeting between the Prime Minister and the Chancellor to review the broad strategy. A meeting would eventually take place after delay, but the discussion would generally be without much focus and invariably without the benefit of previously circulated papers of any substance – Gordon did not want anything written down. There would be an agreement to hold further meetings, with the Chancellor committing the Treasury to prepare papers on specific issues, involving the relevant advisers from No. 10. Nothing would happen – neither cooperation with advisers from No. 10, nor papers would be forthcoming, for example about the plans to alter mainline corporation tax that were under discussion soon after we got into government. On a number of occasions the Prime Minister reminded the Chancellor of the importance he attached to the proper involvement of No. 10 in policy formation, and written instructions were also sent across on at least two or three occasions in the first term. Barely six months after the 1997 election, I drafted a letter that was sent without significant modifications to the Chancellor as a personal memorandum from the Prime Minister. The message could not have been clearer: Gordon was to ensure that his private office made it clear to officials in both the Treasury and Inland Revenue that it was part of their function to discuss issues with the policy unit at No. 10 and papers on important policy areas were to be sent across as a matter of course even if they might on occasions await perusal and decisions by ministers. This had no effect on Gordon Brown, even when the Prime Minister raised the problem again at subsequent meetings or over the telephone. This inevitably affected the way the Treasury itself reacted to advisers and officials in No. 10 and it soon became known throughout Whitehall that, in some areas at least, the Chancellor could defy the Prime Minister with impunity.

In this atmosphere, advisers at No. 10 had sometimes to behave more like investigative journalists than prime-ministerial aides, putting together a picture from snippets of information from officials in the Treasury or Inland Revenue or other 'sources', before offering advice and opinion to the Prime Minister. The only difference was that the Chancellor's team was far more likely to volunteer the contents of budgets and other announcements to journalists than they were to communicate with their opposite numbers next door. Still, sometimes No. 10 did manage to identify problems and get changes made before any damage was done, but it was a time-consuming and roundabout way of doing things. One instance of this was the plan to change corporation tax, which was paid eighteen months after the financial year to which it applied: the plan under consideration ahead of the 1999 budget was to move to 'same-year payment'. This was a sensible step, but the phasing was critical and the Chancellor's initial proposals brought it in too quickly, with damaging effects on company cash flows. For a long time, ministers at the Treasury denied a problem existed. I had a bizarre meeting with Geoffrey Robinson, when he said, 'I haven't told Gordon about this meeting you know,' but he dismissed my concerns about the substantive issue. Afterwards, Geoffrey kindly insisted that he personally see me out of the Treasury and at the exit we bumped into Charlie Whelan, Gordon Brown's press aide and factotum, who was just entering the building, so removing any chance that the Chancellor would be in the dark about Geoffrey's meeting with me.

Tony simply kept expressing his concerns to Brown who eventually recognised changes had to be made. On occasion, the resort to subterfuge got close to farce and briefings had to be arranged surreptitiously. For example, one Friday afternoon officials slipped into the entrance of the Cabinet Office halfway up Whitehall, passed through the connecting door to No. 10, past the office occupied by Jonathan Powell and the private secretaries, up the main staircase that is lined with the pictures of all previous prime ministers and into the White Room on the first floor. Afterwards, they were shown out of the front door of No. 10, which in turn raised the risk of bumping into Gordon coming through the connecting corridor from No. 11. I suggested that next time they should be provided with false beards.

The lack of cooperation went well beyond the spats between No. 10 and No. 11 characterising most governments, and it affected most of my colleagues at No. 10 in one way or another. However, they were generally able to establish working relationships with the departments they were shadowing in a way that was impossible for anyone at No. 10 to do with Gordon Brown's Treasury. As the Prime Minister's principal private secretary, Jeremy Heywood had to cover the whole front of domestic policy. He was the most constant conduit with the Treasury, but he too could be treated cavalierly by Brown's office when following up his remit from the Prime Minister, sometimes in the most petty ways. At the end of October 1999 we had only the haziest notion of what was in the PBR due on 9 November. Gordon and the Treasury presented the economic forecasts underlying the PBR to the Prime Minister on the morning of Thursday 4 November, but still no content. Tony wanted information, but papers hadn't arrived by the weekend, and they only reached No. 10, together with the Chancellor's draft speech, on the Monday morning. However, with rare exceptions, any difficulties had very little to do with officials working in Gordon's departments (Treasury, Inland Revenue and Customs and Excise). Some of these were themselves, 'outside the loop' of the Chancellor's inner circle, and sometimes they were simply 'under orders' not to divulge. And these orders could be very explicit, as was brought home to me when I was dealing with pensions.

By the time of the 2001 election, the Government had got itself into a bit of a pickle over pensions, not least by increasing the basic state pension in April 2000 by a miserly 75p, the minimum required to raise it in line with the rise in prices. This was something forced on the Secretary of State, Alistair Darling, by Gordon Brown. The decision might have been justified in narrow economic terms, but soon afterwards Tony and Gordon both realised the political mistake and said as much at the Labour Party annual conference in the autumn – 'I tell you now, as Gordon made crystal clear yesterday, we get the message'. Ahead of the election, substantial future increases in the basic pension were announced, but there were other serious problems that had to be tackled when Tony was back in Downing Street, and he became very worried about both state and private pension provision.

One of the problems was that the centrepiece for dealing with existing pensioner poverty – the Minimum Income Guarantee (MIG) – meant that it was not worthwhile those on low incomes trying to put away a bit extra for their retirement because quite small amounts of private savings led to cutbacks in benefits. In an attempt to put this right, Gordon Brown came up with Pensioner Credit (PC) in an effort to reduce the loss of benefits suffered by those with small amounts of private savings. But although PC was less of a disincentive to save, it was certainly not an incentive: Gordon Brown presented it as the Government giving sixty pence for every one pound saved, but in fact it was a forty per cent tax on savings, rather than one hundred per cent. A series of meetings took place at No. 10 through the latter part of 2001 with Gordon, Alistair Darling and the Prime Minister that occasionally became quite heated. ('Quite a little firecracker when we let you off, Derek,' said Tony.) At the same time as these concerns were being discussed, traditional occupational pensions were being undermined for a variety of reasons, some at least beyond the Government's control. On top of this the Government's own 'stakeholder pension' aimed at providing those on modest incomes with an affordable vehicle to save for a personal pension, had got off to a bad start. Gordon Brown was reluctant to even recognise the problems in the structure of state provision (though by the end of 2003 the Treasury had begun to acknowledge in private the failings of Pensioner Credit) and wasn't very interested in the intricacies of private provision. Andrew Smith, who took over from Alistair Darling at the Department of Work and Pensions, was aware of the problem, but he wouldn't make any move without Gordon's agreement and occasionally had to be reminded by the Prime Minister that he, not Gordon, was his ultimate boss, but old habits died hard. One morning in the early autumn of 2002, Tony asked Andrew to pop in for a private chat the following day. Before this meeting took place Gordon dropped in to see the Prime Minister on another matter and casually remarked, 'I gather you are seeing Andrew tomorrow.' Andrew had obviously told him about his forthcoming 'private' session with Tony.

The Prime Minister realised that if the Government were to get to grips with pensions the subject had to be addressed in the round; there had been too many instances when governments of both parties had made apparently sensible decisions in one area without appreciating the knock-on effects elsewhere. Tony wanted all the issues to be set out in a planned Green Paper, but the contents had to be watered down under pressure from Gordon and Andrew, and a Pension Commission was set up instead, with Gordon again fighting to dilute its terms of reference. In the end, Tony ensured these were broad enough to be interpreted widely by the chairman, Adair Turner,[23] if he chose to. In the autumn of 2002 there was a series of meetings involving the Prime Minister, the Chancellor and Andrew Smith that brought things to a head. I had spent a lot of time briefing Tony and he had a firm grip of the essentials. He was determined to get what he wanted in the end, showing extreme patience and restraint as Gordon ploughed on regardless of the argument being put to him – a style that Tony Blair once described as Gordon's speaking clock mode. At one meeting, in November 2002, Gordon arrived at the den with no fewer than seven officials (all of whom remained silent), sat down next to Andrew on the sofa with me opposite them in a wing chair to the right of the Prime Minister, leaning back at the side of his desk. The meeting became quite heated and tense with the Prime Minister, Gordon and myself the most combative. However, even after this, there were a lot of issues still to be resolved with the deadline for publication of the long-delayed Green Paper getting very close. The Prime Minister wanted this sorted out and demanded that the expert on social security at No. 10 and I should have the full cooperation of the Treasury, Inland Revenue and DWP. Yet again the Chancellor reassured the Prime Minister that his department would, of course, cooperate fully with policy advisers from No. 10, as always. They could naturally have access to anything they wanted. A meeting with the Treasury and Inland Revenue was fixed up to go through the outstanding questions. When I went to this, however, I was told by the official chairing the meeting that they would listen to any suggestions I might have, but he had been instructed by his political masters not to disclose anything or answer any questions about the pending conclusions of the Treasury or Inland Revenue. This was a pretty extraordinary way to treat the Prime Minister's office and most of the officials were embarrassed, but the message from the top was clear: it was no business of No. 10 or the Prime Minister; Gordon was in control. This particular incident was typical of my time in Downing Street and it continued to the very end. Two months before I left No. 10, after one meeting officials whom I had got to know pretty well apologised for being less than helpful, but they had been under instructions from Gordon's people. We agreed to meet a few days later to sort things out in a better atmosphere, even though they were under instructions not to talk to me. But the pattern for the behaviour of Brown's team had been set very much earlier and sometimes the Prime Minister seemed to fare little better than his advisers in getting his Chancellor to open up.

A month away from the 1998 budget, No. 10 had only the haziest picture of what Gordon was planning, although his team had obviously been trailing an outline with the press, in particular to Larry Elliot on *The Guardian*. The Chancellor was summoned to a meeting at No. 10, arriving with Ed Balls and a senior official. In addition to the Prime Minister, No. 10's team included Jonathan Powell,[24] Alastair Campbell, David Miliband[25] and myself. Clutching a large bunch of papers, Gordon started talking about the problems of controlling public spending the following year – bids from departments were already over £5bn against a contingency of just over £2bn and this, he said, made the budget very difficult. His problems were being compounded by the state of the economy: inflation and earnings were set to rise and he criticised the Bank of England for not raising interest rates. He then launched into a résumé of what he called the difficult international situation. The monologue lasted well over twenty minutes and was clearly designed to delay any discussion of specifics. During a pause, the Prime Minister said gently, 'Gordon, what about the budget?' The Chancellor, pulling his bundle of papers tightly to his chest, growled, 'I haven't made my mind up yet.' The Prime Minister, leaning forward and upward from the couch on which he was sitting, eyebrows raised with a disarming smile and head tipping slightly from side to side in the manner portrayed by Rory Bremner, simply said, 'Give us a hint, Gordon.' Soon after that the meeting broke up as no one from No. 10 could keep a straight face. The No. 10 team reviewed the shambles, with Tony phoning Gordon later in the day. I can think of no other prime minister who would have put up with such behaviour. Certainly, Callaghan would not have tolerated being treated by Healey as Blair tolerated Brown and it would never have occurred to Denis, although by any standards a very big beast of politics, to treat Jim in a similar manner.

In one sense, of course, No. 10 was in constant touch with the Chancellor's thoughts and plans since Tony Blair and Gordon Brown were in communication daily and very often several times a day. A lot of business was conducted when they were alone together or with their closest political advisers. But these sessions, sometimes in the Prime Minister's den or at Chequers, sometimes in the garden at No. 10 and often on the phone, were primarily political and when policy was discussed it was usually at a pretty generalised level. This could all too often leave the Prime Minister unsighted and the Chancellor unchallenged about the details and implications of his proposals. For example, it took a very long time for Tony to wake up to the future public expenditure implications of the Chancellor's extensive programme of tax credits, despite warnings from me and other advisers. At Chequers at the end of 1999, he promised to take on the Chancellor over the issue, but most members of the Policy Unit who were there were sceptical whether this would have much effect and it didn't. Yet Tony was still apparently taken aback by the full public expenditure costs when this finally dawned on him in the second term.

The reluctance of the Prime Minister to insist on more thorough and businesslike discussions with the Chancellor was unfortunate since Tony's instincts on many domestic economic issues were more often right than wrong about the requirements for a properly functioning market economy. However, even the soundest instincts do need to be followed up if they are to have any practical effect, and too often the Prime Minister did not follow up his inclinations or insist on appropriate involvement of No. 10. In these circumstances it was impossible for others to make up the lost ground.

In opposition, Blair and Brown had committed Labour not to raise the rates of personal tax, but beyond that no thought had been given to the principles that should underlie a sensible tax policy. Any principles can serve only as guidelines but, without some framework changes, can all too readily simply add to the complexity of the tax system as a whole. In the summer of 1998, the Prime Minister expressed interest in reforming and simplifying income tax. Within No. 10 he took the view that 'direct taxes need to be cut significantly over the medium term' for the vast majority of the population who were or who aspired to be middle class. In early autumn, the policy unit held an 'away day' with the Prime Minister at Chequers, in the course of which I made a presentation on the state of the tax system and some principles that might guide the Government. These included a bias in favour of tax neutrality (to reduce the number of decisions taken for tax rather than economic reasons) and a preference for a broad base and low rates of tax, a reduction in the marginal rates on income and profits and various other largely uncontroversial suggestions. All pretty standard stuff and in order to stir things up a bit, the bullet points I used for the presentation were taken from a text set out in the last budget 'Red Book' of the previous Conservative Government. I only disclosed this after my colleagues and the Prime Minister had all agreed that the principles seemed to fit the bill, but the point was that the new Government had no clear tax framework at all. Gordon saw tax as something that could be altered and tweaked to meet other objectives that he, or the Government, thought desirable and, moreover, he thought that the British electorate had been brainwashed into thinking that a rising burden of tax is a bad thing. Tony knew that Gordon was further complicating the tax system, but he didn't really resist it. The new ten-pence income tax band, discussed throughout 1998 and introduced in the 1999 budget, was an example of this and I argued that a better option would be sustained effort to take more people on lower incomes out of tax altogether. This could have been done in a way that was consistent with the manifesto and the Prime Minister agreed, but sensed that Gordon was very heavily committed. Gordon did simplify capital gains tax (CGT) by reducing the taper whereby reduced rates of CGT were charged according to the length of time the assets had been held but, since he had introduced the taper in the first place, this hardly counted. Initially a much simpler option would have been a reduced single rate of CGT to match or even a bit below that of the USA, and that is what I pressed for, but Tony went along with the Chancellor and his taper, although afterwards he admitted a mistake had been made.

Some will argue that whatever the difficulties and frustrations, most of the time sensible policies emerged in the end and disasters were avoided. However, greater assertiveness by the Prime Minister might have avoided some specific mistakes and reduced the clutter of microeconomic initiatives that characterised Gordon Brown's tenure at No. 11. The economy could only have benefited.

With some justification, Gordon Brown is considered one of Labour's most successful chancellors, but both he and Tony Blair have been blessed with generally benign economic circumstances. It would have been interesting to see how either of them would have fared if they had had to deal with the conditions that faced some of their recent predecessors: a small or non-existent majority, a political party that was running off the rails, a clapped-out economy, an unreformed trade union movement and an international economy falling apart with oil prices doubling twice in a decade. Certainly, past Labour governments made serious mistakes, but it was not an easy environment for them either. Gordon Brown's economic inheritance in 1997 was better than that of any previous chancellor in living memory. Rightly, he was determined to avoid the mistakes of previous Labour governments, but it was just as important not to invent new ones.

Three key domestic factors were largely responsible for Britain's excellent economic performance in the decade after 1992. These were the liberalising of labour, capital and product markets under Margaret Thatcher ('supply-side reforms'), the decisions taken by Norman Lamont in the wake of the ERM shambles (whatever his mistakes before) and Gordon Brown making the Bank of England independent in 1997. If the new Labour Government had done nothing else at all, the economy would probably have performed rather similarly in the subsequent six years to the way it actually did between 1997 and 2003. Once the fundamentals are on the right lines, momentum can carry an economy along for many years unless the Government does something really stupid, which it didn't (or are very unlucky with the external environment, which was certainly not the case for most of the decade after 1992). The danger is less of a sudden deterioration or a dramatic collapse in the economy, than the effect of cumulative changes building up so that the economic arteries gradually get 'furred-up'. In some respects this makes the job of economic adviser more difficult, since it was rarely possible to argue that any particular decision was enormously damaging to the economy in the short term. The process is cumulative.

The competition regime that Gordon Brown established was probably one of the most liberal (in a free-market sense) anywhere in the industrialised world. If it is maintained, it could have a beneficial effect in ten years or so that will outweigh any other single economic decision he made, except making the Bank of England independent. But in other respects Gordon was too prescriptive. Rhetoric about encouraging enterprise is not the same as having a real understanding of what makes the private sector tick. Judging from a conversation with me at Chequers in the spring of 2002, Tony had simply resigned himself to the fact that his Chancellor had 'a blind spot' on this. In a market economy the emphasis needs to be on keeping the economic arteries open and the blood flowing freely and less in attempting to direct it in particular directions. This encourages economic dynamism and properly functioning markets allow outsiders, be they the unemployed or new businesses, to break in and get established on the economic ladder. Politicians (of all parties) too easily become obsessed with new economic initiatives, schemes and wheezes of one sort or another, that are designed to improve economic growth, raise productivity, boost enterprise or stimulate something or other. Few of these may individually do much harm – and almost none much good either – but cumulatively they can do considerable damage and added up they cost money that might be used better elsewhere. Government programmes to help entrepreneurs are almost a contradiction in terms and, as far as economic policy is concerned, 'I'm from the Government, I want to help you' is a phrase that usually should set alarm bells ringing.

The long-term impact of the Brown-Blair partnership on the British economy remains to be seen since it takes several years for the full impact of policies, for good or ill, to take effect. In the next few years, Britain's economy should continue to outperform many of our nearest neighbours, but there are limits to the length of time public spending can increase at a faster rate than growth in Gross Domestic Product (GDP) without causing some problems and by the time I left Downing Street, Britain was approaching, or perhaps even past, that limit. The regulatory burden had been increased, the tax system become more complicated and the tax burden was rising too. Over the medium term all this matters and it is easier for governments to mess up an economy than it is to improve it.

Tony Blair gave Gordon Brown unprecedented authority over a range of domestic policy, but that was his choice. They were jointly responsible for the economic outcome. Their relationship determined the policies that were pursued. But the strains and irritations over economic policy between 1997 and 2003 set the tone for the very public differences before the five economic tests on EMU were announced in October 1997, the subsequent insistence by the Treasury team that Gordon Brown would be the one to make any decision on EMU, and the proprietary attitude taken by the Chancellor to the assessment itself, an attitude that drifted into farce as the deadline approached in 2003. As will be seen later, the five tests really only addressed second-order questions, but the stresses and strains between Blair and Brown will continue until membership of EMU and the EU constitution is settled one way or another.

However, it is important to recognise that there was no ideological split between the two about the euro, as there had been between John Major and various members of his administration. There were differences of emphasis that periodically came to the fore, which then took on a life of their own and which reflected the complications of their basic relationship. It was other aspects of their relationship that found expression in exaggerated differences on the euro, rather than these reflecting any fundamental differences about the single currency itself, and the political manoeuvrings between the two men on this issue will be addressed later in the book.

CHAPTER TWO

In for a Pound

Politics and Economics in Europe

'Everybody knows that the decision to enter into EMU is a decision to swim in the European sea forever, and with deep intensity.' The language of Romano Prodi[1] might have been too flowery for some tastes but he set out the implications of EMU with more directness than most politicians in Britain have mustered. Tony Blair was more committed to Europe than any previous Labour prime minister and, with the exception of Edward Heath, possibly more than any prime minister of either party, but, unlike Heath, he never acknowledged the wider political significance of EMU and this set him apart from most political and other elites in continental Europe, for whom it was as much about politics as it is about economics. In November 1999, Wim Duisenberg, then President of the European Central Bank (ECB) summed it up: 'EMU is and was always meant to be a stepping stone on the way to a united Europe.'

The politics of Europe have reached an important stage. The six founding members of the European Economic Community have become a European Union of twenty-five, and still more countries want to join. In 2003, member states of the EU were asked to adopt a new constitutional treaty that its authors hoped would last for at least fifty years, and Tony Blair gave it wholehearted support in 2003 and again when negotiations resumed in 2004.

The future development of the EU will have enormous implications for all its members, not just Britain. But the course chosen will affect and be affected by Britain's decision to enter or remain outside EMU. The two issues are tied together. One of the arguments often introduced into discussions on Europe was the charge that those with doubts about EMU or the proposed constitution, wanted to 'disengage' from Europe. That is certainly not my purpose, I voted 'yes' to Europe in the referendum in 1975 and anyone who has glanced at a map or dipped into history knows that Britain is inextricably linked with its neighbours on the continent of Europe. The issue is how best to cooperate in partnership with other countries within the EU and what is the most appropriate political and economic framework for that to take place. Because EMU is part of a broader political project, some people argue that the economics don't matter. This is to miss the point. EMU is clearly a political project and politics and economics are bound up with each other, but the economics are important in their own right for a number of reasons.

First, bad economics makes for bad politics. Any economic framework that is to last must retain political support – apparently robust economic frameworks can be blown away or transformed by political crises which themselves originate in economics.

Secondly, in Britain economics have always played a bigger part in decisions on Europe than elsewhere, with some British politicians playing down the political implications of various steps along the way. The electorate may now be wary of this, so unless the economic case is convincing, political arguments put forward in favour of entry may not carry the British electorate in any referendum.

Thirdly, the majority of those in Britain who advocate entry – even those for whom the decision is entirely political – implicitly and usually explicitly claim at least some economic benefits, either immediately or in the future.

Finally, the Government led by Tony Blair stated specifically that the economics had to be right before the question of entry was put before the British people, and Gordon Brown and most other likely successors to Tony's crown have taken a similar line. The efficacy of the five economic tests that the Government laid down in October 1997 and the nature of the assessment in June 2003 will be considered later, but economics are clearly still seen as fundamental to any decision to adopt the euro. After the Government's assessment in 2003, any attempt to take Britain into EMU seemed a long way off, but in 2004 the Government committed itself to keep the position under review and Tony Blair is, rightly or wrongly, convinced of the political argument for entry, so that the issue is not going to go away and it is important to be clear about the economic arguments on both sides of the case.

The economic case made by proponents of entry puts a lot of emphasis on the increased stability that membership would bring and this will be examined in the course of the book. What does this word 'stability' mean? Clearly being in EMU provides currency stability with other members of Euroland and this has its advantages, but it only does so for the nominal exchange rates with others in the single currency. In economics, the 'real' exchange rate, which takes account of 'real' economic variables such as growth and productivity, is just as, if not more, important. It is pretty well accepted that governments have very little control over a country's real exchange rate in the long run, but it can nonetheless change significantly over quite a short period of time. What if the nominal exchange rate stability within EMU is bought at too large a cost, not only in terms of greater nominal volatility of sterling against the dollar, which is important for Britain, but also at the cost of greater instability of 'real' things like output, investment and jobs?

From the foundation of the European Coal and Steel Community (ECSC) in 1951, the discussion of Britain's relationship with Europe has been littered with references to missing buses and trains leaving stations. Whatever Britain's ambivalence towards Europe it has been said on many occasions that, 'we always join in the end', but there is nothing inevitable about the single currency: the Danes and Swedes have voted against joining and the British people will make their own minds up if the time ever comes for a final decision.

Concern about the economics of EMU is not based on any nostalgic desire to keep the pound as some historical relic of Britain's former glory. It is about the future and the desirability and practicality of any country to retain in its own hands the economic levers that affect the jobs and prosperity of its citizens. If interest rates are to be set at a level to meet the needs of the British economy, the pound has to be free to appreciate and depreciate. This is important enough during the normal course of the business cycle, but from time to time all economies experience disturbing occurrences that are referred to in the jargon of economics as 'asymmetric shocks'. These are events or a series of events that affect real economic variables such as growth and productivity. They may be either benign or malign in their impact, they may originate within or outside a particular country, but the point is they are events that affect one economy more than others. It is now widely recognised that these shocks are best dealt with by appropriate changes in monetary policy, but within EMU this is rarely possible for an individual country so there is much attention devoted to using fiscal policy instead or encouraging additional elements of flexibility into an economy. But fiscal and monetary policies impact on an economy in very different ways. They are not substitutes. And many measures to increase an economy's flexibility are themselves forms of asymmetric shocks.

A decision to swap the pound for the euro raises questions of both political and economic sovereignty. Some people argue that in EMU sovereignty is merely being 'pooled' for greater gains and that the 'globalisation' of the international economy has made it impossible for a country the size of Britain to have an independent monetary policy. Allowing the pound to float is 'just the right to devalue'. However, there is an alternative view that preserving the freedom for the pound to appreciate and depreciate is more important today precisely because of the huge amounts of private-sector capital flowing across national frontiers. Maybe in economic terms EMU would have worked more smoothly in the 1950s and 1960s. Then private-sector capital flows were small, rates of return played little part in investment decisions, economies were more regimented and significant movements of populations (the 'guest workers') were accepted without appearing to threaten national identity. From this perspective, the world has moved on and it is EMU that is dated.

In or out of EMU, an economy will not always run smoothly. Governments and central banks will periodically make mistakes. The important thing is to determine the monetary and fiscal framework that is most likely to reward sensible policies and enable any mistakes to be rectified and later chapters in the book will draw out the implications of this for entry into EMU.

The euro is up and running, but a number of countries in Euroland are facing serious economic problems, including high levels of unemployment and rising budget deficits. The question arises as to the extent to which the single currency can be blamed, if at all, for this state of affairs and the answer will have obvious implications for British entry.

Between 2001 and 2003, the international economic environment became more difficult than at any time for a decade or more and central to this was the state of the American economy. Policy mistakes were made in the long US upswing of the 1990s that contributed to subsequent excesses, and huge imbalances had to be addressed despite the recovery in the US economy during 2003 and into 2004. But any adjustment by the USA had implications for other currency blocs too and the potential turbulence in foreign exchange markets must be taken into account in any decision on British entry to the single currency.

But in some respects at least the desire to emulate the USA was one of the factors behind the ambition of Europe's leaders at the Lisbon summit in March 2000 to make the EU 'the most dynamic modern economy in the world'. The continental economy of the USA reaps clear benefits from a single currency, but as well as having a single market and a single currency, America is a single country too. This may have implications for the political conditions that have to be met if Europe is to benefit from its single currency.

Political union was the ultimate dream for the founders of Europe and remains so for many others today. In the wake of German unification, the leaders of the EU (in particular France and Germany) decided that monetary union should take precedence over political union in Europe, but monetary unions do need political underpinning if they are to last. Furthermore, there are some features of EMU that its proponents suggest will require closer political coordination from the centre, particularly the need for a credible framework for fiscal policy. This will strengthen the argument for further political integration in Europe and it also needs to be taken into account in any decision by Britain to enter.

Where is Europe heading politically? The route followed by the EU – via the original ECSC, the EEC and the EC – is, we are told, towards an ever-closer political union that has an unstoppable momentum. However, it is not clear where this momentum is leading. A largely sceptical electorate is assured by many of its political leaders that the destination is definitely not a nation state (and certainly not a 'super state') or an empire, the only two models for most of modern European history. Europe is unique. On the whole, the lack of precision about the political endgame and its institutional framework has not seemed to matter much until now. At the end of the Second World War, there was a unanimous feeling that a European war should never happen again. The key to this was preventing military conflict between France and Germany. That objective has been achieved and it no longer provides an adequate basis for taking Europe forward. The present form and structure of the EU is the result of particular historical circumstances. These have changed significantly, most notably with the unification of Germany, the end of the Cold War and prospects for enlargement to the east. These and other pressures pose their own challenge to the structure formed in different times for different ends. The peoples of Europe want a structure and purpose for the EU that they can understand and is up to date.

The significance of the constitutional treaty put forward in 2003 was recognised by all shades of opinion and in all countries of the Union. Many people in Britain, across the political spectrum, argued that any new treaty should ultimately be put to the people in the form of a referendum. Others, led by Tony Blair, said the purpose was as much about clarifying and consolidating previous treaties as it was staking out new ground. They argued, and continued to argue when negotiations on the constitution reopened in 2004, against a referendum on the basis that the proposed new treaty introduced less significant changes for the way Britain is governed than some previous ones such as the Single European Act (1986) or the Maastricht Treaty (1992) when there were no referendums. In the end, however, the crude political repercussions of not conceding ultimately persuaded Tony Blair that he should, after all, lend his support to the idea of a referendum on the subject.

Of course, even if the new treaty had simply been consolidating previous treaties without fundamentally affecting the way Britain is governed, it would not in itself have undermined the case for a referendum. There are many people in Britain who were unaware of the contents and implications of the various European treaties that have been signed. Furthermore, some of those who voted 'yes' in the referendum in 1975, endorsing Britain's membership of the EEC, may have become disillusioned with the outcome. Others who voted 'no' then may now be converts and supporters of the EU. People do change their minds. And there are many who were too young to have participated in 1975 and still others not even born then, who have never had a chance to vote on how they are governed within the present structure of the EU. A new treaty that spelt out and codified the implications of the EU for holding our elected representative to account for decisions affecting British citizens is as good an opportunity as any to seek renewed endorsement from the people in a referendum.

However, some of the arguments about a referendum – centring on whether the new constitutional treaty was putting forward new proposals or mainly consolidating previous agreements – missed something that may be just as significant. The proposals set out in 2003 and discussed again in 2004 represented the culmination of a process and the creation of a political and economic structure for the Union that could be traced back to at least as far as the Treaty of Rome (1957).

The real issue to be addressed is whether this structure is any longer appropriate for the EU in the light of its existing and prospective membership and the many other changes that have taken place in the world in the past half-century. Tony Blair caricatured those who opposed the proposed constitution. To use a phrase associated with Mrs Thatcher in a different context: 'there is no alternative' as far as the EU is concerned, it's a matter of 'in or out'. But there were and are alternatives available to the political and economic model outlined in the constitution, should Britain and other countries choose to take them, and ones that might be more in tune with the democratic and economic needs of the modern world. These include a more overtly federal and democratic structure for the EU or alternatively one that has a much less comprehensive political and economic agenda with much of the existing authority of 'Brussels' restored to the democratic accountability of member states. People will have their own views about the desirability of these and other options, but the point is there are alternative routes that Europe could follow to those that have been set out. Some of these will be considered later in the book, but the availability of these alternatives and the ability of Britain to influence the outcome will be critically affected by a decision to enter or remain outside EMU.

Proponents of the single currency argue that Britain will only be able to exert its full influence in the EU when it has adopted the euro. But this can't simply be asserted and there is a contrary view that will also be addressed later, that it is only by remaining outside EMU that Britain can help guide the future political and economic structure of the EU in ways that meet not only the economic realities of the twenty-first century but also the need to bring the EU closer to its peoples.

However, it served the Prime Minister's purpose to suggest that those with doubts about entering EMU wanted to leave the EU and no doubt some did and do, just as other people might join EMU irrespective of the economics. But it does not have to be the case. Likewise it served the Prime Minister's purpose to suggest that those who opposed the constitution were really setting out to secede from the Union. Some may have been, but it does not have to be the case and to suggest otherwise is simply disingenuous. Nobody can doubt that the EU itself needs to adapt and address a different set of problems and opportunities from those that existed when 'the Six' signed the Treaty of Rome in 1957. In 2003 and 2004, most of those opposed to the constitutional treaty in Britain and in other countries were not making a declaration to 'scrap the EU'. They were telling the politicians to go back to the drawing board and come up with a political structure more in tune with the aspirations of Europe's peoples and less designed to meet the inclinations and ambitions of its bureaucrats and politicians.

PART TWO

The Background

CHAPTER THREE

A Vision Takes Shape
The Evolution of Europe

In 1998 Tony Blair concluded his address to the French National Assembly[1] with the comment that, 'Monnet[2] and Schuman[3] and, yes, Churchill had the vision to declare that the world they found was not going to be the world they would leave to future generations. I believe that you in France, share that vision with the British.' What was this vision? Does Britain really share it with France? Does it matter?

Today, nearly half of the legislation passed by the British Parliament originates in Brussels. Through newspapers, television and travel many people are at least vaguely aware of Europe and its institutions that were established with the Treaty of Rome in 1957. For many, however, the history of the European Union is at best a hazy memory and a lot of younger people may be unaware of its origins altogether. But the economic and political implications of Economic and Monetary Union and any future constitutional settlement cannot really be grasped without some understanding as to how the EU came to be what it is today.

Jean Monnet and Robert Schuman are often regarded as the founding fathers of modern Europe and the vision of Monnet (though very different from Churchill's) was clear: 'Cooperation between nations, while essential, cannot alone meet our problem. What must be sought is a fusion of the interests of the European peoples.'[4] The EU structure today is recognisably that of the founding fathers. Periodically there have been setbacks and diversions along the way, but the overall direction during the last half-century has been towards deeper integration and an accrual of authority or 'competence' away from individual member states to the Union, in practice the EU Commission. As to the interests of Britain and France, alluded to by Tony Blair in 1998, it is true that on occasions the two countries have appeared to use the same language, but 'a common vision' has, so far, not been much in evidence.

The idea of a united Europe has a very long history, going back at least to the year 800, when the Pope crowned Charlemagne as Holy Roman Emperor. The Frankish Empire that Charlemagne ruled (rather briefly) covered most of what are now France, Switzerland, Austria, southern Germany and the Benelux countries, quite close to the boundaries of the original six members of the European Economic Community, Germany, France, Italy, the Netherlands, Belgium and Luxembourg. At the Treaty of Verdun (843), Charlemagne's empire was divided between his three grandsons. Charles the Bald got the west, which became France; Louis 'the German' got the land east of the Rhine; and the eldest, Lothair, got the long thin middle kingdom stretching from Friesland to the borders of Calabria. This middle kingdom straddled the linguistic dividing line between the Latin and Germanic parts of the empire, and the whole of subsequent European history can in some ways be seen as a struggle between the heirs of Charles and Louis to control the kingdom of Lothair. It is probably no coincidence that some of the key figures in reuniting Europe after 1945 came from this historically disputed territory, most notably Konrad Adenauer,[5] Alcide de Gasperi[6] and Robert Schuman.

The desire for a specifically federated Europe has a shorter pedigree, but the notion was widely discussed in the nineteenth century and was given new impetus by the traumas of the First World War. In 1924, the first Pan-European Manifesto was launched in Vienna and, six years later, Aristide Briand[7] set out the French Government's proposals for a European federation just as Hitler – a man with his own ideas about forging a European union – was enjoying an election triumph in May 1930.

After the Second World War, the federalist cause enjoyed a resurgence that was stimulated from an unlikely quarter. In September 1946, Winston Churchill made a speech in Zurich in which he called for a 'United States of Europe'. All manner of people have called Churchill's speech in aid of their cause. Churchill was certainly not a federalist and definitely not a 'Little Englander', and he saw the British as 'friends and sponsors' of the new Europe rather than participants. However, his call for reconciliation between France and Germany was bold coming barely eighteen months after the end of the war and his speech had a dramatic effect. It led to the Hague Congress in 1948 that was attended by all the 'great men' (they were mainly men) of Europe.

The Hague Congress led to the formation of the Council of Ministers and a Consultative Assembly that met in 1949 for the first time in Strasbourg under the presidency of the Belgian federalist Paul-Henri Spaak.[8] In May 1950, the

French Foreign Minister, Robert Schuman, launched his plan – mainly designed by Jean Monnet – to fuse the coal and steel industries of France and Germany. Coal and steel would cease to be controlled and sold by their respective governments, but would be subject to shared decisions. These decisions would be made not by national governments acting as sovereign powers, but by a new organisation: the High Authority. This can be seen as the precursor of what later became the European Commission and other institutions of the present EU can also be traced back to the European Coal and Steel Community (ECSC), including the Council of Ministers, the Parliamentary Assembly and the Court of Justice. Germany and France were joined in the ECSC by Italy, the Netherlands, Belgium and Luxembourg and collectively they became 'the Six'. The agreement was signed at the Treaty of Paris in April 1951.

The High Authority involved ceding sovereignty to a supranational body for a limited purpose, but the wider federalist aim was embodied in Schuman's declaration in May 1950: 'This proposal will lay the first foundations for the kind of European federation that is indispensable for the preservation of peace.' Monnet and Schuman saw federation coming step-by-step, sector-by-sector. They were certainly unclear about its eventual structure, but the overall intention was never in doubt.

The European Defence Community (EDC) – the so-called Pleven Plan after its author Rene Pleven[9] – was an attempt to apply the Schuman Plan's principles to the integration of defence. The background was the need for German rearmament in the light of the growing tensions of the Cold War. The French were very worried about rearming their old foe, and for them the EDC was a way of placing German rearmament within the scope of a European army, the proposed European Defence Force (EDF). The British watched with some concern. Labour's Foreign Secretary, Ernest Bevin, saw it as diluting NATO and, after the election in 1951, Churchill's antipathy to the European army was expressed even more graphically on account of its supranational (or what he labelled 'metaphysical') features. Nonetheless, with the Cold War getting icy, the Americans, particularly Secretary of State John Foster Dulles, were keen on the idea and the Six signed up for the EDC in May 1952. But the decision then had to be endorsed by the parliaments of the six signatories.

While all this was going on, the Council of Ministers of the ECSC asked an assembly to draw up a treaty of political union. The result was a draft treaty for a European Political Community (EPC) that was presented to the governments of the Six in March 1953. It was a quasi-federal structure incorporating the ECSC and the EDC, and was driven by those who wanted to introduce federalism more quickly than the step-by-step approach of Monnet.

The political union outlined in the EPC included a parliament with two chambers, a 'Chamber of the People' (directly elected) and a 'Senate' (elected by national parliaments) that would be the legislature of the European

Community. There was to be a European Executive Council that was to 'oversee the Government of the Community'. Some of the proposals in the EPC were taken up subsequently in the Treaty of Rome and others still later, for example electing the European Parliament. Other ideas in the EPC remain in abeyance, but were still being argued for in a modified form at the Convention of the Future of Europe half a century later. For example, the EPC created a very powerful executive and a central role for its president that found echoes in the proposals for a strengthened EU Commission and more authoritative president put forward by Romano Prodi and others during discussions on the new constitution at the end of 2002.

However, fifty years ago the future of the political union envisaged in the EPC depended on the ratification of the defence arrangements set out in the EDC and although this was adopted in five parliaments it fell at the final hurdle. There were continuing concerns in France about rearming Germany, and the Fourth Republic was riddled with a succession of unstable governments. In August 1954, the French National Assembly rejected the EDC and with it fell the political framework of the EPC. This was a significant set back for those favouring a 'fast track' to a federated Europe and for a time at least cut short the notion of a 'political community'. Despite this, the cause of integration was soon to be given new momentum.

In June 1955, the foreign ministers of the Six met at Messina to re-launch the Community in the economic sphere. Defence and external affairs, which had featured in the EPC plan for political union, were dropped, at least for the moment. The meeting at Messina adopted a proposal 'to work for the establishment of a united Europe by the development of common institutions, the progressive fusion of national economies, the creation of a common market, and the progressive harmonisation of their social policies'.

A committee of experts, again chaired by the Belgian Foreign Minister, Paul-Henri Spaak, was charged with charting the way ahead and the subsequent report of May 1956 bearing his name is an important document in the history of Europe. It set out an approach to economic integration that has continued ever since and was the basis for the two Treaties of Rome signed in March 1957, one setting up the European Economic Community and the other the European Atomic Energy Community (EURATOM).

The EEC had a similar administrative structure to the ECSC, setting up a series of the institutions that are still familiar today, including a Council of Ministers (where member states were consulted and common decisions taken); the Commission (responsible for administering the Treaty and watching over the development and functioning of the common market); the Court (to consider treaty violations); and an assembly (to exercise some parliamentary oversight).

The goal of the EEC treaty was 'an ever-closer union of the peoples of Europe'. The treaty committed its signatories to the creation of a common market within twelve years by gradually removing all restrictions on internal trade, setting a common external tariff for all goods going into the EEC, reducing barriers for the free movement of people, services and capital among member states. There were to be common agricultural and transport policies. A European Social Fund and a European Investment Bank were to be created too. Any disagreements would be set aside for later discussion: the Common Agricultural Policy (CAP) was agreed only in 1969.

At this stage, several phases of European integration can already be identified. Immediately after the war there was enthusiasm for an overtly federal Europe. Nonetheless, the first practical step towards European integration – the ECSC – reflected a more pragmatic approach to a federated Europe. This was confirmed after Messina and the setting up of the EEC after the bolder supranational projects – the EDC and the EPC – had run into a wall. The next project – the Fouchet Plan – was an attempt to go in another direction entirely.

General de Gaulle was thoroughly sceptical about European integration, ridiculing the EDC and playing a significant role from the sidelines in its defeat in the French National Assembly. If he had come to power a bit earlier France might well not have signed the Treaty of Rome, but de Gaulle had to deal with the world as it was and he knew what he wanted in Europe and he thought he knew how to get it. 'Europe is France and Germany; the rest are just trimmings' was just one of his very explicit comments to Adenauer. De Gaulle wanted an intergovernmental union ('Europe des patries') and he got his trusted aide Christian Fouchet[10] to draw up the text for such a proposal. The existing communities (EEC and EURATOM) would be subject to a new political authority and the capital would be in Paris. Macmillan remarked later, after de Gaulle's visit to Birch Grove in 1961, that, 'He talks about Europe, and means France.'

In the summer of 1960, de Gaulle told Adenauer of his plans at Rambouillet. They disagreed about the need to transform NATO, a vital part of de Gaulle's objective to break the ties between Europe and America. Nonetheless, Adenauer did see the Franco-German link as the cornerstone of European security and the German Chancellor went along with de Gaulle because he saw it was a way of bringing him round to at least a confederation of Europe.

The preliminary talks on the Fouchet Plan began in October 1961 and descended into a clash between the French and those who favoured supranationalism. In an attempt to overcome these difficulties, Fouchet and his opposite numbers in the Six were asked to draw up statutes for a political union characterised as a 'Union of Peoples'. The main institutions of the Union were to have been the Council, the Assembly and the Political Commission. The Council, made up of Heads of Government or by Foreign Ministers, was normally to meet three times a year and its decisions were to be made by unanimity. This can be seen as a precursor of the European Council that came into operation formally in December 1974. The Assembly was to be made up of delegations from the national parliaments and was essentially consultative. The real government of the Union would be the European Political Commission that would sit in Paris and be made up of senior civil servants from each of the member states and be accountable to their governments.

The only real opposition came from the Dutch and (later) from the Belgians. The Netherlands, always wary of the Franco-German steamroller, would not countenance the Fouchet Plan unless Britain was first admitted into the planned political union but, in early 1962, de Gaulle hardened the French position. He suggested that the Council's decisions should not be binding for a country that had taken no part in them and he put a line through four words covering defence that referred to 'strengthening the Atlantic Alliance'.

De Gaulle was not looking for agreement. He announced his veto of the British application to join the EEC on the morning of 14 January 1963, taking even his foreign minister by surprise. On the afternoon of the same day, the Netherlands formally vetoed the Fouchet Plan. A week later, de Gaulle concluded the Elysée Treaty between France and Germany that he had always wanted and had been discussing with Adenauer all along. With that in the bag, de Gaulle no longer needed the institutional framework – 'the trimmings' – provided by the EEC.

Soon after, France withdrew from Europe, embarking on what became known as the policy of the 'empty chair', adopted for a variety of reasons but primarily over a dispute about financing a common agricultural policy. The empty chair effectively paralysed the EEC for two years until the so-called 'Luxembourg compromise' of 1965, enshrining a national veto in most areas of activity, and this remained in place until 1986. The motor of political union had stopped and economic integration had stalled too.

By the early 1980s, although the planned customs union was in place, all sorts of barriers remained to the creation of the common market envisaged in the Spaak Report and the Treaty of Rome. In response, two of the most important steps in the process of integration were introduced: the launch of the European Monetary System, which will be addressed in the next chapter, and the Single European Act (SEA).

The key driving force was Jacques Delors, who became President of the EU Commission in 1985 and who thought that the single market could only be completed with institutional reform that reduced the power of the veto on the Council and strengthened the power of the supranational Commission. The Commission issued a white paper in 1985 and the following year the Single European Act (SEA) was signed, coming into force in 1987 after ratification by national legislatures.

The most important goal of the SEA was to complete the single market (which was why Mrs Thatcher supported it, as will be seen in Chapter 5). The aim was the creation of 'an area without internal frontiers in which the free movement of goods, persons, services and capital is ensured'. This was to be completed by the end of 1992 and involved the removal of all remaining physical barriers (such as customs and passport controls at internal borders), fiscal barriers (mainly in the form of different levels of indirect taxation) and technical barriers (such as conflicting standards, laws and qualifications). This meant that the Commission and the Council of Ministers had to agree to a massive amount of new law that then had to be applied at the national level. In the event, the deadline came and went without all the proposals being implemented. Nonetheless, the single market went into force in January 1993 with the understanding that the backlog of legislation would be cleared as soon as possible. In practice, the single market still awaited completion a decade later.

But the SEA had wider implications too since, although it only increased the powers of the European Parliament and the Commission to a small degree, it did involve a large extension of qualified majority voting (QMV) in the Council of Ministers on single market issues. The SEA also gave Community institutions responsibility over new policy areas such as the environment, research and development and regional policy that had not been covered in the Treaty of Rome. It gave legal status to European Political Cooperation (an informal process that had sought to promote foreign policy coordination) so that member states could work towards a European foreign policy and cooperate more closely on defence and security issues. The SEA also made economic and monetary union an objective.

Delors also pushed forward the social dimension of Europe: the Treaty of Rome had provided for the development of a Community social policy, but this had been left in the hands of member states and very narrowly defined. This changed and, in 1989, the Charter for the Fundamental Social Rights for Workers – otherwise the 'Social Charter' – was adopted. This emphasised general social-policy goals and it was subsequently attached as the 'Protocol on Social Policy' to the Maastricht Treaty that was signed in February 1992.

The Maastricht Treaty represented a change in the integration of Europe. The power of the centre increased. In addition to agreeing a timetable for the single currency by January 1999 and extending EU responsibility over a number of areas, including consumer protection, public health policy, transport, education and social policy, the Maastricht Treaty created a European Union (EU) with three 'pillars' (something that was to be dissolved in the proposed constitution drawn up in 2004). The first pillar was the 'European Community' and brought together the three pre-existing communities (EC, ECSC and EURATOM). The second and third pillars consisted of two areas in which there was to be more formal intergovernmental cooperation: a Common Foreign and Security Policy (CFSP) and Justice and Home Affairs (JHA).

In the first pillar, the Commission had the monopoly on the right to initiate legislation; there was widespread use of qualified majority voting (rather than unanimity) in the Council; there was an active role for the Parliament and uniform interpretation of Community law by the Court of Justice. The second and third pillars were retained within an intergovernmental framework where the Commission's right of initiative was shared with member states or confined to specific areas of activity, the Council generally acted unanimously, the European Parliament was purely consultative and the Court of Justice played a more limited role too.

However, although the second and third pillars were apparently squarely based on intergovernmental decision-making, the centre continued to accumulate further power. This came about in a number of ways, through modifications to the Treaty: the 'Protocol on Social Policy' was incorporated in the Amsterdam Treaty (1997); further extensions of qualified majority voting; the Nice Treaty (2001) extended this to about thirty new areas; or transfers from one pillar into another. For example, the Amsterdam Treaty transferred asylum and immigration from the third or intergovernmental pillar to the first or Community pillar. As a result, the third pillar covered 'police and judicial cooperation in police matters' with a facility that allowed member states to transfer areas of competence. This process was complex, but its existence meant that in time all areas concerning justice and home affairs might be brought within the Community framework.

On top of this, continued extension of community power or 'competence', the method of intergovernmental cooperation was modified. The Amsterdam Treaty introduced the concept of 'enhanced cooperation'. This allowed a group of countries to cooperate with the national veto (the 'emergency brake') removed except in foreign and security matters. The provisions for enhanced cooperation provided cover for sub-groups of the EU to undertake deeper integration among themselves without the approval of all member states, at least in the first and third pillars.

The Treaty of Nice increased the scope for further Community involvement into areas previously in the competence of member states with the attachment of the 'Charter for Fundamental Human Rights' (CFHR). This was a very sweeping document, putting into a single text such traditional rights as the freedom of assembly and the right to property with other more narrowly focused ones such as the right to 'a high level of consumer protection' and 'the right to good administration' and many others. The Nice Treaty also included a 'Declaration on the Future of the European Union', calling for a 'deeper and wider debate about the future of the Union'. At the European Council meeting in Laeken in December 2001, a 'Convention on the Future of Europe' was established. It deliberated for sixteen months, finally delivering a 'Draft Treaty for establishing a constitution for Europe' to the governments of the EU who considered it at an intergovernmental conference in Brussels at the end of 2003. This broke up without agreement but discussions on the constitution were resumed in the spring of 2004.

The implications of the proposals outlined in the EU constitution for the way Britain is governed were controversial and will be addressed later in this book. What is not in dispute is that in addition to breaking some new ground, the draft constitution consolidated the closer economic and political integration that has been a feature of Europe ever since Robert Schuman and Jean Monnet launched their plan for the European Coal and Steel Community. Over most of that time Britain had sought to resist the prevailing trend, initially by staying out of the ECSC and the EEC and later as participants, by swimming against the tide of further integration. One effect of the draft constitution and the discussion it provoked in 2003 and 2004 was to make people in Britain more aware of what had been agreed on their behalf by their political leaders since they were last consulted in the 1975 referendum.

Chapter Four

The Birth of a Currency

Earlier Proposals
for Monetary Integration

In October 1997, Gordon Brown said, 'In order for monetary union to be right for Britain, the economic benefit should be clear and unambiguous.'[1] In June 2003, when the Government announced its economic assessment, Tony Blair said that, 'When we come to say that this is the right thing to do for this country, it will be on the basis that we have done the economic analysis.'[2] Economic and Monetary Union and the desire to create a zone of currency stability within Europe have a long history, but the political implications have never been in much doubt. As the Bundesbank has noted, EMU 'needs a more far-reaching commitment in the form of a comprehensive political union for it to be permanent'.[3] But EMU has also been political in another sense: in the process of achieving the long-standing goal, the actual operation of monetary policy became intensely politicised – while in Britain the trend has been the other way since 1997 – and it is important to know why since, as will be clear in later chapters, the desire to politicise the operation of monetary union remains prevalent in Euroland.

When the EEC was founded, currency stability among its members was based on the Bretton Woods Agreement of 1944 and the linchpin was the dollar (convertible into gold) against which other currencies were permitted to fluctuate within margins of +/- one per cent of agreed central parities. These parities could be altered from time to time if economic circumstances demanded it, but in essence participating European currencies were stable against each other.

The Bretton Woods system came under increasing pressure in the late 1960s, in essence because the dollar liabilities of the USA continued to expand while its gold assets remained constant or in decline. The result was that either the USA curbed its balance of payments deficit, which would damage world growth, or the deficits would continue, undermining confidence in the system itself. Both the French and German currencies suffered considerable turbulence on the foreign exchange markets, proving unable to stay within the fluctuation margins around the dollar. This produced large swings in parities within Europe and, against this background, the European Council decided that economic and monetary union (EMU) should be a long-term Community objective and the European Commission took the initiative, with Raymond Barre, the Commissioner responsible for economic and financial affairs, bringing forward specific plans. The 1969 Barre Report proposed that macroeconomic coordination be increased and that the fluctuation margins around the currencies of the Six should be eliminated as the first step towards fusing them into a single entity.

Early differences emerged between the French (and Barre in Brussels) and the Germans. The former favoured the rapid freezing of exchange rates, arguing that this would itself promote the degree of convergence between the different economies that was necessary for a single currency. Germany argued the opposite case, proposing convergence as a precondition to a later locking of exchange rates. These two contrasting views remained in place thirty years later, as will be seen in Chapter 13.

In March 1970, a study group was set up under Pierre Werner, the Prime Minister and Finance Minister of Luxembourg and a well-known advocate of closer monetary integration, and the subsequent Werner Report set out the path to monetary union in three stages, beginning in January 1971 to be completed by 1980. The first stage would be directed at getting the economic underpinnings right and preparing the ground for any institutional development that might be necessary. The second stage would consolidate the economic and institutional progress of the first, leading in the third stage to the irrevocable fixing of exchange rates and finally the adoption of a single currency. During the first two stages, the domestic economic policies of member states would be increasingly closely coordinated and there would need to be 'an economic centre of decision' but spelling out what exactly this meant was deemed beyond the remit of the Report. In parallel, there would be a progressive narrowing of currency fluctuation bands.

Gaullist opposition meant that France only went along with first stage (1971–1974) but in March 1971 the Council of Economic and Finance Ministers (Ecofin) duly agreed to complete EMU 'during the coming decade', though only the first phase was elaborated. Member states committed themselves 'from the beginning of the first stage and on a permanent basis' to intervene to ensure that their currencies fluctuated against each other by less than the existing margin allowed against the dollar.

The new arrangements were known as the 'snake' as the currencies were tied to one another and not just the dollar. In May 1971, the continued weakness of the dollar forced Germany and Holland to float their currencies despite the opposition of other members of the EEC, especially France. In August 1971, the dollar itself became a freely floating currency, and the whole Bretton Woods system of cross-rate parities against the dollar effectively collapsed.

The Smithsonian Agreement at the end of 1971 was a last-ditch effort to shore up the edifice. It widened the range of agreed margins against the dollar and would have allowed intra-European currencies to fluctuate against each other by about nine per cent (since they could move plus or minus 4.5 per cent against the dollar). However, this was deemed excessive and a number of European governments determined to tie their currencies more closely together by limiting their margins against the dollar to 2.25 per cent. Since the 'snake' was still wriggling within a tunnel derived from the Smithsonian margins against the dollar, the system was known for a time as the 'snake in the tunnel'. Within a year, the currencies of four countries (Britain, Ireland, Denmark and Italy) had withdrawn from the system and the reduced 'snake' lost its 'tunnel' when Bretton Woods finally imploded in 1973. For a time there was an attempt by some countries to limit currency fluctuations within Europe by sticking to the 'snake', but it didn't last. The French franc left in January 1974 (returning in July 1975 only to quit again in March 1976) and Werner's goal of establishing EMU by 1980 was officially abandoned in December 1974.

The 'snake' ended as a collection of smaller currencies, including some non-EEC countries, linked in what was effectively a deutschmark zone and even within this grouping there were several changes in parities. Western Europe was thus split into two camps. On the one hand, those countries around Germany (Benelux, Denmark, Norway and Sweden) that had agreed to restrict movements of their exchange rates against each other (their 'bilateral rates') within a margin of plus or minus 0.75 per cent and, on the other hand, the rest. For Germany this helped protect its competitiveness when the dollar was weak but the effect was limited because the three other biggest economies in Europe were not part of it.

The idea of a 'zone of currency stability' in Europe was revived in 1977 by Chancellor Helmut Schmidt and President Giscard d'Estaing, and given an important push by the President of the EU Commission, Roy Jenkins. The result was the proposal for the European Monetary System (EMS), the formal framework containing the Exchange Rate Mechanism (ERM). At the core of the latter was the aim of limiting fluctuation between any two currencies to plus or minus 2.25 per cent around a central parity. Policies of the countries concerned had to respond if bilateral fluctuations between their currencies tested the agreed limits.

Before the new system could get underway, however, two issues needed to be resolved between Germany and France. One was the proposal for the European Monetary Fund. The details of the EMF were never spelt out, but it was seen by the French as a forum to monitor exchange rate arrangements. However, the Bundesbank was concerned that this would lead to the gradual politicisation of monetary policy with more pressure on the strong currencies than on the weak ones to bear the burden of exchange rate adjustment. A compromise was agreed whereby the EMF and its role would be held in abeyance until a second stage of the EMS that was scheduled to start at most two years after the inception of the system. In the event, when the time came and despite the clear agreement of the European Council in December 1978, to the fury of the French, Chancellor Schmidt was too weakened by political and economic problems to overcome the opposition of the Bundesbank and the potential threat of a challenge in the constitutional Court. The EMF proposal came to nothing, but the inclination to 'manage' currency markets remains a feature of French policy today.

The second difference between France and Germany centred on the role of the European Currency Unit (ECU) in the ERM. Essentially, the ECU was a composite 'basket' of currencies in the EMS system weighted according to size of the participating economies. The French wanted to express exchange rate obligations in terms of the ECU rather than in terms of exchange rates against the deutschmark, as this would downplay the Bundesbank's leadership of the system. This was unacceptable to Germany and Holland. At a Franco-German summit at Aachen in September 1978 it was agreed that compulsory intervention would be triggered, as in the 'snake', only if the bilateral limits between two actual currencies were reached. The ECU would be described as the 'centre of the system' and all central rates would be expressed in terms of ECU: a feature that was meaningless in practical terms but important symbolically for the French.

The ERM came into operation in March 1979. The original members were Germany, France, Italy, Holland, Belgium, Luxembourg and Ireland; these countries were joined later by Spain in 1989, by Britain in 1990 and by Portugal in 1992.The history of the ERM can usefully be divided into four phases: 1979–1983, 1983–1986, 1987–1992 and 1992–1993.

The first period was characterised by divergent economic policies and high rates of inflation with substantial differences between countries. There were frequent currency realignments, no fewer than seven changes of central parities in four years. The first, involving France, was in 1981 following the election in May of François Mitterrand, who had talked of 'making a clean break with capitalism' during the election campaign. Not surprisingly, when he was elected capital flowed out of France and the franc was devalued in October 1981. However, in several respects the process set a pattern for the future. First, the decision was taken at a political level between France and Germany rather than the Monetary Committee of the EMS, which was formally responsible for running the system and which was essentially presented with a fait accompli. Secondly, the change was presented as primarily a deutschmark revaluation rather then a devaluation of the franc. Thirdly, in the person of its Finance Minister, Jacques Delors, France insisted that the franc was not singled out for devaluation, so the lira followed suit (although it had devalued alone only a few months earlier) with Italy's government given little say in the matter.

However, French domestic policy – which some commentators have described as 'socialism in one country' – didn't change and budget and current account deficits deteriorated. Further devaluations followed in 1982 and again in 1983. The latter was presented as a 5.5 per cent revaluation of the deutschmark and a 2.5 per cent devaluation of the franc. The reality was that there had been a thirty per cent devaluation of the French franc in the space of about eighteen months and, under pressure from Germany, France adopted targets for its current account deficit, bringing about a massive turnaround in French domestic policy.

This ushered in the second phase of the ERM, roughly from 1983 to the end of 1986 or early 1987. In this period in the lexicon of the Mitterrand Government, 'socialism' was replaced by 'Europe' and a key element holding the link between the French franc and the deutschmark, a policy that became known as the *'franc fort'*. This policy was stuck to, with two exceptions following the National Assembly elections in March 1986 that led to a period of 'co-habitation' between the Socialist in the Elysée and Jacques Chirac at Matignon. Prime Minister Chirac devalued the franc, first in 1986 and again in early 1987.

The ERM was formally symmetrical in that its main feature was the bilateral parity grid. If one currency reached margins of plus 2.25 per cent (or six per cent in the case of Italy and later Spain, Britain and Portugal) against another, the second had by definition reached a margin of minus 2.25 per cent against the first. However, although the duties, rights and obligations of the strong currency were formally identical with those of the weak, the strong currency was always under much less pressure to react. In practice the ERM worked asymmetrically and, by the end of 1986, the ERM had become an undeclared deutschmark zone: the other currencies simply pegged their currencies to the deutschmark. The Bundesbank thus provided the monetary policy 'anchor' to the system. It called the shots.

The French wanted to change this and attempted to do so during the next phase of the ERM. In early 1987, the French pressed for technical 'improvements' in the ERM arguing that the resources available to central banks for countering speculation had to be increased. France wanted regular monitoring of exchange rates and interest rates, as well as other economic policies in Europe and in the rest of the world. This led to the Basle-Nyborg Agreement of September 1987. In principle this agreement somewhat reduced the asymmetry of the system, so that France could claim some vindication for its point of view. However, the agreement also established a presumption that when a currency came under pressure the first step would be for the relevant country to take measures to keep it within the appropriate bilateral band. If necessary, this might be followed by an adjustment of interest rate differentials between the two countries concerned and only in the last resort by intervention in the foreign exchange markets with central banks buying the weak currency.

Between 1987 and 1990, there were no realignments in the ERM and in June 1988 the EU agreed to complete the liberalisation of capital movements by June 1990. However, despite the appearance of calm and stability, beneath the surface there was an intense struggle between the Bundesbank and those who wanted to dilute its power over monetary policy in Europe, notably the French.

One problem for the Bundesbank in 1987 was the Louvre Accord, under which the finance ministers of the G7 (USA, Japan, Germany, France, Britain, Italy and Canada) agreed to 'stabilise' the weak dollar, through a series of target zones with other major currency blocs, the deutschmark and the yen. From the Bundesbank's perspective, this brought too much 'politics' into its sphere of activities and could undermine its leadership in the ERM.

Faced with what it saw as a worrying growth in German money supply, the Bundesbank raised interest rates in early October 1987 for the first time since 1981. This provoked a strong reaction in the USA from James Baker (the Treasury Secretary) and led to fears that US interest rates might have to rise, adding to other problems preoccupying financial markets. Wall Street and other stock markets around the world crashed and the US Federal Reserve pumped huge amounts of liquidity into the markets. The fall in the dollar and the initial (misplaced) fears that a stock market crash would lead to recession led to strong downward pressure on the French franc against the deutschmark.

This faced the Bundesbank with a dilemma, since the French were determined not to devalue. To defend the franc, the Bundesbank could reverse the rise in interest rates or alternatively intervene on a large scale in the foreign exchange market (selling deutschmarks and buying francs). The former would be a climbdown and the latter would risk further boosting German money supply. In November 1987, the Bundesbank reduced interest rates and the French raised theirs. The Bundesbank could justify the move as a reaction to effective appreciation of the deutschmark against the dollar, but in other respects the coordinated response to the franc's weakness represented an end to its period of undisputed leadership of the ERM.

A further indication of the way the wind was blowing was Chancellor Kohl's agreement to set up a Franco-German Economic and Finance Council (EFC) where the two countries' finance ministers and central bank governors would meet twice a year, with the first meeting in March 1988, to discuss matters of common interest. Two months later, the French Finance Minister, Edouard

Balladur, presented the Council of Economic and Finance Ministers (Ecofin) with proposals for a European Central Bank, in effect replacing the Bundesbank with a joint (essentially Franco-German) central bank with power well beyond the consultative EFC. This set the background to the Hanover European Council in June 1988 that established a study group of experts, including central bank governors, under the chairmanship of Jacques Delors. The result was the 'Report on economic and monetary union in the European Community', better known as the Delors Report. It stated that EMU would 'require further major steps in all areas of economic policy-making.' More coordinated or common policies would be necessary because economic and monetary union 'would eliminate an important indicator or policy inconsistencies among Community countries and remove the exchange rate as an instrument of adjustment'.

The Report recommended that EMU should be established in three stages and it was only in the final one that currencies would be permanently locked together and a single currency adopted. The first stage was aimed at producing greater convergence of economic performance through strengthening economic and monetary coordination within the existing institutional framework. The prime responsibility for coordination would be the Ecofin meeting, when appropriate, with the Chairman of the Committee of Central Bank governors. The Delors Report suggested there should be a clear indication of the timing of the first stage (and that this should be no later than July 1990 when capital controls were due to be removed) but it did not set deadlines for the other stages. A new European institution, the European System of Central Banks (ESCB), was to take responsibility for the common European monetary policy. It would be independent of instructions from national governments and would have two main parts: a central body, the European Central Bank proper (although the name is not in the Delors Report) and the existing national banks that would be responsible for carrying out the decisions of the ESCB council.

The Delors Report accepted that within EMU there would be scope for independent policy-making by national government, but argued that there must be limits to this if the whole system was not to be destabilised. These limits would apply particularly in the area of fiscal policy where binding rules would be required for budget deficits and borrowing. The Delors Report was forwarded to Ecofin in May 1989 and the next month the European Council in Madrid agreed to convene an Inter-Governmental Conference (IGC) – to be held at Maastricht – to discuss amendments to the Treaty of Rome in order to implement the Report's recommendations.

The Delors Report appeared to offer the prospect of a smooth transition from the ERM to monetary union, a 'glide path' as it came to be called, particularly after the 'informal' European Council in Rome in October 1990 that set out a timetable for the second and third stages of EMU. Paradoxically, this glide path made the system more brittle and thus played a part in the demise of the ERM in

1992. Prior to this, the ERM had been a system that tolerated realignments and so could bend under strain, but after Delors the perception grew that realignments were no longer part of the system. This created problems for all participants: but particularly for those that were or were about to become uncompetitive within the system. In the next few years their predicament worsened and in response to the emerging crisis, the special relationship between France and Germany was consolidated.

In November 1989, the Berlin Wall fell. The opening of the borders between East and West Germany constituted an asymmetric shock to Germany.[4] East German workers and their families would travel to the West, many of these would be well educated and mostly more enterprising and all would speak German. They would have to be housed and would want to buy western cars and consumer durables. This would put pressure of demand on the resources of West Germany. Increased demand and improved labour supply would raise the rate of return on capital in West Germany and lead to an investment boom that would put further pressure on available resources in the short run. The deutschmark was bound to appreciate in real terms either through a nominal appreciation or higher inflation in Germany.

Then, at the beginning of 1990, Chancellor Kohl announced that the deutschmark would be the currency for the whole of Germany and that ostmarks would be converted into deutschmarks, one for one. Since the unofficial rate had been about seven to one this meant that the wages and welfare payments of East German families were suddenly worth seven times as much in terms of West German goods and services as they previously had been. This was bound to create further demand for goods and services in the new Germany, yet the output of the union as whole would fall since East German firms were made even more uncompetitive by the one for one rate of exchange.

The net impact would be a rise in inflationary pressure in Germany as a whole. Normally, the policy response would have been a rise in interest rates and an appreciation in the deutschmark nominal exchange rate to switch demand from overstretched German sources of supply to foreign ones. This was certainly what the Bundesbank favoured, but Chancellor Kohl had agreed with Mitterrand that the bilateral exchange rate between the deutschmark and the French franc was sacrosanct and the Bundesbank knew this. For example, in October 1989, the then President of the Bundesbank, Karl Otto Pohl, said that realignment within the ERM was desirable, but acknowledged that Germany's 'most important partners' within the system (in practice that meant France) had ruled out the use of the exchange rate as a means of adjustment (that is Germany's). A little later, Hans Tietmeyer (State Secretary at the German Finance Ministry and already scheduled for the Bundesbank directorate at the beginning of 1990) said there would be no realignment, at least not within the narrow band, effectively calling for a devaluation of the peseta and the lira.

With realignment ruled out, the inevitable real appreciation of the deutschmark following unification could only take place through a rise in German inflation above the rates of inflation in its trading partners. That's exactly what happened. However, once Chancellor Kohl was re-elected in 1990, the Bundesbank determined that the absolute rise in German inflation had to be brought under control and reversed by raising interest rates. Within EMU the only way to secure a real appreciation of the deutschmark was if Germany's main trading partners had even lower inflation. If the French would not allow a deutschmark revaluation, then they would have to endure the recession that would reduce their inflation rate. This was bound to have distressing economic implications for France, where inflation was already below Germany's, but even more for those countries that needed to improve their own competitiveness – countries such as Britain, Spain, Portugal, Italy and Denmark. The final phase of the ERM had begun.

On 2 June 1992, Denmark failed to ratify the Maastricht Treaty and this shattered the idea of a steady glide path to EMU. Money had flowed into Spain and Italy, in anticipation of a convergence of bond yields between the 'periphery' and those of the 'core'; it now poured out again putting the peseta and lira under pressure. That increased when the Bundesbank raised its discount rate in July to a record 8.75 per cent. The differential between short-term interest rates in the USA (where rates were at levels not seen since the 1960s) and Germany inevitably put further downward pressure on the dollar and upward pressure on the deutschmark (taking others in the ERM in its wake). The severe monetary squeeze on other countries in the ERM that were already in serious economic trouble became intolerable.

The unravelling began from outside the ERM but spread to the core. On 8 September, the Finnish Government floated the markka (which had been pegged to the ECU for 15 months) and it immediately fell thirteen per cent against the deutschmark. This put pressure on the Swedish krona (also pegged to the ECU) and Sweden's central bank put up short-term interest rates despite the fact that its economy was in the third year of recession, trying to cope with a banking crisis and speeding towards a crisis in its public finances.

Faced with this unravelling, the German and French governments were determined to ring-fence the lira and the Bundesbank agreed to unlimited intervention, well beyond any obligations of the ERM, to defend the French franc if it came under attack from currency speculators. On 13 September, there was a realignment of the lira by seven per cent when the Italian Government had wanted fifteen per cent. After a brief respite, the lira came under renewed pressure and the pound became exposed too after an interview in which Helmut Schlesinger, President of the Bundesbank, had said the realignment of lira was not enough to restore order to the system.

On 15 September, the Italian lira dropped below its new central ERM parity, sterling fell to its lowest level against the deutschmark and the Spanish peseta slipped below the central ERM rate too. On 16 September, sterling was under huge pressure and the Bank of England intervened on a massive scale, putting interest rates up to twelve per cent and then a proposed fifteen per cent. The stock market rose on the news, indicating that it did not think such a policy was sustainable and a little later the pound was suspended from the ERM. The day became known as 'Black' or 'White' Wednesday, depending on whether the eventual exit of sterling was seen as a 'bad' or 'good' thing. The Italian lira followed the next day. The Spanish peseta was devalued by five per cent within the ERM on 17 September, and the French franc, Danish krone and Irish punt all came under heavy pressure. On 19 September, Britain announced that it would not return to the ERM until 'fault lines' had been reformed. It did not return. On 20 September, France narrowly approved the Maastricht Treaty but unemployment was twelve per cent, public finances were deteriorating and the French economy was on the edge of its deepest recession since the Second World War. Three days later, just one week after the exit of the pound, massive pressure on the French franc was only fended off by virtually unlimited intervention from the Bundesbank buying Francs and selling Deutschmarks.

On 19 November 1992, Sweden abandoned pegging the krone to the ECU and four days later the Spanish peseta was devalued again, this time with the Portuguese escudo, both by six per cent. On 10 December, Norway abandoned its peg with the ECU. On 1 February 1993, after a cut in rates in Britain, the Irish punt was devalued by ten per cent in the ERM. This put further pressure on the French franc. The Bundesbank provided some relief to Paris by cutting German interest rates, although German inflation was over four per cent, but on 13 May the Spanish peseta was again devalued, followed by the Portuguese escudo, by eight per cent and 6.5 per cent respectively. In the summer, there was renewed pressure on the Danish krone (Denmark's unemployment was twelve per cent and rising) and the French franc (despite the defeat of the Socialists in elections to the National Assembly) and heavy intervention by both the Bundesbank and the Banque de France to support the French currency. In July, the markets were selling all the weak currencies against the deutschmark, so tensions spread to the whole system. This intensified when the Bundesbank failed to cut interest rates at its meeting at the end of the month with particularly heavy selling of the French franc. To counter this, the Banque de France intervened heavily in the foreign exchange market, buying francs. But the game was up.

On the weekend of 31 July–1 August 1993, various meetings took place to shore up the edifice. These included a stormy one between the German and French finance ministers and central bank governors in Paris, Waigel and Schlesinger on the one hand and Alphandery and de Larosiere on the other. The next morning, Sunday, the Monetary Committee met and later in the day so did all finance ministers and central bank governors in the EMS, including the recently appointed British Chancellor of the Exchequer, Ken Clarke. This gathering seriously considered dissolving or suspending the ERM, but in the end decided, with Ken Clarke in support and opposed to suspension, that ERM bands would be 'temporally widened' to plus or minus fifteen per cent and the central rates maintained: the ERM 'en vacances'. The meeting also reaffirmed the commitment to the Maastricht timetable for EMU.

The Maastricht Treaty (1992) built on the proposals set out in the Delors Report, but it set a clear timetable for each stage of monetary union. The first stage (membership of the ERM) was assumed to have begun. The second stage was scheduled for January 1994 and this 'transitional' phase was set out in some detail. In particular, from 1994, a European Monetary Institute (EMI) was to be set up to promote the coordination among national central banks on technical matters related to monetary union. During stage two, member states also committed themselves in general 'to endeavour to avoid excessive government deficits'. However, countries that wanted to go ahead with stage three had to achieve a 'high degree of sustainable convergence' with reference to four specific economic criteria: a national budget deficit of less than three per cent of GDP, a public debt less than sixty per cent of GDP, a consumer inflation rate within 1.5 per cent of the average in the three countries with the lowest rate, long-term interest rates (bond yields) within two per cent of the average in the three countries with the lowest rates, and a record of keeping their exchange rates within approved ERM fluctuation margins for two years.

At the Madrid Council in December 1995, EU leaders decided to call the new currency the euro and agreed that countries would be assessed for entry on these economic criteria in May 1998. When the time came, in theory all countries had met the budget deficit goal, though there was considerable massaging of figures, especially those of Italy and France. Germany was particularly concerned about the lack of budgetary discipline and at the Amsterdam Council in June 1997 got agreement to the Stability and Growth Pact (SGP) that was intended to set up a procedure to prevent 'excessive deficits'. But Maastricht included a clause that allowed countries to qualify if their debt-to-GDP ratio was 'sufficiently diminishing and approaching the reference value at a satisfactory pace'. In the event, despite the fact that the national debt in Belgium and Italy was nearly twice the target, all members of the EU apart from Britain, Denmark (both of which had met all four criteria), Greece (which joined in 2001) and Sweden, announced their intention to adopt the euro.

On 1 January 1999, the euro was officially launched and participating countries fixed their exchange rates and the new European Central Bank began overseeing the single monetary policy. The final stage began on 1 January 2002, when euro notes and coins became available and national currencies ceased to be legal tender in Euroland on 1 March 2002.

CHAPTER FIVE

The Odd Man Out

Shifting Attitudes in Britain towards Europe

Towards the end of 2001, Tony Blair said that, 'the history of our engagement with Europe is one of opportunities missed in the name of illusions.'[1] This familiar theme implied that only a Colonel Blimp mentality had prevented Britain being fully engaged in Europe from the start.

Illusions of one sort or another have no doubt played a part in Britain's relationship with the rest of Europe, but from the very beginning there have been some real differences of interest and perspective that can't be dismissed. Furthermore, the political, economic and monetary integration that has taken place in Europe during the past fifty years, outlined in the previous two chapters, had political reverberations in Britain, including the shifting allegiances of individual politicians as well as within and between the main political parties, and these may themselves be worth recalling briefly to put current political alignments into perspective.

To explain Britain's ambivalence towards Europe it is necessary to go back to the beginning. At the end of the Second World War, Britain was in a very different position to that of most other countries in Europe. On the continent there was revulsion at what had happened in the 1930s when national democratic regimes had been incapable of resisting fascism. In 1945, all the countries of core Europe had suffered military defeat and occupation in, or as a result of, the Second World War. Britain was in a very different position. It was not a failed state that had been defeated and occupied, though it had paid a very heavy price for defending the rest of Europe, and there was no lack of faith in its political institutions.

This affected Britain in at least two ways. First, supranational solutions that reduced national sovereignty had much less appeal than elsewhere in Europe. Secondly, after the Second World War, British politicians had very little confidence that they could rely on the countries of Europe to provide an adequate defence against the new threat to Britain's security. Very soon after the end of the war, Russia rather than Germany became the main European problem for Britain, but in France foreign policy continued to be dominated by the German question. This different perspective was reflected in discussions on the aborted European Defence Community (see Chapter 3). For France, the EDC was primarily a way to address the problem of the rearmament of Germany by placing it in the context of a European army. For Britain, the EDC was a means to another end: the creation of a Western European force, including Germany, which Britain would not only join but which could, along with the USA and therefore NATO, help defend Europe against the Soviet Union. When the EDC project collapsed in 1954, Britain swiftly moved to put in place arrangements that ended allied occupation in Germany and provided for direct German membership of NATO.

By 1954, the *Pax Americana* had provided the security assurances that Western Europe needed, and it was obvious that there would not be any fighting between the countries of the region. Furthermore, the democratic regimes installed after the war appeared well rooted, and Western Europe enjoyed increasing prosperity. Despite this, the desire for further political and economic integration with supranational rather than national emphasis continued and this was something that Britain was still reluctant to embark on.

What worried the British Government in 1955 was that the Messina Conference (see Chapter 3) had thrown up the possibility of a new politically united bloc that was probably protectionist. Between 1956 and 1958 the aim of the British Government was to create a free-trade area encompassing the whole of Western Europe. There would be no supranational institutions and politically the area would remain anchored firmly to NATO and the Atlantic Alliance. However, the Six had other ideas (though in Germany Ludwig Erhard[2] favoured a free-trade zone, including the British, rather than the European Economic Community) and France was particularly hostile to a free-trade area. Faced with the impossibility of constructing a Europe-wide free-trade area, Britain opted to set up an organisation separate from and alongside the Common Market. This came into being in 1959 as the European Free Trade Area (EFTA) or 'the Europe of the Seven' (Britain, Switzerland, Sweden, Denmark, Norway, Austria and Portugal). But although the arrangements in EFTA were purely economic, its role, as seen by Britain, was political: it was the way that Britain hoped to resurrect its idea of a wider free-trade area, through some form of association between EFTA and the Common Market. However, the idea of association got nowhere with the Six (with the French notably hostile to the idea), and the Prime Minister, Harold Macmillan, grew more and more concerned about the political as well as the economic threat to Britain from the EEC.

As a consequence, Macmillan announced the Government's intention to seek Britain's entry to the EEC in the summer of 1961 and serious negotiations began in October, but there was not the slightest chance that France would agree as long as de Gaulle was in power. In pursuing his objective of keeping Britain out de Gaulle was supported, implicitly if not always explicitly, by the Chancellor of the Federal Republic of Germany, Konrad Adenauer. Adenauer was not anti-British, though he did find 'difficulty in seeing Britain as a European state'.[3] Adenauer was a German patriot who distrusted Prussian values and saw Prussian militarism as responsible for the rise of Hitler. As a Catholic Rhinelander, Adenauer looked west and to some extent this explained his ambiguous attitude to German unification after the Second World War. In the years after the First World War, Adenauer periodically gave support to the idea of a Rhenish Republic and at one time he put forward the notion of a West German republic, incorporating land on both sides of the Rhine, though support for both abated as the threat of French annexation receded. At the end of the Second World War, even before the western zones of occupation had been brought within one control, Adenauer held a series of secret (and strictly speaking illegal, since Cologne was in the British zone) meetings with French officials about cooperation between the Rhineland and France. None of this made him the poodle of de Gaulle (or anyone else), but both men believed that the Franco-German relationship was unique. As de Gaulle told Adenauer at Rambouillet there was 'no European reality other than France and Germany; the others mean nothing, they don't count'. Adenauer's loyalty to and support for the General allowed France to take a tougher line with Britain when it sought entry to the EEC than would otherwise have been the case. De Gaulle's 'non' was possible only because of Adenauer's implicit 'nein'.

De Gaulle's veto in January 1963 was inevitable. Tony Blair has said that 'nothing could be more misguided' than the notion that de Gaulle was anti-British. In fact, he said, de Gaulle:

> was an admirer of Britain and grateful for our support in World War II. But he had painstakingly given France back her dignity and self esteem. He mistrusted American intentions and saw Britain as a Trojan horse for the United States and a brake on the necessary strengthening of Europe. So, even though, ironically, he was closer to Britain in his conception of what Europe should be than virtually anyone else, he blocked Britain.[4]

This interpretation of de Gaulle was amazing. For a start, Britain's preoccupation with extending free trade was anathema to de Gaulle. It might have been true that the General was grateful for Britain's 'support' – 'liberation' might be a better word – in the Second World War, but he had a pretty odd way of showing his gratitude. In fact, de Gaulle was imbued with a heavy dose of Anglophobia that even his biographer suggested was the 'result of excessive attachment to a past in which Hastings, Agincourt, Waterloo and Fashoda loomed large'.[5] De Gaulle's childhood was clouded by French humiliation at the hands of the British at Fashoda eight years after his birth. His rejection of Britain in 1961 was brutal and motivated by historical revenge. When Paul Reynaud, de Gaulle's champion in 1940, wrote protesting at de Gaulle's treatment of the old ally and friend, he received an envelope addressed to him personally in the General's hand. There was nothing inside, but on the back were the few words: 'If absent forward to Agincourt or Waterloo.'[6] The notion that de Gaulle's view of Europe was close to Britain's, other than in an entirely superficial way, is fantastic. The Fouchet Plan (see Chapter 3) was designed to exclude Britain, undermine NATO, and confirm the Franco-German directorate with the administration based in Paris. For de Gaulle, the purpose of Europe was clear: 'Europe is a means for France to regain the stature she has lacked since Waterloo, as the first among the world's nations.'[7] De Gaulle began his memoirs with the phrase, 'All my life I have kept alive a certain idea of France.' He also kept alive a certain idea of Europe: founded on French hegemony, with Germany a junior partner. To argue that de Gaulle might have changed his attitude and Britain entered Europe if London's policy had been different amounts to suggesting that Britain should have abandoned its history and interests for those of France.

While Macmillan was trying to take Britain into the EEC, the Labour Party, led by Hugh Gaitskell, was in principle agnostic and in spirit largely hostile to entry, though it included a core of passionate pro-Europeans, including Roy Jenkins, who were amongst Gaitskell's closest friends and supporters. The Labour Party's attitude stayed on similar lines after Harold Wilson defeated the pro-European George Brown for the leadership after Gaitskell's death. Labour's 1964 manifesto had 'five conditions' for entry, rather as it has five economic tests for EMU forty years later, and in government Wilson remained very cautious about the issue. However, buttressed by a large majority after the 1966 election, Wilson started to shift his ground towards Europe, though opposition within the Cabinet and Labour Party remained strong. Wilson and George Brown toured the capitals of Europe between January and March 1967. In May 1967, with unanimous Cabinet support, Wilson announced a second application for Britain to join the EEC. In November, de Gaulle delivered a second veto.

However, de Gaulle disappeared from the political scene in 1969 (after losing a referendum on the role of the Senate and the regions). This produced a temporary reaction in Paris under President Pompidou against his rigidly Franco-German approach, helped by an apprehension that Willy Brandt was taking Germany on a more independent line than any other post-war Chancellor. This brief departure from the traditional French line coincided with an equally brief period in office of a British Prime Minister, Edward Heath, who was anti-American and right from the start went out of his way to distance himself from any notion of a 'special relationship' with the USA.

Heath had prepared the ground well and his personal commitment to Europe certainly carried weight with the Six. The Conservative manifesto in the general election in June 1970 promised only to negotiate: 'no more, no less'. Talks began immediately after Heath entered No. 10. (Wilson had also been planning to have another try and most of the official team in Whitehall that Heath used had been set up by Wilson.) After strenuous negotiations, Heath signed the Treaty of Rome in January 1972 and Britain entered the European Economic Community in January 1973, but both the main political parties were divided on the issue. In the crucial vote on accession in January 1972, the official position of the Labour Party was to vote against entry, but sixty-nine Labour MPs, led by Roy Jenkins, together with the Liberals, voted with the Government. This offset a rebellion in the other direction by a number of Conservatives and accession was agreed in the House of Commons by just eight votes.

Edward Heath also endorsed the Werner Report (see Chapter 4) and he would have signed up to it when Britain entered the EEC had it been necessary, and to that extent Edward Heath, not Tony Blair, was the first Prime Minister to embrace the principle of economic and monetary union. But a year after taking Britain into Europe, Heath was out of office.

Wilson returned to No. 10 in 1974: in both the February and October general elections Labour pledged to 'consult the people through the ballot box' after new terms of membership had been agreed. Wilson wanted Britain to remain in the EEC but he was still faced with the threat of Labour splits. The renegotiations were largely face saving and got through Cabinet by eleven votes to seven (after much arm twisting). When the Cabinet decision was put to Parliament it received a large majority as a result of Conservative votes: 145 Labour MPs were against and only 137 in favour, with thirty-three abstentions. Wilson contrived to hold the Labour Party together by holding a referendum that allowed members of the Labour Party, including the Cabinet, to campaign for or against entry. During the 1975 referendum campaign most of the political establishment as well as most of the business community and press was lined up in favour of remaining in the EC. In June, the electorate voted to stay in Europe by a large majority (sixty-seven per cent voted 'yes' and thirty-three per cent 'no').

When Jim Callaghan took over from Wilson as Prime Minister in 1976, he avoided any major new engagement in Europe. In 1977, the Government introduced legislation to allow direct elections to the European Parliament, though for Callaghan this was a necessary deal with the Liberals during the

'Lib-Lab pact' more than a matter of principle and more Conservatives voted for the bill (229 out of 280) than Labour members (132 out of 308). Margaret Thatcher, who succeeded Heath as leader of the Conservative Party in 1975, was one of these and she had supported Macmillan's first application to join the EEC in 1961 showing no qualms about the impact on Britain's sovereignty. 'Sovereignty and independence are not ends in themselves. It is no good being independent in isolation if it involves running down our economy and watching other nations outstrip us both in trade and influence.'[8] Mrs Thatcher voted for accession in 1972 and in opposition gave little hint of the later hostility towards Europe, going so far as to accuse Callaghan of being insufficiently *communitaire* at the Paris summit in March 1979, just before the election that brought her to power: 'It would be more to Britain's advantage if he and his colleagues dropped their abrasive and critical attitude towards our Common Market partners.'[9] Some of this could be put down to the tactical considerations ahead of an imminent election and Mrs Thatcher was surrounded by pro-Europeans in the shadow cabinet. Nonetheless, the contrast in tone with what came later when she was Prime Minister, is striking. Europe conflicted with many of her natural instincts, particularly her support for liberalising markets, but when Jacques Delors became President of the Commission she apparently thought that his commitment to what he called 'les quatre libertes' – free movement of goods, services, capital and people – was consistent with her idea of the Community as essentially a free-trade area.[10] Thatcher signed up to the Single European Act, which brought about a large extension to the use of qualified majority voting (see Chapter 3), apparently under the impression that if countries gave up their vetoes, it would be possible to construct a single market open to competition and cleansed of much government interference and regulation. But the use of qualified majority voting was extended well beyond the bounds that Thatcher had expected and, as one of her biographers comments, 'The fact is that Mrs Thatcher "gave away" more sovereignty in 1985 than Heath in 1973 or Major in 1992.'[11] The reasons for this are unclear; it is difficult to believe she did not know what she was signing since it is incredible that she would have done so without reading and understanding the Act. Bernard Ingram, her press secretary, has said that she knew what she as doing: 'I think she knew at the time that she was taking risks… She was taking a calculated risk with a very clear mind.' Jacques Delors recalled that she hesitated and asked for an extra few minutes to think about it before she signed.[12]

When Mrs Thatcher resigned in November 1990, John Major became Prime Minister largely thanks to perceptions of him among Tory MPs that he was less pro-Europe than either of the other candidates and that he was the most likely candidate to defeat Mrs Thatcher's 'assassin', Michael Heseltine. Nonetheless, it was John Major who in his latter years in office found himself under attack from the Eurosceptics in his own party after he had signed up to the Maastricht Treaty.

The political credibility of the Major Government was blown apart in September 1992 (see Chapter 4) by the exit of the pound from the Exchange Rate Mechanism which Major, as Chancellor, had persuaded Thatcher to enter in 1990. In 1979, Margaret Thatcher had chided Callaghan's decision not to enter the ERM as a sad reflection on the performance of his government, and the position of the Conservative Government after the May 1979 election was that it would join the ERM 'when the time was ripe' or 'right' as it eventually became. The new Chancellor, Sir Geoffrey Howe, was one of those most opposed to entry. Britain was self-sufficient in oil and the price of oil had shot up for the second time in a decade, doubling between 1978 and 1980. This was bound to have a different impact on the economy and currency of Britain to those of most other countries in Europe. Furthermore, the new Government's decision to remove exchange controls made an exchange rate target even less appropriate.

In the autumn of 1981, there was a discussion on ERM between Thatcher and Howe followed by a more formal meeting involving other members of Cabinet in January 1982. However, neither the Chancellor nor the Chief Secretary (Leon Brittan, who later became an EU Commissioner and advocate of joining EMU) favoured entry though, according to her memoirs, Mrs Thatcher accepted, 'that when our inflation and interest rates moved much closer to those of West Germany the case for joining would be more powerful'.[13]

One person who had become convinced of the case for entering the ERM was Nigel Lawson and, as a journalist, he had set out his position in a number of articles including several in the (now defunct) *Financial Weekly*. After the election in 1979, as the Financial Secretary, his initial enthusiasm cooled, with him apparently taking the view that with inflation rising sharply, the level of the exchange rate was best determined in the markets. By 1981, he had resumed his previous position and was urging the case on his reluctant boss, the Chancellor. However, Lawson was made Secretary of State for Energy in September and only returned to the Treasury, as Chancellor, after the election in 1983. He took up the issue again, but did not raise it with the Prime Minister until 1985, by which time Geoffrey Howe, Foreign Secretary, was also keen to join. Two key seminars on ERM took place at No. 10, on 30 September and 13 November 1985, and at the latter the Chancellor, Foreign Secretary and Governor of the Bank of England argued the case for joining, but the Prime Minister was not persuaded.

Mrs Thatcher's economic arguments had long been bolstered by the views of her economic adviser, Alan Walters (see Chapter 1). He thought that the ERM was fundamentally flawed – developing what became known as the 'Walters critique' – so that there could be no 'right' time to join. In the end, Walters' very public criticisms of Lawson's exchange rate policy became too much for the Chancellor, who resigned in October 1989.

However, before that, Lawson and Howe had made another attempt to change the mind of the Prime Minister. The Madrid summit in June 1989 was due to consider the implications of the Delors Report and, on the eve of the summit, the Chancellor and Foreign Secretary submitted a joint memorandum to Mrs Thatcher. It argued that Britain should undertake to join the ERM by the end of 1992. This was apparently intended to provide Britain with a stronger base for arguing in Madrid that the second and third stages of EMU be postponed for further examination. Mrs Thatcher was unconvinced by that strategy and did not want to commit herself to an entry date. After a meeting at No. 10 and a further shorter joint memorandum, Lawson and Howe confronted Thatcher on the Sunday morning of her departure for Madrid, and both threatened to resign unless a more conciliatory line was adopted at the European Council the next day. The Prime Minister was forced to tack. At the Madrid Council she made clear her opposition to the three-stage process of the Delors Report, but she made no attempt to kill it. The British accepted stage one, in which all countries were enjoined to enter the ERM.

Howe was sacked from the Foreign Office a few weeks later, taking up the post of Leader of the House of Commons and Deputy Prime Minister. In November 1990, Geoffrey Howe left the Government but by then sterling had joined the ERM under John Major's stewardship at the Treasury, following Lawson's resignation, and he was in a powerful position: Mrs Thatcher had had one Chancellor resign and she was not in a sufficiently strong position to risk another. Major believed that entry to the ERM would be a beneficial anti-inflation anchor and increase Britain's influence on stage two and three of EMU which, like the Prime Minister, he opposed. By March 1990, he was convinced of the case for going into the ERM and through the summer persuaded the Prime Minister not to resist entry, although the timing had to be agreed.

The economic effects of ERM membership and any possible implications for a decision on EMU will be set out in Chapter 10, but the political fall-out was dramatic. Sterling entered the ERM on 8 October 1990 only to exit a little under two years later. By that time, Mrs Thatcher had been forced out of office in the wake of Geoffrey Howe's resignation and John Major had replaced her in No. 10. Against expectations, he won the 1992 election and subsequently negotiated an 'opt-out' from EMU at Maastricht. However, the Conservatives' reputation for economic competence never recovered from the pound's ejection from the ERM in September 1992, although the Labour opposition was equally committed to the system, and the Tories were swamped by Labour's landslide victory in the 1997 general election.

Labour's manifesto stated that any decision about joining the single currency would be 'determined by a hard-headed assessment of Britain's economic interest'. It emphasised the importance of 'genuine convergence' but suggested there were dangers in excluding membership forever. However, any decision by the Government and Parliament to recommend entry would have to be endorsed in a referendum. In October 1997, the new Government set out 'five economic tests' that had to be met before it would recommend sterling entering EMU and effectively ruled out the prospect of entry during the parliament. Labour's 2001 manifesto promised that the five economic tests would be assessed 'early in the next parliament'. This was done in June 2003 and the decision was to postpone recommending entry, but it remained an objective.

Tony Blair's approach to Europe will be set out in Chapter 14, but by the time he had become leader, the Labour Party itself had undergone a transformation in the short time he had been in Parliament. In 1983, the careful handling of Europe by Wilson and Callaghan had broken down. With Michael Foot as leader, Labour committed itself to withdrawal from Europe altogether and it was only under the leadership of his successors, Neil Kinnock and later John Smith, that the party's position altered again. By the time Blair took over, the position of the two main parties had been transformed: Labour was the pro-European Party and in government Blair's objective was to put Britain on an equal footing with Germany and France within the EU, but history suggested that that was not going to be easy.

In the 1950s, the Six represented an acceptable, indeed desirable, configuration of Europe. For France, it was the recreation of the Empire of Charlemagne and an ideal way of taming and using Germany's economic power without having to involve the USA or Britain. For Germany, it held out the prospect of a *Mitteleuropa* (extended to include France) and a way of retaining the idea of a German-influenced Western Europe. For the Benelux countries, the Six reduced the perceived risk, however unlikely, of renewed Franco-German military conflict. Italy was happy to tag along with anything that provided an avenue for its presence in the European Concert of Nations. Italy was also desperate to ensure guaranteed rights of migration to other European countries for its surplus, long-term unemployed workers who might otherwise provide material for a Communist, or at least anti-Christian Democrat, revolution.

The first enlargement of the EEC in 1973 that brought in Britain depended on the fortuitous conjunction of circumstances following de Gaulle's fall from power; Ireland and Denmark joined in Britain's wake. The second enlargement in 1981 brought in Greece, as a bulwark for its return to democracy after the fall of the Colonels, quickly followed in 1986 by Spain and Portugal for similar reasons. This was followed in 1995 by the third accession of Sweden, Austria and Finland.

The striking thing was that de facto Franco-German control of the EU had been unaffected throughout these successive enlargements: any policy that was opposed by both had no chance of materialising and any policy that was supported by both became reality. Sometimes personalities had been important and there had been serious differences between the two countries, indeed periods of disharmony between France and Germany had sometimes been as important as periods of harmony in determining the path that Europe followed.

There were differences even over the introduction of EMU, but it represented a triumph for attitudes that had been predominant in both countries since 1945. France was determined to tie down Germany, particularly its economic power. Chancellor Kohl went along with this because of his own concern about the potential economic power of the new Germany and the ghosts from the past that it might reawaken. However, despite changing personalities and differences from time to time, the fact remained that within the EU, the Franco-German relationship was something more than a typical bilateral relationship, it was 'special'; and despite its ups and downs, it remains so.

In 2004, ten new countries of the former Communist bloc joined, which took the membership of the EU to twenty-five and could alter the political balance within the EU; but enthusiasts in Britain for entering EMU suggest that it is only by joining that Britain will achieve equal status and influence with France and Germany. The validity of this claim and that of the central issue of influence will be assessed later in the final section of the book after the economics of EMU have been examined thoroughly.

PART THREE

The Economics of Europe

CHAPTER SIX

You Can Be Serious

The Case for Entering EMU

Most proponents of Economic and Monetary Union believe there are political as well as economic advantages from entry, but the two are at least analytically separate, and this chapter only sets out the economic case that is put forward; the politics will be dealt with later in the book.

For the sake of simplicity, the economic case for Britain's entry can be grouped under three headings. First, the macroeconomic benefits, secondly the microeconomic and supply-side advantages and finally the view that, in one way or another, membership of EMU gives Britain more 'influence' within the EU and in the wider international economy.

The macroeconomic case for entry often starts with the historical performance of the British economy since the Second World War. When the fighting stopped, Britain was effectively bankrupt, but its economy was still the biggest and strongest in Europe and living standards were higher than anywhere else on the continent with the exception of Switzerland. Once the immediate post-war economic crisis had been surmounted with the help of the Marshall Plan, economic recovery gradually got underway in Western Europe and gained pace through the 1950s and 1960s.

These have been called the 'Golden Years'. In much of the world there was a period of unprecedented economic growth, generally low inflation, high levels of employment and rising living standards. Britain shared in this, but slipped down the league table. Other European economies had faster rates of growth in GDP and attempts to match them in Britain were held back by balance of payments 'constraints' or were brought to a shuddering halt by regular sterling crises or periodic devaluation. From the mid 1960s, Britain's standard of living was overtaken, first by Germany and then by other countries in Europe.

If this was bad, there was worse to come. In the 1970s, the international economic framework established at Bretton Woods fell apart. The world was hit by two major oil shocks, inflation accelerated and GDP growth slowed. Unemployment rose to levels not seen since the 1930s and, despite the discovery of oil in the North Sea, Britain seemed to do worse than most. Inflation reached twenty-five per cent and the IMF had to be called in to bale the country out in 1976. The characteristic volatility of the British economy continued in the following decades. There were two deep recessions in the early 1980s and early 1990s, and a boom in between that took inflation into double digits. To bring the economy back under control, interest rates were stuck at fifteen per cent for a whole year.

For the proponents of entry to EMU, the lessons are clear: those responsible for managing Britain's economic affairs had produced one of the most volatile economies in the industrialised world. Rates of economic growth and living standards had fallen behind others in the EU. Much of the country's manufacturing industry had disappeared. Britain's economic sovereignty didn't amount to a row of beans and would mean even less with the growing integration of the world economy. The removal of capital controls made it impossible for a country the size of Britain to defy the whims of the international capital markets or face down the currency markets in which $1,200 billion crosses the exchanges each day. An independent monetary policy was just 'the right to devalue'.

EMU appears to offer a stable alternative. More than half Britain's trade in goods is with the economies of the EU. Within EMU this would be carried out in what would in essence be a domestic currency as, of course, it would be for all participants. This would encourage the growth of intra-European trade and in turn help bring about faster growth of national income and living standards.

Arguments about cyclical divergence between Britain's economy and Euroland are dismissed. These are reckoned to be no greater than already exist between some participating members and, in so far as they exist, are best reduced by closer integration with the economies in EMU. It is argued that joining EMU would lead to mortgage finance shifting to the continental model of a fixed rather than floating rate basis, thus reducing the importance of housing in interest-rate policy decisions, making it easier for Britain to adapt to the same interest rate as the rest of Euroland.

Within a single currency, Britain would benefit from low and stable inflation. The Bundesbank achieved this in the past and, since it was the model for the European Central Bank, similar success can be expected from the new bank in

Frankfurt. Low inflation and the removal of the exchange rate risk, by reducing the premiums demanded by investors, would also help to ensure that both short-term and long-term interest rates were lower inside EMU than outside. Some proponents of entry argue further that interest rates will be more stable because they will reflect the average monetary conditions across Euroland rather than the particular conditions of individual countries.

Finally, because it will be part of a large, continental-sized economy, Britain will be free of balance-of-payments constraints and therefore much less vulnerable to external shocks such as the Asian crisis in 1998 and any slowdown in the USA.

Whatever the macroeconomic gains in the form of greater stability claimed for EMU, most proponents view them as merely the basis for more significant microeconomic benefits and these can be summarised briefly. The single currency reduces the cost of converting money from one national currency to another, the so-called 'transaction' cost. The single currency also makes it easier to spot price differences for the same goods or services than when there are separate currencies. This increased 'price transparency' will benefit consumers in lower prices and put pressure on businesses to cut costs and restructure to become more efficient. The removal of currency risk encourages trade across frontiers and enables companies, big and small, to invest with greater confidence not only within domestic markets but to plan their operations on a pan-European basis. The result should be faster rates of economic growth, more efficient businesses, higher productivity growth and rising living standards. For its supporters, the single currency underpins the single market and in particular the single market for capital. As the latter develops it is envisaged that it will bring its own benefits in cheaper finance for those trying to raise capital and broaden the investment horizon for both individuals and institutional investors. If Britain remains outside EMU, it is argued, the country will miss out on these benefits. And this implied threat to its prosperity and standard of living is accentuated by two characteristics particular to the British economy: success in attracting huge amounts of foreign direct investment and the importance of the financial services industry in the economy as a whole. Both these two features are seen to be especially vulnerable if sterling stays out of EMU.

The single currency certainly does cut transaction costs. For British tourists or business travellers, this may have been their first experience of the euro. Anticipating these benefits before EMU was launched produced some bizarre calculations involving the apocryphal tourists who travelled through each European country in turn exchanging an original £100 for each successive currency. By the time they returned home, after spending nothing except the commission on exchange transfers, they would have barely half the amount. Even enthusiasts for EMU saw that this is pretty eccentric behaviour, given the wide availability of credit or cash cards and it is not a significant part of their case. However, because it is a 'benefit' that is easier to get across than some others, it plays a part in the propaganda war by proponents of entry. Of course, if there are other reasons for not adopting the euro, British travellers to the continent have the best of all worlds. They keep the economic benefits of an independent monetary policy, but can change pounds into just one currency for travel anywhere in Euroland.

However, for companies operating across national boundaries, savings in transaction costs are real enough. Generally speaking, the cost is small for large companies that enjoy the benefits of scale, but can be large for small and medium-sized businesses. Estimates on the overall savings vary, but most reckon it to be around 0.2 per cent of GDP, not insignificant but probably less than the cost of conversion to the euro, though these costs are a one-off while the purported benefits are ongoing.

As already noted, however, proponents of entry do not put forward the savings in transaction costs – which are themselves being reduced by technological change – for business or tourists as a strong reason for Britain's entry. Most enthusiasts of the euro see greater potential in the increased price transparency that it introduces. In EMU, it will be easier to compare prices across national markets and this, it is argued, will benefit both consumers buying the end products or services and those making or providing them, since it will be easier to identify the best sources among suppliers. Even before EMU, a lot of this was happening already and would have continued without the single currency. Individual consumers can use the internet to find the prices for a whole range of goods such as books and cars, and it is not very difficult to make the calculations to compare prices across different countries, but so far the biggest impact of the internet has been business to business rather than business to consumer. Businesses use it to seek out suppliers as well as a marketing tool. EMU, it is argued, could help this process along within Euroland, even though it is part of a wider picture, not least because business and consumers often want to make comparisons outside Euroland, with the USA, the Far East or Eastern Europe.

It is generally accepted that within Euroland greater price transparency is unlikely to make much difference to smaller, cheaper items. However, proponents of entry argue that the impact could be significant in the case of consumer durables like washing machines and cars, though even for some basic durable goods there are different local or national consumer preferences that can lead to some surprisingly segmented markets.

Even with separate national currencies it has always been relatively easy for people living close to national frontiers to compare prices for goods and to travel the short distances to take advantage of any marked differences. It is argued that a single currency should accentuate this effect.

The euro's proponents argue that it will increase trade and investment. Investment decisions can concentrate on the underlying worth of a project and not be distracted by fear that the gains will be wiped out by swings in the value of the currency. This will not only make businesses more confident about investing in their domestic economy, but also make it easier for them to think of broadening the scope of their activities beyond traditional boundaries.

All sorts of businesses will be affected by the euro, but some are thought more likely to benefit than others. Beneficiaries should include companies with long-lived assets, which will include much of manufacturing, since there is more chance of currency fluctuations during the period these assets are being used. Financial businesses and the trading sector more generally, are also exposed through their investment but to a lesser extent. Smaller and medium-sized firms should also benefit, since for them the cost of attempting to manage currency risk and cash management involving several currencies can be disproportionately large. Of course, big or small, these purported benefits of EMU only apply to companies primarily trading in European markets. For companies whose trade is more internationally dispersed, the benefits of eliminating intra-European currency uncertainty will be less clear.

For its supporters, therefore, the single currency completes the single market. The euro reinforces competitive pressures and accelerates the process of industrial restructuring as businesses consolidate their activities in the most productive plants and genuinely start to regard the EU as a single market. Companies will compete with each other head-on without currency barriers. Price lists will be increasingly pan-European. The more competitive market that this creates will lead to opportunities for operating across a much larger customer base, whether as a large or a niche player, but it also poses threats. The inefficient or unresponsive company will find itself under pressure from the more intense competition. There will be winners and losers with some companies going to the wall. Over time, the effect will be to reduce the issue of country as a factor in decisions about investment or location, bringing about the geographical concentration of certain industries in particular regions, similar to the USA. In the EU, these may stretch across national boundaries, but if economic forces are allowed to operate there is no reason why some industries need have any presence in some countries at all.

Proponents of EMU see particular scope for restructuring in banking and financial services. The presence of many currencies has acted as a barrier to competition: a bank wishing to enter the market of another member country needed to establish systems allowing it to operate in the other national currency, and this raised the cost of entry. By removing this barrier, EMU is seen to strengthen competitive pressures among the various national banking systems. This will lead to incursions by banks across national borders into markets previously dominated by domestic banks. The loyalty of the local customer-base to familiar names will not be eroded quickly, but in the medium to longer run, stronger competition is expected to transform the European banking system. Within Euroland, efficient banks will expand both by organic growth and by mergers and takeovers; inefficient ones will reduce their activities or be taken over. Proponents of EMU anticipate the emergence of a pan-European banking system in which rationalisation will provide cheaper and more efficient service with wider choice, the ultimate beneficiary being the customer, whether household or business.

Larger businesses are expected to benefit from the development of a single market for capital that will reduce the cost of raising finance and give investors, whether individual or institutional, a wider choice of assets in which to invest their savings.

Many investment funds are understandably cautious about the foreign-exchange composition of their investments relative to their liabilities. To limit their exposure, they retain a domestic currency or home bias. EMU should alter this because it enlarges the area where funds can invest without exposure to foreign currency risk.

There has already been an impact in bond markets and this is expected to continue. It is easier to compare relative value in fixed-income markets than in equity markets and in any case equity culture is not well established in much of continental Europe among either institutional or private investors. But, proponents see the gradual integration of equity markets brought closer by EMU. As businesses operate more and more across the EU they will want to raise capital on a pan-European basis too and this will encourage the development of genuinely pan-European equity markets and exchanges.

Against this background, enthusiasts argue that Britain has much to gain from participating in EMU, and much to lose from staying out. If Britain stays out, it is said, it will miss out on the benefits to growth and trade, just as it missed out on the benefits of the EEC when tariff barriers were brought down. British companies will be challenged on at least two fronts. First, some of the large UK-based companies will gradually come to see the euro area as 'home' with implications for future investment. Secondly, the anticipated restructuring within Euroland will lead to larger and stronger EU companies that UK firms will find it harder to compete with in the domestic market.

Proponents argue that the important thing is to join up. The need to enter is reinforced by two features that are particular to Britain. First, Britain has succeeded in winning a large share of foreign direct investment. This has revolu-tionised parts of manufacturing. Some of the highest-profile investment has been in car production, but the phenomenon goes well beyond this into high-tech and all kinds of services, particularly banking and financial services. This, it is argued, has been the result of Britain being a member of the EU and would be put in jeopardy if investors thought that Britain would not enter EMU.

The second feature peculiar to Britain is the contribution of financial services to the economy and the status of the City of London as the dominant financial centre in the European time zone. This is seen to be at risk on two fronts. First, the 'natural' economic effect resulting from not being in the dominant currency of the EU and the likely shift to financial centres, like Frankfurt, that are. Secondly, the inability to influence decisions outside EMU with the result that regulatory and other changes might make London a less attractive place to do business.

Proponents of entry put a great deal of emphasis on 'influence'. They deny that Britain surrenders any important degree of economic sovereignty by entering EMU. Rather, they emphasise the advantage of what is called 'pooling' sovereignty which they claim increases the ability to influence events. This reflects the view that, in the modern world, national economic sovereignty for an economy the size of Britain is an illusion.

Entry to EMU would remove the freedom of the Bank of England to set interest rates for Britain, which would be set by the ECB in Frankfurt, but there would be a representative from the Bank of England on the ECB. Britain would surrender the ability to set its own interest rates but gains the opportunity to have a voice in setting the level of interest rates across Europe and, as one of the largest economies in Euroland, the views of Britain's representative on the ECB would carry weight. For enthusiasts, this would be more important than whether or not the decision was one that would be judged appropriate had it been made by an independent Bank of England free to set interest rates on domestic criteria. Of course, the two could be the same but that would be a coincidence that is irrelevant to the case made by those arguing for Britain's entry.

In addition to being a participant of the ECB, membership of EMU is put forward as a means to increase Britain's influence in other ways too. Europe's finance ministers meet regularly in the EU's Council of Economic and Finance Ministers (Ecofin) and this is one of the most powerful ministerial committees in the EU. Ecofin members include countries in and out of EMU, but since the start of the euro the finance ministers of participating countries have met together in the euro group before the full meeting. It is early days to judge the impact of this, but it is expected that the inner core will gradually establish a dominant position within Ecofin and that the 'ins' will decide on a policy line that will be very difficult for the 'outs' to resist.

It is further argued that membership of EMU will give Britain greater clout on the international economic stage as part of a currency bloc that will challenge the international role of the US dollar. In the future, proponents of entry to EMU see the international financial system being run by a group of three: the USA, Japan and Euroland. If it remains outside the single currency, Britain will be marginalised. Inside EMU, Britain will have a voice in decisions affecting the international economy.

A further influence is also claimed for membership of EMU. Joining means being a full member of the European club, so Britain will be better able to affect the outcome of EU policies across the board. There is no specific area where being member of EMU brings extra authority in terms of votes, for example, but the argument is that, by ceasing to be a 'semi-detached' member, Britain's voice and economic size will have more authority and influence within the EU.

For enthusiasts for entry, dithering over the timing is just part of the familiar pattern that has characterised Britain's dealings with Europe since the 1950s. Britain always joins in the end but, by doing so late, it denies itself the opportunity to influence the course of events at a formative stage, and the claims for EMU have not been understated. Less than two years after its launch we were told that, 'the euro is ushering in a golden age of European prosperity' and 'outside the euro, we lose power, influence and sovereignty.'[1]

This sounds very heady stuff but, for proponents of EMU, the macroeconomic benefits are real but secondary. However, it is the macroeconomic framework claimed for EMU that creates the conditions for the microeconomic gains. It is the greater stability provided by the single currency that allows the other purported advantages – for growth, investment and jobs – to come through. If, however, EMU does not produce greater stability, the case for Britain's entry is holed too. This will be addressed later, but first, a slightly different but related argument needs to be considered. It is said that in an era of mobile capital, economic sovereignty has no meaning for a country the size of Britain: it will be tossed about like a cork on the waves between the major currency 'blocs'. The attempt is futile. 'An independent monetary policy (both interest rate and exchange rate) is a diminishing asset in a world which is becoming increasingly interdependent'.[2] This proposition is central to the case put forward by proponents of EMU and the next chapter will examine it in detail.

CHAPTER SEVEN

Back to the Future

The Implications of Globalisation

It is a popular view that the world's economies are more integrated than at any time in history. In many respects this is true. For example, the speed of travel and communications today is unprecedented. It is, though, only fair to point out that the nineteenth century saw some big strides too; for example, the fall in transport costs following the spread of railways after 1860 and the large-scale introduction of steamships from 1870. But in other respects the degree of integration has only recently regained levels last achieved before the First World War.

In the nineteenth and early twentieth centuries, international trade was the engine of economic growth, but it was not the only force bringing economies together. As new areas of the world were opened up and settled, there were huge opportunities for borrowers and lenders of capital to earn potentially very high rates of return on their investments.

During the latter decades of the nineteenth century, vast amounts of capital flowed from the older industrialised countries of Western Europe, especially Britain and France. It was attracted to the developing countries of the 'periphery' like the USA, South America, Russia and many other regions of the world where new discoveries and opportunities were unfolding.

For the last third of the nineteenth century, much of the world was also brought together by its monetary system: the Gold Standard. Gold had long been used to provide the basis for coinage in certain countries, but it was only after 1870 that it triumphed over silver and became the international norm and involved countries defining their currencies in terms of gold, maintaining fixed exchange rates against each other. During this period, there were huge returns to be had and capital flowed across the world to take advantage of the opportunities presented as countries and continents opened up to commerce and settlement. It was a very turbulent time economically and with exchange rates fixed it was only the massive shifts in population between continents that allowed the international economy to adjust as well as it did. There was more voluntary migration in the century after 1815 than at any time in history, before or since. About sixty million people left Europe for the Americas, Oceania and south and east Africa, and the bulk of these movements took place in the second half of the century with particular surges in the 1870s and 1880s. Even with these flows of population, economies periodically came off the rails and the Gold Standard was suspended and, to that extent, investment boomed and prosperity spread despite fixed exchange rates, not because of them.

The interconnected economic system was brought crashing down by the First World War. In between the two world wars, trade integration was pushed back and the stream of private sector capital dwindled to a trickle, and the weakness of fixed exchange rates was exposed in an aborted attempt to return to Gold. Some countries held on longer at lower fixed exchange rates, but this merely exposed the difficulty within any system of fixed exchange rates of deciding what is the right level for a currency.

After the Second World War, the Bretton Woods conference set up institutions to facilitate international trade and investment but in a framework that restricted private-sector capital flows, and these remained almost non-existent despite the steady growth of world trade in the forty years or so after 1945. Only gradually were controls on capital movements removed and offshore financial markets expanded under the impetus of the oil crisis in 1973. International capital movements accelerated in the early 1980s under the influence of the administrations of Ronald Reagan and Margaret Thatcher and financial markets became truly global in the early 1990s after the collapse of the USSR.

Essentially, the last twenty years of the twentieth century saw the re-emergence of a genuinely international form of capitalism that constituted a key feature of economic 'globalisation'. To that extent, the year 2000 was more like 1900 than 1950. Today, private-sector capital flows are huge and this has transformed the economic parameters for everyone. Of course certain other aspects of nineteenth-century capitalism are intolerable today and the policy mistakes of the 1920s and 1930s are also now better understood, but politicians of all persuasions have to understand the implications of what has happened in the past twenty years.

Capital flows in search of the highest rates of return, and the most significant development to arise from the re-emergence of large movements of private capital was that 'rates of return' were restored as an economic discipline for the first time since the outbreak of war brought the last period of genuine international capitalism to an end in 1914.

After 1945, not only was private capital not free to move from its home country in search of higher returns elsewhere but, even within individual countries, with the partial exception of the domestic USA, 'rates of return' had very little practical role. For a long time, capital markets hardly existed in the countries of continental Europe and most technological change came from the USA. European societies put great store on solidarity and cohesion and this was understandable in the wake of the Second World War and in the face of the Cold War, but it meant that much business was conducted in the absence of what would now be regarded as properly functioning markets. Much investment was carried out by the state beyond any market framework and improving the efficiency of markets was not a priority. Some of the more obvious forms of central planning were eliminated, as when price controls were removed by Ludwig Erhard in the western zones of Germany, but more often varieties of controls, regulations and interventions distorted and disguised the true rate of return on investment.

This changed in the mid 1980s. Not everyone embraced liberal economics or globalisation with enthusiasm, but there was a widespread removal of capital controls and private capital was set free to flow from one country to another in search of the highest rates of return.

Apart from restoring the importance of rates of return in economic decisions, freely flowing capital has had other effects. First, the relationship between the anticipated rate of return on investment and the anticipated real rate of interest re-emerged as the driving force for economies. Secondly, the freedom for nominal exchange rates to appreciate and depreciate becomes the pivot for stabilising output and jobs within and between individual economies.

At its most basic, capitalism is driven by expectations. Decisions are made on the basis of views about the future, though, of course, the anticipated outcomes may or may not be fulfilled. The distinction between anticipated (ex-ante) returns and actual outcomes (ex-post) can be confusing. However, it is critical to understanding the significance of the re-emergence of huge international flows of capital and the role played by exchange rates in stabilising individual economies. When there is a rise in the realised rate of return, profits rise. It is therefore natural that anticipations of future rates of return lead to similar expectations as well as providing the incentive to borrow to finance investment. This may seem obvious in the case of firms, but it is also rational for households. When there is a rise in the rate of return, there will be a rise in the rate of productivity growth and with it real earnings. It thus makes sense for consumers to purchase durable goods in anticipation of higher future incomes.

It is the borrowers that get the investment cycle going; business and households borrow to invest. However, those with responsibility for investing the world's savings also have to make decisions in advance of the results. Savers and investors are brought together in the market place and after the event, as an accounting identity, investment always equals total (domestic plus foreign) saving. Whether this result is achieved at levels of investment and savings consistent with internal balance in a particular economy – neither recession nor overheating – is a matter of monetary policy. If interest rates vary appropriately with rates of return, internal balance can be maintained when rates of return change. But for interest rates to be free to move appropriately, the exchange rate must be free to move up and down. This important conclusion can be taken in stages:

- The implications for interest rates of the free flow of capital;
- the impact of changes in rates of return on the appropriate level of interest rates;
- the implications for the exchange rate and hence for those deciding monetary policy.

Sometimes people say, 'I don't mind the euro, but we want to be able to set our own interest rates.' This is not an option. It is only by retaining the freedom for its currency to move up and down that a country can set its own interest rates. A single currency, the same money for all countries, means a single interest rate and the removal of the means of bringing supply and demand into some sort of balance or equilibrium.

In a world where there is no currency or inflation risk it is easy to see that interest rates in any one country cannot diverge from the world level. Assuming some sort of overall balance between economies, a rise in interest rates in one country would attract flows of capital from others which would then be obliged to raise their own interest rates to stem the tide. Alternatively, if a country cut its own interest rates, money would flow out and it would be forced to reverse the decision and put its rates back up to the world level. This is obviously artificial, but serves as an illustrative first step on the way to important conclusions for the world that most certainly does exist.

In the real world, inflation rates differ between countries. Investors take this into account when forming their views about the profile of 'real' interest rates (interest rates adjusted for anticipated inflation) over a particular time ahead. But the principle is the same as in the illustrative example. Arbitrage is relatively straightforward in fixed-income markets that are liquid so that the anticipated real rate of interest will be equalised across the whole market, and for this to happen it does not require investors to have the same view about the future profile of inflation nor is it essential that the expected rate of inflation of any particular investors be confirmed.

The only way for the anticipated interest rates in one country to be above or below the anticipated world level is if views on the path of a currency are taken into account. Investors 'risk-adjust' their views on the profile of future interest rates in the light of their expectations for the path of the currency over the same period.

This means that if the anticipated real rate of interest in one country is to be above the world real rate of interest, then the currency must be expected to fall. In this case the anticipated currency loss will be offset by a higher anticipated real interest rate. Similarly, the only way that the anticipated real rate of interest in one country can be below the world real rate of interest is if the value of the country's currency is expected to rise. The lower anticipated real interest rate would be offset by the higher anticipated currency gains. The conclusion therefore is that for the anticipated real rate of interest to rise or fall it is necessary for the currency to be free to appreciate and depreciate, and this is very important. The reason being that when there is a rise or fall in anticipated rates of return, the ex-ante real rate of interest needs to be able to move too if an economy is to adjust reasonably smoothly.

A variety of factors influence the anticipated rates of return on capital. These include new discoveries, technological change, changes in the political and legal framework, or reforms in the structure of markets and in attitudes towards them, but when there is a rise in the expected rate of return, certain consequences follow.

First, the impact will be uneven. As noted earlier, anticipated results are not always reflected in actual outcomes. When there is a rise in expected rates of return it very often starts in particular sectors of the economy or perhaps within individual firms. Even if there is a more general cause, say a dramatic shift in business taxation or freeing up of labour markets or the development of some new natural resource, it is unlikely that the actual returns will be the same across the whole economy.

Secondly, expectations are cyclical. A rise in the anticipated rate of return will be followed by a fall. The anticipation of higher returns leads to an increase in investment, but as this is put in place the additional gains from each extra 'unit' of capital spending will decline. There is a fall in the marginal return on capital. When this happens people will anticipate a fall in future returns.

Thirdly, expectations about the future become critical and investment is driven by a sense of optimism. The most successful economies are probably the most optimistic ones too, but optimism can get out of hand.

These three consequences have implications for the appropriate level of interest rates. When there is a rise in the anticipated rate of return, businesses and households are encouraged to spend and borrow to invest. They do this because they expect higher profits or real income growth. This is a rational response because if profits and incomes are expected to be higher in the future, investment in plant and machinery or in consumer durables can sensibly be undertaken without curbing current expenditure. The debt can be financed from future incomes and profits. However, as the money starts to circulate, this 'optimism' is liable to spill across the economy to areas where it turns out there are no improved rates of return. This excessive optimism will lead to unwise borrowing, that is borrowing that will turn out not to be supported by future profits or real income growth, by companies and households. Unless measures are taken, this will lead to an asset price boom (particularly equities and housing) and overinvestment.

This can go on for some time: people get carried away and at this stage in the cycle market commentators can be heard 'explaining' why traditional valuations are old hat and giving rationalisations that 'it's different this time.' However, eventually it becomes obvious that expectations about future returns are unrealistic and businesses and households realise that they cannot finance their unwise borrowings by likely profits and earnings. The trigger for this change in perception is unpredictable, but when it happens it is liable to produce an undue pessimism about future returns to mirror the excessive optimism on the upswing. This deepening gloom may cause more retrenchment than is really required to unwind the overinvestment accumulated in the upswing. The boom is followed by bust.

The important point is that the equilibrium real rate of interest changes during the course of the cycle. As its name implies the equilibrium rate of interest is the one that keeps the economy in overall balance, encouraging the growth of employment and output while keeping the rate of inflation at an acceptable level, neither too high nor too low. When there is a rise in the anticipated rate of return it leads to a rise in the equilibrium real rate of interest. In the same way, there is a decline in the equilibrium real rate of interest when anticipated rates of return decline in the wake of investment coming on stream. During the upswing, therefore, the aim will be to bring about a rise in the average real rate of interest, putting up the average overall anticipated cost of borrowing. This will influence investment decisions since these are affected by shifts in the anticipated cost of borrowing and the anticipated rates of return. But the impact will vary between sectors. It will have no deterrent effect on the more dynamic areas where anticipated rates of return remain high and above the new equilibrium real rate of interest, but it will have a dampening effect on some of the less productive sectors.

This has two big benefits. First, it brings about a better allocation of resources – employment and investment – by shifting them to relatively more productive assets, leading to higher profits and real incomes. Secondly, it helps smooth investment over the cycle. Investment that is postponed when there is a rise in the equilibrium real rate of interest will become an economically worthwhile proposition when this falls in line with expected rates of return as investment during the upswing is put in place.

A rise or fall in expected rates of return brings about a rise and fall in the equilibrium real rate of interest. But, as noted, real rates of interest are set in international capital markets and the only way that the rate of interest in one country can be higher than the world level is if investors expect a fall in the currency of the country in question. However, this is only possible if the currency has previously risen to a level that is in some sense seen as 'unsustainable'. So for an economy to adjust as smoothly as possible to a rise in the anticipated rate of return, the 'spot' value of the currency has to rise too. Similarly, when there is a fall in the anticipated rate of return, a decline in the anticipated real rate of interest is needed. For this to occur there has to be a view that the currency will rise which means that it first has to fall to a point that is 'unsustainable'. When the expected rate of return falls, so too should the 'spot' value of the currency.

The freedom for the nominal exchange rate to appreciate and depreciate is thus essential if the equilibrium real rate of interest is to adjust appropriately to changes in anticipated rates of return, changes that will be a feature in a dynamic economy. It is the relationship between these two variables – rates of return and rates of interest – that drives economies when capital is free to flow across frontiers. And the more dynamic the economy, the higher the expected rates of return, the more important is the freedom for a currency to appreciate and depreciate at appropriate stages in the business cycle.

Of course, markets will always adjust in one way or another but, if a currency is not free to move up and down, the adjustment comes at a price that is much more damaging to output and jobs. If the nominal exchange rate is not free to move up and down, neither can the equilibrium real rate of interest respond to changes in the rates of return. The upswing will spill over into a boom and the downswing into a bust. If the nominal exchange rate can't adjust, the 'real' exchange rate will through higher inflation in the upswing, risks of deflation on the downswing.

The role of currency appreciation and depreciation in keeping economies on a reasonably even keel can be shown in a different way. When the balance between supply and demand is changing within an economy, having an exchange rate that can move up and down allows this to take place in ways that maintains high levels of overall demand to the benefit of output and jobs.

When higher rates of return are expected, businesses and households spend more in advance and in anticipation of higher profits and wages in the future. Domestic savings fall short of domestic investment and the result is a current account deficit. Because of improved expectations about the performance of the domestic economy, the world capital markets are willing and able to provide the necessary lending. Viewed from abroad, high rates of return attract foreign savings. Capital flows in and there is a capital account surplus to match the current account deficit.

From a domestic perspective, households and businesses increase spending in anticipation of higher profits and incomes. The additional spending on

investment goods by firms or by households on houses and consumer durables
leads to an increase in domestic demand. But domestic supply cannot suddenly
adjust – plant and machinery has to be built and installed before it can produce
the output to supply the goods and services.

There may be spare capacity – plant and machinery or labour – that can
meet this additional demand but when this is used up, or if domestic capacity
is limited, the increase in domestic demand will have to be met by imports.
This ensures that some of the excess domestic demand is met by overseas
supply and this diverts inflationary pressures since it is not demand that
leads to inflation but the interaction of (rising) demand and (temporally static)
supply. In this phase of the cycle, imports must rise relative to exports to fill
the inflationary gap. The next phase is different. Additional supply is installed
when new investments are put in place and firms get into their stride, but once
this investment is installed, the demand from businesses and households for
investment goods decreases. Supply increases as demand falls away.

This switch in the supply-demand balance reflects the fact that while the initial
impact of higher rates of return is reflected in increased demand for investment
goods, once in place these create increased supply, a rise in potential output.
In this subsequent phase of the cycle, exports must rise relative to imports to
ensure that there is sufficient total demand to take up all the potential increase
in available output and prevent a deflationary gap developing in response to
the relative rise in potential supply.

A shift towards a current account deficit (capital account surplus) is thus a
natural feature for a developed economy that experiences a rise in the anticipated
rate of return. As the investment cycle progresses, the current account deficit
will swing the other way. This is not to say that a current account deficit is in
itself a good thing. A deficit can become unsustainable: this is not simply a
function of its size, but of the extent to which it alters the relationship between
the rate of interest and the rate of return. This will be covered in more detail in
Chapter 9, particularly as it has affected the USA. For the moment, simply note
that a current account surplus is not necessarily a sign of economic strength
and in a dynamic economy attracting capital it is bound to deteriorate.

How does all this work out in practice? Obviously, real life is a bit messier
than the theory, but the general principles and framework of the theory hold.
Enthusiasts for the euro argue that massive flows of capital have made national
economic sovereignty redundant. In fact, as will be clear from the chapter so far,
the opposite is the case and there is also considerable misunderstanding about
the impact of such flows on currencies. Although there certainly are massive
amounts of capital flowing across the exchanges, a country the size of Britain
can still implement an independent monetary policy with success.

An economy will be helped to adjust if its currency can appreciate and
depreciate and it is only this freedom that allows interest rates to move up

and down. However, the way in which a currency responds to a particular move in interest rates – in extent, timing and even direction – will vary with circumstances. These include the credibility of the particular central bank, views about domestic and foreign interest rates and inflation as well as the efficiency or otherwise of the foreign exchange markets. And the latter can vary from time to time, even in deep liquid markets such as those for the dollar, sterling, yen and euro. However, if a central bank has market credibility, it is more likely that movements in interest rates will be associated with movements in exchange rates in the 'right' direction.

The issue is not whether there is an absolute interplay between interest rates and exchange rates in the sense that a cut/rise in interest rates by a central bank will be followed by an immediate depreciation/appreciation of the currency. Even the textbooks only envisage this with 'other things being equal', a phrase that hides many important and far from innocuous assumptions. The really important thing is the freedom to focus monetary policy – the combination of interest rates and the exchange rate – on domestic conditions.

Prevailing conditions in foreign-exchange markets will affect the balance between interest rates and the exchange rate, but there are some things that a particular central bank can't do anything about. Success – or lack of it – must be judged on results. How this relates to Britain and participating members of EMU will be addressed in subsequent chapters, but for a decade after 1992 the British economy experienced an unprecedented period of stability – decent growth, low inflation and low unemployment – and this was at a time when sterling was free to float.

Currency markets adjust to equalise the rate of return on assets across countries. So if the Bank of England raises interest rates the pound moves to a level where investors expect a future depreciation just large enough to make them indifferent between holding sterling and foreign-currency assets. This means that if the market anticipates interest rates in Britain above those overseas they will price in a depreciation of sterling consistent with this view. It is this expectation of future depreciation/appreciation that allows interest rates in one country to be higher/lower than the world level of interest rates. An exchange rate appreciation takes place because higher domestic rates, relative to interest rates on equivalent foreign-currency assets, make sterling assets more attractive to international investors.

However, it is important to be clear about the process. When the Bank of England raises interest rates the market makers will mark up the price of the pound because they know that sterling assets will be more attractive. It is not the flows as such that are driving the exchange rate. The information that is published on capital flows says very little about their impact on the exchange at least in liquid markets for the main currencies. This can be illustrated by a simple example.

Suppose a government decided to introduce measures to make labour markets much more flexible or restructure and reduce company or capital taxation. Any of these measures would clearly lead to a rise in the anticipated rate of return on investment. But market makers would be just as capable of drawing appropriate conclusions, as would potential investors, so they could mark up the price of the relevant currency before a single flow had crossed the exchanges. The central bank would also be able to judge the implications, and raise interest rates, though the timing of any response would depend on the initial position of the economy. For example, if there was a great deal of spare capacity, the central bank might delay raising interest rates even after clear signs that rates or return had risen, until the gap between actual output and potential output – the output gap – had been closed.

Of course, rises and falls in anticipated rates of return cannot be observed directly and are rarely as clear cut as in the illustrative example above. A central bank may make a judgement about whether or not there has been a change in rates of return, as Alan Greenspan did in the long upswing in the US economy in the 1990s. However, the central bank can really only observe changes in rates of return indirectly, particularly by the pattern of investment spending. And as we have seen the optimism that is generated by higher anticipated rates of return can spread to sectors of the economy and encourage spending by businesses and households where returns do not materialise. Thus any decision on interest rates will be based on views as to whether the overall growth of domestic demand is consistent with maintaining the economy in some sort of overall balance.

Capital flows may impact on the demand for a currency if an investor borrows in one currency to purchase assets in another, or sells assets in one country and then transfers the proceeds into another currency – for example, if an American investor in New York wanted to invest in the UK and borrowed dollars to buy the pounds to make the purchase. However, the investor might just as easily decide to borrow in the same currency as the assets. So the same American investor might decide to borrow sterling to purchase UK assets so that there would be no impact on the pound exchange rate. And it is very easy to borrow currencies like the dollar or pound, yen and euro, because these markets are very liquid.

In illiquid markets it is a different story. In 2001, for example, international investors were attracted by prospects of very high rates of return in the Czech Republic. Capital flowed into the country. Because the market was illiquid, investors could not borrow korunas; they were forced to borrow in foreign currency and buy the koruna, which rose dramatically and for a sustained period even though this was not matched by any new news affecting fundamentals. In other words the currency overshot.

In efficient markets, changes in supply and demand – flows – should not affect the price unless it is associated with news that alters the underlying value. The size of the flows is not the issue. This can be illustrated by a more mundane example. Most people have stood in line at market stalls, perhaps for oranges (or a turkey at Christmas). Sometimes we may be at the head of the queue and at other times perhaps there may be twenty people in front, but prices are not affected by the number of people in the queue or the flows of orders. At the end of a day's trading (or late on Christmas Eve in the case of the turkey), prices will drop. But this is not because of the length of any queue, but due to the fact that by the next day the produce is less fresh (in the case of the turkey perhaps even worthless) so there has been a change in the fundamental value.

In financial markets, price movements caused by non-news can be put right by those operating in the market on the basis of fundamental value. In the earlier example of the koruna, the central bank would be the best bet since it has access to potentially unlimited amounts of its own currency. In liquid markets where borrowing is easier, it is best left to the private sector.

This is important, since the case for retaining an independent monetary policy is not based on a naive assumption that financial markets, including foreign exchange markets, are always efficient. Over the long term, the evidence is that currencies do tend to reflect the economic fundamentals of their respective economies, though no one can be certain about the exact level of an exchange rate that would appropriately reflect them. But it is also very clear that over the shorter term – which can in practice last for quite sometime – exchange rates can and do move a long way from levels that reflect any conceivable interpretation of fundamentals. A currency can overshoot on both the upside and downside, but we need to be clear about the reasons and draw the right conclusions.

First, the policies of governments can play a part in creating conditions for currencies to overshoot. The way in which the mix of policies should be chosen, in particular the balance between fiscal and monetary policy, was the subject of pioneering work by Professor R.A. Mundell.[1] Policy mistakes can have the effect of altering fundamentals and thus the appropriate level of the exchange rate, but some swings in currencies have gone much further than warranted by any credible assessment of fundamentals, with one example often quoted being the surge in the dollar in the first half of the 1980s.

Secondly, many examples of overshooting have followed attempts to fix, 'peg' or otherwise manage exchange rates since, under these sorts of currency regimes, economic imbalances build up until they are unsustainable. The fundamentals are altered. The dam breaks under the pressure – usually recession – and as the fixed exchange rate regime cracks, the markets take the currency well beyond even the new fundamentals. But, more than anything else, it is the attempt to fix that creates the conditions for the currency to overshoot. Two obvious examples of this were the dramatic fall of sterling in September 1992 and the collapse of the Argentine peso in December 2001.

The most authoritative academic work on 'overshooting' is probably that of the late Professor Rudi Dornbusch.[2] In very simplified terms, his starting point is familiar enough. For example, a cut in domestic interest rates lowers the return on domestic assets, thereby making the holding of foreign assets more attractive. In order to keep foreign and domestic assets equally attractive, the price of the foreign currency must increase sufficiently to generate an expectation that it will fall. This future decline in the price of the foreign currency reduces the total expected return on foreign asset holdings and brings it into line with the return on domestic assets.

However, Dornbusch introduced a second-round effect that creates a currency overshoot. This is induced by the fact that the prices of goods do not adjust as quickly as those of financial assets. This means, for example, that an increase in nominal money supply associated with the initial reduction in officially determined interest rates will give rise to an increase in the real money supply. The result is an increase in liquidity that further reduces market-determined interest rates and induces further outflows of capital. The reverse process takes place if there is an increase in official interest rates.

These influences provide useful insights into what might cause currencies to overshoot, but Dornbusch explains overshooting as a rational consequence of price stickiness and so provides no argument to support sterling entering EMU. Indeed, Rudi Dornbusch was very much opposed to British membership of the single currency on both theoretical and practical grounds, commenting that, 'If there ever was a bad idea, EMU is it,'[3] a view he repeated in much stronger language to me in Boston when I met him for breakfast a few months before his death: 'It's crazy, you don't want to join the bad people!'

On the other hand, one advocate of sterling's entry is Willem Buiter,[4] who takes the view that damaging currency volatility is induced simply by the existence of exchange markets: speculation runs rife so the market (for separate currencies) should be shut down. But the same logic would suggest banning stock markets too. A better response is to ensure that the markets work as efficiently as possible and this means acknowledging the nature of the market and the motivations of those operating in it.

The psychology of currency markets is such that traders react to a plethora of influences or fads and the herd instinct periodically takes over. But there are essentially two types of people involved. There are some whose activity is based on an analysis of past, backward-looking data, to spot trends, the so-called chartists. These also respond to day-to-day 'noise' in the market, including rumours, statistical releases and various interpretations of current 'news', hence the term 'noise-traders'. Then there are the fundamentalists who take a view of the underlying economics, and in practice many financial institutions – including hedge funds, the infamous 'speculators' – combine elements of both.

In many respects, large and liquid financial markets are far more efficient than other markets such as those for goods and labour. But in a truly efficient market, as noted earlier, prices react quickly and correctly to a change in demand and supply that is associated with information or news about fundamental value and do not react to non-information that should not affect fundamental value. Of course real markets do not always behave like that, but speculators can play an important part keeping markets more in line with fundamentals. There are many different types of speculators, but in the current context the most important are the so-called 'macro-funds' that focus on macroeconomic developments in the various economies and they have an important role to play in the foreign exchange market, incidentally making most money when central banks or governments attempt to maintain non-market exchange rates.

In order to carry out their function, speculators need to borrow and they can only do this on a sufficient scale in the large liquid markets. They need to be able to borrow large amounts, since they need to be able to ride out the risk that prices may move even further away from fundamental value before being corrected. The longer the time horizon of the speculator and the more aggressive the trading, the more likely prices are to revert to fundamentals. But if speculators cannot borrow enough to enable them to take positions based on their assessment of fundamentals, they will be forced to second-guess the noise-traders and in the process reinforce the trend away from fundamentals.

As noted earlier, there is no necessary relationship between published information on capital flows and the exchange rate, but many commentators often believe that 'flows' do have a direct impact on currencies. One only has to glance at the financial pages of newspapers to see ex-post rationalisations of currency movements. If noise-traders act on similar beliefs, and they do, it will have an effect on the currency. For example, foreign-exchange traders might easily mark up a currency in the wake of news about flows associated with mergers and acquisitions, even though such activity may involve no net purchase of foreign exchange and reflect no change in the fundamentals of the economy concerned. If the speculators, who understand the nature and impact of flows, are able to take a position on fundamentals (in this case selling the currency short) they can make a profit for themselves and at the same time bring the currency back into line with fundamentals. However, if they are unable to operate in this way they will take a less risky route and in the process reinforce the move away from fundamentals and help establish a trend. In this case, the speculator knows that traders will mark up the currency on news about flows so the speculator will go 'long' the currency, pushing it further away from its underlying value.

This is merely a simplified illustration of a wider issue. It is the absence, rather than the presence of appropriate speculative activity, that moves currencies away from fundamentals and periodically causes them to overshoot.

And one of the problems after several macro-hedge funds were wiped out 1998 in the wake of the Russian and Asian crises was the lack of speculative activity by macro-funds. It is no coincidence that this was accompanied by sustained currency misalignments, particularly the yen.

It is clear that currencies can overshoot and it is in everyone's interest that this be reduced, since at certain times this can have some detrimental effects on particular economies. However, in looking for remedies there is need for clarity about the causes. These include prior attempts at fixing exchange rates, domestic policies that are unsustainable – in that they are incompatible with combining any semblance of internal and external balance – as well as the periodic emergence of conditions in the foreign-exchange market that reduce the influence of those taking positions on fundamentals. Whatever the apparent drawbacks, allowing currencies to appreciate and depreciate still helps economies adjust more smoothly than would otherwise be the case. This is particularly true when huge amounts of private-sector capital are free to flow to where anticipated rates of return are highest. And in this environment, the more dynamic the economy, the more attractive it is to capital, the more important that its exchange rate be free to appreciate and depreciate if this dynamism is to be combined with overall economic stability. It is this that membership of EMU prevents and which is the fundamental economic issue at stake.

CHAPTER EIGHT

Mind the Gap

The Impact of EMU
on Its Members

The start of Economic and Monetary Union in January 1999 coincided with
an economic upturn in France and with an upswing in some of the peripheral
economies of Euroland that had been going on for longer. Germany remained
in the doldrums, growing just under two per cent in 1999,[1] but for Euroland
as a whole in the first year of EMU there was solid if unspectacular growth of
just below three per cent, and 3.5 per cent the following year. The acceleration
in 2000 could be explained by the fact that both the two largest economies
achieved decent rates of growth: Germany just over three per cent and France a
little above four per cent. In fact, what Euroland experienced in 2000 was little
more than a cyclical pick-up in Germany and France – the core of Euroland
– that was long overdue and, particularly in the case of Germany, short-lived.
In 2001, Euroland GDP grew just over 1.5 per cent; in the following year under
one per cent; and in 2003 about 0.5 per cent. This meant that in the first five
years of EMU, GDP growth averaged a little below two per cent. In the latter
part of 2003, prospects for Euroland's economic growth improved, but this and
its continuation in 2004 was dependent on the pick-up in demand in the USA
that was generated by low interest rates and a large fiscal stimulus. In his final
days as chief economist at the International Monetary Fund, Professor Rogoff
said that if the Europeans wanted to see an economic recovery, they would
have to watch it on television. This may have overstated Europe's predicament,
but it was not far off the mark.

Much economic commentary about Euroland is expressed in terms of averages for the area as a whole. Data set out in this way is obviously going to be more stable than that for particular countries, but it can also give a distorted picture as to what is happening within individual economies, and within EMU stark divergences have developed, particularly between Germany and some of the peripheral countries. This has produced a convergence of sorts, but different from that envisaged by the proponents of EMU.

It is important to recognise that the Euroland economy does not really exist as a single entity. There are only the twelve separate economies of the countries participating in the system. The ECB sets a single level of short-term interest rates, but individual countries still have to adjust to differing economic circumstances. Enthusiasts for EMU say sometimes that the cyclical divergence between the British economy and Euroland is no greater than divergences within it. This is probably true, but in no way strengthens the case for Britain's entry and the lack of adequate convergence between existing members is one of the reasons that the single currency has already caused problems for some of them. If an economic cycle in one country is more advanced (or behind) others its currency should appreciate (or depreciate) above (or below) its equilibrium level if overall economic stability is to be enhanced. The theory outlined in the previous chapter would suggest that in EMU the adjustment in individual counties would take the form of relative inflation and deflation and an exaggerated business cycle and a general lack of economic dynamism across the continent. What happened in practice?

Certainly, the biggest economy performed indifferently in the first years of EMU, and this was not a new story. Germany has enormous strengths and huge potential, but with the exception of a few years surrounding unification, the rate of GDP growth has averaged less than two per cent per annum for over thirty years. For some of this time its competitive position in Europe was helped by relatively high inflation elsewhere (that is to say there was an appreciation of other countries real exchange rates or a depreciation of the real deutschmark exchange rate). However, this became more difficult from the mid 1980s when its major trading partner, France, determined to get inflation down to and even below German levels while at the same time ensuring that with the ERM the parity between the French franc and the deutschmark were unchanged.

Of course, unification caused its own problems for Germany, but this one-off occurrence itself highlights the economic difficulties created when nominal exchange rates cannot appreciate and depreciate. The initial effect of unification was a positive asymmetric shock (see Chapter 4) bringing an investment boom and a rise in Germany's real exchange rate. Inside the ERM, an appreciation in the deutschmark was ruled out because of a political deal between Kohl and Mitterrand, so the rise in the real exchange rate came through an acceleration of inflation instead. After Kohl's re-election in 1990, the Bundesbank was determined to get German inflation under control, raising interest rates. However, these were inappropriate for a number of other countries in Europe, and with nominal exchange rates fixed within the ERM, the response of the Bundesbank spread recession to the rest of the EU (and eventually to the collapse of the ERM).

However, although the initial effect of German unification brought an appreciation in the country's real exchange rate, the ultimate burden worked in the opposite direction and this was to cause its own problems in EMU. By including the low-productivity former East Germany, unification depreciated the long-run equilibrium real exchange rate for the unified country. There had also been massive subsidies from the West German Government to keep East German firms in operation and large transfers to unemployed East German workers so that the cost to the German budget was enormous. Germany needed a depreciation of its real exchange rate. However, in neither the ERM nor EMU could there be a fall of the nominal exchange rate so the necessary depreciation in the real exchange rate could only take place by differential rates of inflation or deflation between Germany and its trading partners. Since German inflation was already very low (under two per cent per annum between 1995 and 1997 and under one per cent in 1998 and 1999), the partial restoration of German competitiveness could only be achieved by an acceleration in relative inflation elsewhere. This is what happened in the second half of the 1990s as first the Bundesbank (within the ERM) and latterly the ECB (in EMU) set interest rates in an attempt to accommodate the needs of the German economy, but these were not appropriate for some other countries.

Even its proponents recognise that in EMU the level of interest rates is bound to be less suitable for some countries than others. Within EMU, it is inevitable that during the upswing of the economic cycle, there will be countries for which the nominal interest rates set by the ECB are too low for their own domestic conditions. These will be countries that require a higher equilibrium rate of interest than Euroland as a whole to keep their economies in overall balance. Inside EMU, such countries will experience a pick-up in relative inflation, and the process will be reinforcing since high relative inflation means that real (inflation-adjusted) interest rates are lower at precisely the time they should be higher than elsewhere in Euroland.

In the downturn, the position will be reversed. The rate of decline in inflation will be faster in those countries where the rise had been greatest. The result is that even if the ECB is cutting nominal rates, the rate of decline in real interest rates in these countries will be behind the rest of Euroland at the very time they should be falling more quickly. And countries caught in this position will still be losing competitiveness from their higher inflation so that the decline in domestic demand will be exacerbated by a reduction in the contribution to overall economic growth from net exports. Thus, in both the upswing and the downswing, EMU will increase the volatility of the business cycle for those countries that are landed with an inappropriate level of interest rates.

In theory, the ECB has to set interest rates on an assessment of the state of Euroland as a whole but, in practice, the bias of ECB policy has to focus on conditions in the weakest economy. If this happens to be a large economy – as with Germany at the start of EMU – it may get relatively prompt attention. Smaller countries with less weight may have to wait a bit longer, perhaps until there are several in similar predicaments, before they will be able to attract sufficient attention of the ECB. The weakness of Germany at the start of EMU resulted in interest rates being set lower than appropriate for the periphery, albeit not as ideal for Germany as if the Bundesbank had been setting interest rates. In its Annual Economic Review, the EU Commission has made its own assessments on the basis of the so-called 'Taylor Rule'. This is one of the most widely used methods of calculating the appropriate level of interest rates, using factors such as the output gap (the gap between actual and potential output) and the actual and targeted rates of inflation. The Commission concluded that, in 2001, Germany, France and Italy would all have benefited from interest rates on average 0.5 per cent lower, relative to the rest of Euroland, and also that significantly higher rates would have been appropriate for the smaller countries. It was estimated that in Ireland interest rates should have been three per cent higher (four per cent in 2000), 1.5 per cent in Holland and one per cent in Portugal and Finland. If anything, this understated the misalignment of interest rates since the Commission's report was based on GDP forecasts for 2001 that were far too optimistic, particularly about Germany. The result was to reinforce the already strong upswing in a number of countries and their inflation accelerated.

Increased variability in inflation rates is at odds with the stability EMU was supposed to provide, but there are those who see differential rates of inflation as part of the natural process as poorer countries catch up with richer partners in the EU. This is known as the Balassa-Samuelson effect, after Bella Balassa and Paul Samuelson. This is based on the observation that productivity gains tend to be concentrated in manufacturing and hence trading sectors of the economy and the potential for rapid rates of productivity growth are particularly marked during phases of catch-up. These sectors, where prices are determined by international competition, can therefore pay good wages while still remaining competitive. However, these wages will tend to spread to other (non-traded) areas of the economy where prices are determined by a mark-up on costs (particularly wages) so domestic inflation will rise. But this process is not seen as harmful, since external competitiveness is maintained by the pressures from international competition and the fact that (say) the price of a haircut (a non-traded service) is higher in one place than in another doesn't matter. Of course, even if this thesis is accepted, inflation in the non-traded sector of the economy will have its costs: high levels of inflation impede the efficient allocation of resources and have distributional impact too since it will hit those on fixed incomes, including the elderly. Furthermore, if monetary policy is inappropriate, there is more chance that inflation in the domestic economy will be higher than 'warranted' by the spillover effects from the high productivity traded sector. However, this is not the real issue, there is a more fundamental point that the focus on the price level misses: under a regime of fixed exchange rates, like EMU, it is not possible to align real interest rates with rises in the rate of return on investment so that, if there is a rise in the rate of return, it will lead to asset price bubbles (particularly in equity markets and housing), overinvestment and the unwise expansion of credit – the road to boom-bust.

In any case, some of the countries in which inflation rose within EMU were not catching up in the way described above, certainly not Holland and probably, today, not Ireland or Spain. The experience of Holland is particularly interesting and not only because it is clearly a developed economy that did not have to catch up. It is also sometimes argued that membership of EMU will increase the economic integration among its participants and thus make any problems stemming from a single interest rate transitional. The guilder had been linked to the deutschmark since the 'snake' in 1972 (see Chapter 4), Holland has particularly close trade links with Germany and it has historically been one of the most determined inflation fighters in Europe: exactly the sort of economy that is supposed to benefit from EMU. Yet during 2000 and 2001, inflation accelerated to 5.5 per cent and in 2001 average inflation was more than twice the rate of Germany (5.1 per cent compared to 1.9 per cent) and remained so in 2002 as well (four per cent against 1.3 per cent). This inevitably made the downturn sharper than would otherwise have been the case and, in Holland, GDP growth was about 0.2 per cent in 2002 and it actually fell in 2003.

Ireland has felt the impact of EMU too. Some have suggested that the Irish economy's dynamic performance in the 1990s can be attributed to financial transfers from Brussels. Clearly these have helped Ireland in a number of ways, including in its infrastructure, but these transfers are not new and for many years they did not prevent Ireland's economy performing badly: slow economic growth (given its relative opportunity for 'catch-up'), high inflation, large budget deficits and high unemployment. This was transformed by the collapse of the ERM and the adoption of market-oriented policies. After 1992, Ireland's economic performance was spectacular: strong GDP and employment growth, low inflation and large budget surpluses, underpinned by the repatriation of the Irish Diaspora and a huge inflow of capital attracted by high anticipated rates of return. This was the 'Celtic Tiger'. However, towards the end of the decade problems built up because entry into EMU meant that interest rates were kept lower than if they had been set by Ireland's central bank. As noted earlier, the EU Commission reckoned that interest rates in Ireland were at least four per cent lower than required in 2000 and three per cent in 2001. In the course of 2000, inflation accelerated to six per cent and the average rate of Ireland's inflation in 2002 was 4.7 per cent compared to 1.3 per cent in Germany. Rates of economic growth declined sharply, though remaining stronger than most of Euroland, and there was a sharp deterioration in the public finances. Trade with Britain and America is still very important for Ireland, and the buoyancy of these two economies supported Ireland's growth in 2003 and into 2004, but these same connections mean that Ireland would be significantly affected by a rise in the euro (against the dollar and sterling). Furthermore, Ireland's economic vulnerability would be exposed if US GDP growth were not to be sustained.

But Holland and Ireland were not alone. During 2000 and 2001, inflation was over four per cent in Spain and just over five per cent in Portugal. In the later part of 2002 and early 2003, inflation in Portugal and Spain was again hovering either side of four per cent (when it was about two per cent in France and one per cent in Germany). And higher inflation not only distorts the economic upswing, but also makes the downswing sharper than otherwise would be the case for reasons summarised earlier. At the end of 2003, Spain had performed better than most countries in EMU, but in Portugal the problems were more obvious and as the effects of one-off emergency measures faded, the budget deficit was again heading towards four per cent of GDP. The EU Commission[2] saw this happening throughout 2004 and 2005, and even it was forced to acknowledge that the assumed slowdown in expenditure growth in Portugal was an 'ambitious target', which was Commission-speak for 'unachievable'. Portugal's current account deficit was also deteriorating fast and there were increasing concerns about the credit risks to domestic and overseas banks that had financed business activities stimulated by the low level of interest that EMU had brought. The political implications of all this for Portugal and the EU will be addressed in Chapter 13.

When an economy has lost competitiveness and its public finances deteriorate in a serious way, one way or another the real exchange rate has to fall, but the single currency rules out nominal depreciation. Nonetheless, a country inside EMU that becomes 'uncompetitive' can still only restore its position if it improves its inflation and labour costs relative to others. Unless inflation and labour costs rise elsewhere – the route that provided some relief for Germany as noted above – within the single currency, inflation and labour costs have to be forced down below those of other economies by deflating the uncompetitive economy. If a country gets into this position in EMU, fiscal policy will have to be tightened, expenditure cut, or taxes raised. As time goes by, the squeeze on the economy will force inflation down to the level of competitors, but it has to go further than that to make up for the initial loss of competitiveness. Inflation and wages have to fall below the level of competitors by a significant amount and for a substantial period. The result is an even more depressed economy, rising budget deficits and ultimately the risk of an economic and political crisis.

This is essentially what happened within the ERM when the French embarked upon the so-called *franc fort* policy (see Chapter 4). This entailed maintaining an unbreakable link between the French franc and the deutschmark whatever the cost and, with the exception of a couple of devaluations in 1986, this policy was maintained from 1983 until the start of the single currency. The squeeze on the economy forced French inflation down to the German level and below, but as German interest rates set the floor for nominal rates within the ERM, this meant that real interest rates in France were higher than in Germany. High real interest rates in France depressed consumer and business confidence and reduced domestic demand. The shortfall in domestic demand meant that overall economic activity could be restored only if net exports were spurred by competitiveness gains. But with the nominal exchange rate fixed, competitiveness could only improve through more relative deflation. That in turn be could be achieved only through recession – and once achieved translated into even higher real interest rates, creating a vicious circle of more and more deflation.

France did improve its competitiveness with Germany under the *franc fort* policy. One result of this was that France out-performed Germany in the cyclical recovery in the last years of the 1990s, but this 'success' was gained at the cost of a prolonged period of lost output and employment. The French economy did have three years of strong GDP growth between 1998 and 2000 (averaging over 3.5 per cent), but this followed almost a decade in which growth was below two per cent every year, and even this short and belated spurt in growth came to an abrupt end in 2001. In 2002, GDP growth in France was less than 1.5 per cent and in 2003 under 0.5 per cent with unemployment stuck at close to ten per cent. As with other countries in Euroland, France's economic outlook for 2004 remained heavily dependent on what happened in the USA.

Jean-Claude Trichet, then Governor of the Banque de France and now President of the European Central Bank, described the *franc fort* policy as 'competitive disinflation', but its economic purpose was in fact the same as the so-called 'competitive devaluation' for which the British were pilloried after the exit of the pound from the ERM. That purpose was to produce a needed improvement in competitiveness for an economy in serious trouble. The difference was that 'competitive disinflation' had its effects over a much longer period than did exchange rate depreciation, and it produced those effects only by contracting the market for France's partners. Of course, the policy of the *franc fort* was political not economic, but the French only avoided economic catastrophe for two reasons. First, thanks to political agreements between Mitterrand and Kohl, the French obtained some influence on the monetary policy of the Bundesbank. Secondly, and more importantly, France was rescued from its predicament by the strengthening of the dollar in the second half of the 1990s. Even so, the French economy fell into recession and public finances deteriorated. The budget deficit rose to six per cent of GDP in 1993 and it remained close to that figure for three years.

In EMU, as economies slowed in 2001, a similar deterioration in public finances was experienced. And one characteristic of systems of fixed exchange rates is that apparently robust budgetary positions can change quickly and, when EMU began, a number of countries started off with their public finances far from robust. Through 2002 and 2003, the only economic convergence that took place in Euroland was towards slower rates of economic growth, deteriorating public finances and a growing threat to the banking and financial sector. Of course the slowdown in the US economy in 2001 and turmoil on the world's financial markets affected all economies, including Britain and those in Euroland, but at the time several leading figures in Euroland expressed the view that it would be protected from events in America. In January 2001, the Governor of the Banque de France said, 'It used to be said that when the US got a cold, Europe got pneumonia. Those days are over.'[3] In the same month, Belgium's finance minister, Didier Reynders, proclaimed, 'We are not afraid of the evolution of growth in the US. We are armed to resist a slowdown.' Not much of that has been heard since and most of Euroland's economic problems are in fact homemade, with any recovery largely on the back of America. However, public finances cannot be put to rights and budgets can't be consolidated without economic growth or at least the prospect of growth, requiring appropriate monetary policy.

This has some important implications for the ambitious ten-year programme of 'economic reform' launched at the Lisbon summit in 2000. The objective was nothing less than to make the EU 'the most competitive and dynamic knowledge-based economy in the world by 2010'. For some, the problem in implementing the policies to produce this outcome is seen to be the lack of political will, and that was absent in a number of countries, but within Euroland there was a more fundamental problem. Economic reform can best be implemented effectively if monetary policy is appropriate and the exchange rate is allowed to play its proper role in smoothing economic adjustment. In EMU this can't happen, so that, far from stimulating economic reform, the single currency actually makes economic reform more difficult.

Economic reform is an example of an asymmetric shock – an event or series of events affecting real variables (output and productivity) in one economy to a greater extent than others. For example, the discovery and development of North Sea oil was an asymmetric shock affecting the British economy. The impact of such shocks can either be positive (in which case there is a rise in the equilibrium real exchange rate) or negative (when there is a fall). When North

Sea oil was discovered and oil prices rose there was a positive shock to Britain relative to other countries, but when oil prices collapsed in 1986 there was a negative one. Economic reform is a form of positive asymmetric shock to the country that embarks on it.

Economic reform can take many forms and different economies may have particular priorities, and the implementation of economic reform is bound to reflect the differing cultural and political traditions in Europe. It does not have to mirror all aspects of what is called Anglo-Saxon capitalism, in either its American or British guise. But whatever form it takes and whatever else it does, economic reform must result in a rise in rates of return on investment, without which it has no economic meaning at all. This has implications for the appropriate path for the exchange rate (see Chapter 7).

The initial impact of economic reform often appears to make things worse as unproductive capital is closed down and labour is laid off, and this needs to be offset as far as is possible by a slacker monetary policy. However, as underused capacity is taken up and the benefits of reform come through, monetary policy needs to adjust if the rise in anticipated rates of return generated by economic reform are not to spill over into a boom. In EMU, it is not possible for an individual country to adjust its monetary policy in this way, either in the initial phase of reform or later, when the benefits of higher rates of return are starting to come through.

There is huge opportunity and need for economic reform throughout Euroland and probably nowhere more than in Germany. Labour markets are very inflexible, there is a lot of capital tied up in the myriad of cross-holdings that characterise much of German industry and large parts of its potentially employment-generating service sector are in the dark ages. So far, the attempts at reform have been tentative and, as elsewhere in parts of Europe, there is a great deal of emphasis placed on consensus and solidarity. In the end, it may well be that radical change to the so-called European social model is impossible, but in principle German capitalism could take off if the right steps were taken. If and when Germany embarks on economic reform it will result in a rise in anticipated rates of return on investment and an appreciation of the equilibrium real exchange rate. If interest rates are not adjusted at an appropriate stage in the business cycle and the nominal exchange rate can't appreciate, the adjustment in the real exchange rate will come via higher inflation, as happened in the initial phase of German unification. Given this, economic reform in Germany would pose a dilemma for the ECB. If the ECB did not respond to German reform there would be a serious risk of boom and bust in Germany undermining business and consumer confidence in a way that made further reform more difficult. Alternatively, the ECB might respond to the new dynamism in Germany and set interest rates accordingly. In which case they would be too high for other countries in Euroland where reform had not taken place or where it had already advanced, so that a rise in anticipated rates of return could not be expected to match those created by belated reform in Germany. In 2004, these concerns were a long way from Germany's preoccupation with the slow growth and high unemployment and economic conditions may well have to get worse before they get better. However, at some stage the German electorate will decide they have had enough and change will occur and when that happens Germany and the rest of Euroland will be made even more aware of the implications and contradictions of EMU.

Attention has focused on Germany, since the scope for reform there is very great and it is difficult to imagine the economies of Euroland being collectively strong unless the biggest one is performing well. But the same principle holds for all, as noted already in the case of Ireland. The ECB may be able to ignore the initial implications of reform in the smaller economies of Euroland since their 'spillover effect' will be less (though if Poland ever entered EMU, it would be a relatively big one and that might create further problems for the ECB). However, this means that the problems will increase and be that much more difficult to put right when they are eventually addressed, particularly if a number of small countries are caught in similar predicaments. If an individual country embarks upon reform without the ability to set monetary policy on domestic criteria, it will ultimately run the risk of an accelerating rate of inflation. And the more radical the reform, the greater the risk, since the greater will be the change in anticipated rates of return and the greater the capital inflows into the country. Of course, the more policy allows an economy to become unbalanced in the upswing, the more painful the adjustment in the downswing. In other words, in that overused phrase, the greater the risk of boom and bust.

If reform is slow and grudging or confined to the smaller countries, the result may simply be that the economic cycles of countries participating in the single currency are exaggerated because EMU results in real interest rates being inappropriate for some countries in both the upswing and the downswing. However, if economic reform were to be taken seriously, particularly by one of the big countries, particularly Germany, there will ultimately be boom and bust in the country concerned or deflation elsewhere. Either way, the process is as likely to discourage as it is to encourage economic reform or liberalising measures to complete the single market.

In practice, perhaps the most likely outcome may be a bit of everything, belated and reluctant reform, interest rates neither one thing or the other and a continental economy lacking any real or consistent dynamism. In such circumstances, the only way in which the level of interest rates set by the ECB could be in any sense appropriate for Britain would be if its economy were performing in a similar way. If Euroland does push ahead with economic reform it is equally important that Britain be in a position to run a domestically oriented monetary policy.

To illustrate the point, suppose economic reforms were pursued vigorously in a single large country, for example Germany, or even two, and the ECB did respond in an appropriate manner by raising short-term interest rates and allowing the euro to appreciate. The level of interest rates would not be appropriate for other countries so that the necessary depreciation against the reforming economy would be brought about by domestic deflation. And that would apply to Britain were it to be in EMU at the time. But outside EMU with a domestically oriented monetary policy, the pound could depreciate, thus allowing output to be maintained at a much higher level than would otherwise be the case.

Some people suggest that these problems for Euroland could be eliminated if all countries moved together on the agenda of economic reform. But, in economic terms, this would not resolve the difficulties unless all countries were starting from the same base in terms of economic structure and productivity (which they are not and getting to the same level would itself involve a series of asymmetric shocks) and they then proceeded at the same rates (which they will not).

The single currency has been working for only a short time. But already the tensions created are recognisably similar to those seen in the ERM – slow growth, recession and deteriorating public finances; despite their differences, and for the same reasons: both prevent exchange rates playing their proper role in helping economies adjust to changing circumstances. Although the ERM started in 1979 it was not until 1983 that the system really got underway. A decade later it was blown apart and after this happened all sorts of myths and not a little paranoia gathered around the role of so-called speculators. In fact, speculators were not the cause of the ERM's difficulties, but at a certain stage they did take advantage of economic conditions that were judged, accurately, to be unsustainable, to attack particular currencies. Of course in EMU there are no separate currencies to be attacked as there were in the ERM. There is only a single currency and a single interest rate so that there is no question of imposing devastatingly high interest rates to defend a particular currency. But that is not really the issue; if economic pressures build up, they will seek their own channels and if some are closed, others will be found.

In the ERM, high interest rates served as market signals flashing warnings about the nature of the problems in particular countries. EMU has taken away separate interest rates for participating economies, so there will not be any interest rates flashing 'red'. But when problems arise in particular countries they will still have to be addressed – they don't just disappear. To change the metaphor, the thermometers have been thrown away but the patients can still get ill. If strains are not reflected in interest rates, they will be seen in other ways and ultimately the most likely symptom of sickness will be deteriorating budget deficits and rising debt (and ultimately a political crisis).

EMU is different, and any economic and political tensions will be reflected in different ways and seek release in different channels. The political response and the impact on the EU will be outlined in Chapter 13, but first the impact of the euro on the international economy.

CHAPTER NINE

Wham, Bam, Uncle Sam

EMU and the World Economy

The United States of America is a monetary union broadly similar to Euroland in terms of the overall size of its market. In 2001, the US population was around 285 million, and Gross Domestic Product (GDP) reached more than $10 trillion; compared to a population of around 305 million in Euroland and a GDP close to $6 trillion. For proponents of the single currency, EMU not only helps create a huge domestic market for its participants but also provides some cushion to a hostile external economic environment and, as with America, members of EMU are thought able to be relatively relaxed about the external value of the currency. US imports are huge in absolute terms but relatively small in relation to the total economy and this comparatively small external exposure means that the domestic price level is relatively unaffected by movements in the external value of the dollar. Washington has to pay attention to the interplay between domestic demand and output (supply) but, for most of the time, the level of the dollar against other currencies is of secondary importance. Likewise in Euroland, although most of the component economies are pretty open, a high proportion of trade is between member states and imports from outside are a relatively small proportion of total Euroland GDP (about fifteen per cent, very similar to the USA, but lower than Britain, about thirty per cent). This means that, as in the USA, the domestic implications of currency movements are comparatively slight.

Those advocating entry to EMU argue that if Britain stays out, not only will it be more at risk from any deterioration in the wider international economy, but also sterling will be vulnerable to movements between the two continental currency blocs, the euro and the dollar: the pound will be 'tossed about like a cork' with damaging economic repercussions.

This chapter makes three main points. First, despite a resumption of US economic growth in 2003 and 2004, the outlook for the international economy became potentially more uncertain and currency movements more volatile than had been the case for most of the 1990s. Secondly, although it was not the only cause, the single currency was an important contributory factor in creating this more threatening outlook. The structure of EMU made it more difficult for the US and international economy and currencies to adjust in an appropriate way and at the same time made Euroland more vulnerable. Thirdly, far from strengthening the case for entry into EMU, a more volatile international economy reinforces the case for Britain retaining an independent monetary policy.

For most of the 1990s, the single most constant feature of the world economy was the strong economic performance of the USA. What was also striking about this long upswing was that in some respects it was more typical of the economic cycles of the nineteenth century than those in the decades after the Second World War. It was led by investment.

Perhaps it is not surprising that the most capitalist country, America, performed best with the re-emergence of a form of genuinely international capitalism, reflected in the massive increase in private-sector capital flows. It took time. However, a combination of technological and structural improvements that began in the mid 1980s led during the next decade to a rise in the anticipated rates of return and an increase in investment spending by both businesses and households in America.

Chapter 7 looked at the implications of this in detail and need only be summarised briefly here. In effect, with the rise in the anticipated rate of return, there is a rise in the equilibrium real rate of interest, that is the rate of interest that keeps the economy in some sort of overall balance, but to put this in place the exchange rate needs to rise, and at some stage in the economic upswing it is necessary for a central bank to raise short-term interest rates. Unless this happens, excessive 'optimism' can lead to overinvestment.

This is what occurred in the latter stages of the upswing in the USA. The US Federal Reserve (the Fed) did raise interest rates, but later than needed and not by enough. Making these judgements is never easy and there was a complicating factor in 1998, when the Fed felt obliged to cut interest rates to prevent further contagion from the Asian crisis, the threat of Russian default and fall-out from the collapse of Long Term Capital Management (LTCM). Nonetheless it was about this time that things went wrong. Various upward revisions were made to estimates of the underlying growth rate of the economy, euphoria over new technology and its impact on underlying productivity growth gained momentum. The Fed did not reverse the cuts in interest rates made in 1998 very quickly and only began to raise them from the middle of 1999. The task was completed in May of the following year, by which time interest rates had risen from five per cent to 6.5 per cent.

This had its effect: the economy did slow down and there was a reappraisal of the rates of return that had been built into investment decisions by businesses and stock-market valuations. As noted in Chapter 7, in the course of business cycles excessive optimism is often followed by exaggerated pessimism. By the end of 2000, the Fed was looking to lower interest rates to head off the threat of recession, a threat reinforced by the repercussions from the attack on the World Trade Center on 11 September 2001. However, the failure of the Fed to tighten earlier had two important consequences. First, the rise in the stock market got out of hand so that the cost of raising capital was pushed very low at the very time that anticipated rates of return became excessive. Secondly, the dollar did not appreciate enough. The result was overinvestment, over-consumption and a large increase in the levels of private-sector debt.

The overinvestment took two forms. First in the dynamic sectors – particularly new technology – where expected rates of return had risen, but which became excessive, there was simply too much investment for it all to be profitable. Secondly, the investment took place earlier in the cycle than would have been the case if the exchange rate had appreciated more during the upswing. This primarily involved sectors with low import content such as residential construction. This is investment that takes place at the 'wrong time' in the sense that if it had taken place later it would have helped smooth the cycle. In the jargon of economics there is an 'inter-temporal misallocation'. This sort of investment does not have to be wiped out or liquidated in the downswing since a proportion of it would have happened anyway, albeit later in the cycle. For example, new residential housing does not need to be flattened and sites cleared. However, for new investment to take place it is necessary for the anticipated real rate of interest to be below the natural or equilibrium rate and for that to happen there must be an anticipation that the dollar will appreciate. For that to be possible it must have fallen first, so there could be no increase in investment in these areas of the economy without a fall in the dollar.

In those sectors where there was simply too much capacity the position was rather different. Quite a lot of it did have to be liquidated in the downturn. Corporate America had invested too much, stocked up too much and had taken on too much labour in the upturn. It then began cutting back at a much earlier stage in the downturn than in most post-war economic cycles and this created macroeconomic problems that could have been stabilised by a fall in the dollar. It would have assisted supply to adjust by reducing real wages. At the same time, it would have helped maintain overall demand by offsetting domestic weakness with an improvement in net trade.

A depreciation of the dollar would thus have helped to stabilise the economy, dealt with some of the excess created in the upswing and laid the foundation for solid recovery in the USA. But not only America would have gained. A fall in the dollar would have brought benefits to Euroland, at the time (through 2000) enjoying a healthy cyclical upturn but importing some inflationary pressures. A stronger euro would have curbed these and would have made it easier for the European Central Bank to cut rates, thus strengthening domestic demand and reducing unemployment in Euroland, while at the same time assisting the world economy to adjust.

Unfortunately, for the USA and for the rest of the world, the dollar did not fall at the time. In those circumstances, with companies cutting investment and shedding labour, the Fed had to keep pushing short-term interest rates lower to underpin consumer spending and between the beginning and end of 2001 they were cut from six per cent to 1.75 per cent. If household spending had collapsed on top of everything else, there certainly would have been a deeper recession: bad for America, but bad for others too. A deep recession in the USA would have made the downturn in Europe much worse than the one that actually took place in 2001, but the course taken left the US economy more unbalanced than it might otherwise have been with implications not just for America, but for the rest of the world too.

Why didn't the dollar fall when the Fed was cutting interest rates from the end of 2000 and through 2001? At its most basic, if the dollar was to fall, something else had to rise and although the smaller currencies – such as the Swiss franc and the pound – could play a part, the bulk of the adjustment in the dollar had to be via the bigger currency blocs, the yen or the euro.

However, if one feature for most of the past decade has been the strength of the world's biggest economy, the USA, another was the weakness of the second biggest, Japan. There are many factors behind this and one was the attempt to prevent exchange rates adjusting. The Louvre Accord in 1987 was designed to put a floor under the dollar and as a result Japan kept interest rates far too low for its domestic needs. It led to an asset price bubble, the consequences of which Tokyo was still dealing with fifteen years later. However, there were other problems in Japan too, including demography and lack of immigration, political cronyism, the state of its banking system and the public finances. This is not the place to analyse the predicament of Japan, but in 2000 and 2001 with little investor confidence in Japan or its currency there was only the euro to offset the desirable depreciation of the dollar. However, even though the Fed cut interest rates aggressively through 2001, the dollar was higher against the euro at the end of the year than it was at the beginning and there were probably two main reasons for this: policy mistakes by the Fed and the lack of investor confidence in EMU. The result was to leave both America and the rest of the world facing more troublesome times.

The mistake that the Fed made was that when it started to cut interest rates at the beginning of 2001, it was not aggressive enough. This is easy to say in hindsight, though there were some commentators urging much bigger moves at the time, but it is important in understanding why the dollar followed the path it did. One reason that the Fed was not more aggressive may have been because it did not fully understand the nature of the economic cycle and it probably never envisaged that the USA would have to cut interest rates by anything like the amount that turned out to be necessary. In fact, if the Fed had been more aggressive initially and the dollar had fallen, the cumulative cut in interest rates would have been less than that made necessary by the gradual approach that was actually adopted. Among other things, this would have avoided the rise in consumer debt that subsequently occurred.

In the last few months of 2000, the dollar did weaken when it became evident that a slowdown was underway, for example it fell by about nine per cent against the euro between the beginning of November and the end of December. If the Fed had made a larger initial cut, there is little doubt that the dollar would have weakened further. What the Fed actually delivered was a series of regular cuts in interest rates that soon developed into a predictable pattern. One of the effects of this was to open up huge opportunities for capital gains in US bond markets and as a result there was a massive inflow into them, particularly into corporate bonds.

The other feature creating problems for the international economy was the weakness of the euro. Sometimes careless remarks from politicians didn't help; for example, in September 2000 Chancellor Schroeder said that he was not bothered by the weakness of the euro, since it helped German exports. However, these incidents were rare and despite the US slowdown during 2001 (GDP growth in the USA was under 0.5 per cent, while in Euroland it was just over 1.5 per cent), several factors continued to undermine the euro. First, the Fed retained more credibility than the ECB. Secondly, markets continued to see the USA as a better place to invest and do business. Thirdly, there was no political will in Europe to implement the necessary structural changes and, in any case, for reasons set out in the previous chapter, the single currency made it very difficult for individual countries – let alone Euroland as a whole – to implement economic reform. Yet this was essential if rates of return were to rise and capital was to be attracted to the area. Finally, interest rates set by the ECB were inevitably inappropriate for some countries, so the value of the euro was almost bound to be lower than would be a basket of the separate currencies if all had set interest rates at the optimal level for their domestic economies.

With the Fed cutting interest rates and the Government cutting taxes and increasing spending, the US current account was bound to deteriorate, reaching about four per cent of GDP in 2001 (and continuing to deteriorate throughout 2002–2004). But it is important to be clear that this deficit is a symptom of the scale of the adjustment required. It is not the cause of the problem. The popular view is that a current account deficit somehow reflects the inability of a country to 'pay its way' and the bigger the deficit the worse it is. But it's not that simple in a world where capital can flow freely. In a country in which rates of return are expected to rise, domestic optimism about a strong economic performance and future income growth leads to high rates of investment, but also to high levels of consumption. Thus domestic savings fall short of investment resulting in a current account deficit. Viewed from abroad, high rates of return attract foreign savings, capital flows in and there is a capital account surplus. This does not mean that a country – even one with a dynamic economy – can continue to run up a current account deficit without limit. However, the constraints are not those that existed in the decades after the Second World War when exchange rates were fixed and there was no pool of international savings to tap. The constraints today are different and have less to do with the size of a deficit than the way in which it changes the relationship between the rate of return and the rate of interest.

This can be illustrated by a simple example. Suppose someone takes out a mortgage to build a house and then rents it out. Provided the rental return remains greater than the rate of interest it is perfectly rational – and sustainable – to go on borrowing to build more and more houses, even though in every period investment exceeds savings and there is a deficit financed by borrowing. Of course, if everyone is borrowing to build houses it is unlikely that the rental income they receive or the rate of interest they have to pay will remain unchanged. At some point it will no longer be profitable for anyone to borrow to build more houses: if they were to carry on borrowing they would become insolvent.

There are similarities in a current account deficit. As noted in Chapter 7, real rates of interest are determined in international capital markets, but they can be affected by the demand for savings by an economy as large as the USA. However, more significant were the changes in rates of return during the US economic cycle. The capital that flowed into the USA was attracted by expectations of high rates of return. For much of the upswing this was justified and the same factors were driving the dollar upwards and causing the current account deficit to widen. Far from being a sign of weakness, the widening deficit was a sign of strength. But in the latter stages of the upswing, expectations about rates of return became excessive and when these collapsed the current account had in a sense reached the position analogous to the illustrative example when the rental income could no longer be sustained. By 2003, the US current account had to adjust and the only question was how far and how quickly.

Policy-makers in America did all they could to generate economic recovery and in 2002 GDP grew at about 2.5 per cent, more than twice the rate in Euroland, and in 2003 interest rates were cut to one per cent. In a sense this did the trick. Through the course of 2003, US economic activity picked up strongly, equity markets recovered some confidence and this fed through into Euroland, where some recovery was anticipated in 2004, albeit from a depressingly low base. But maintaining the more optimistic outlook for the USA (and thus Euroland) beyond 2004 was less certain.

When interest rates are down to one per cent, as they were in 2003, and taxes are cut and expenditure increased on the scale seen in America in the previous couple of years, there really would be something to explain if the economy did not rattle along for a while, but how long could it last? Perhaps several quarters, perhaps a year, may be even a bit longer, but significant economic imbalances that had built up for the reasons set out in this chapter, including the lack of investor confidence in the euro, still had to be addressed.

As noted earlier, the US upswing in the 1990s and the subsequent downturn were both led by investment. To that extent the most recent US business cycle has been more like those in the latter part of the nineteenth century than those in most of the post-1945 era. Analysis of traditional business cycles puts a lot of weight on so-called 'Keynesian multiplier accelerator mechanisms', which in essence argues that the more people spend today, the more they will spend tomorrow. But unless there is a rise in the rate of return on capital associated with business investment opportunities that are profitable at 'normal' levels of interest rates, the more people spend today the less they will have available to spend tomorrow. And the less they will actually spend tomorrow unless the timing of spending is altered by abnormally low interest rates or other mechanisms – tax rebates or accelerated depreciation allowances, for instance, that cause spending to be brought forward.

It is true that if more spending today means higher employment than otherwise tomorrow, there will be more income and more spending the day after tomorrow, but this is a question of timescale. When the USA went into the downturn in 2001 it was perfectly possible for a demand-management response to put a floor under the economy and that is what happened. And, for a while, it could continue to happen. But unless the rate of return picked up, stimulating investment and thus raising expectations of future growth in productivity and incomes, the future difficulty of maintaining acceptable balance sheets would restrain spending, and this effect would be all the greater the more that current spending had been previously maintained. In short, policy had to keep running even faster to stand still.

A fall in real wages can contribute to a rise in the rate of return on capital as long as it does not crush demand. If lower real wages do crush demand, then the downward dynamic in the economy will push prices down, preventing a durable fall in real wages and also raising real interest rates, further damaging demand. A large real depreciation in the dollar was in principle a way of coordinating a reduction in real wages and supporting aggregate demand for US output. In 2002 and 2003, the dollar did weaken and this accelerated in the latter part of 2003 and into 2004 as stronger growth numbers paradoxically reinforced concerns about the sustainability of US domestic demand for the reasons outlined above, and from the standpoint of the USA, the dollar's trade-weighted index probably needed to fall to something around 75, implying something around 1.40–1.50 against the euro. In 2000, at least, Euroland had been enjoying a belated but healthy recovery and could have withstood an appreciation in the euro that depreciation in the dollar would have brought about (though if it had happened earlier, the necessary depreciation in the dollar would have been less). However, the problem later on was that the rest of the world, and Euroland in particular, was not in any state to be able to produce a sufficiently large and durable real appreciation against the dollar. In a sense then, even a dollar depreciation might not get the USA permanently out of the hole because it would crush output in the rest of the world. And in these circumstances the impact of a rise in the euro on the economies of Euroland would be very different from an appreciation that reflected new dynamism within its own economies.

Far from being immune to developments in the USA or emulating the rates of economic growth in America, Euroland has shown itself very vulnerable to slowdown on the other side of the Atlantic and incapable of providing an alternative 'motor' for the world economy. The problem with comparing Euroland and the USA, and the benefits it derives from a single currency, is that America is also a single country and this affects the way it performs as an economy. In the Fed it has a single monetary authority whose policy is focused on the domestic economy (with periodic obligations to the international financial system). And there is a genuine single market with a broad socio-political culture that is committed to risk-taking and enterprise and markets. Euroland is not like that at all. The ECB is charged with setting interest rates for Euroland, but it is not a single economy, only the several economies of its participating members. Euroland remains well short of a genuinely single market – and for cultural, linguistic and historical reasons will always remain less integrated than the US internal market – and there is an underlying suspicion of markets. Euroland is collectively weaker than would have been the case had its individual countries been free to run domestically oriented monetary policies within the single market and very much weaker than would be the case if independent monetary policies were combined with a liberalised and genuinely competitive single market. The result is that Euroland lacks internal momentum and dynamism, leaving it rather like a slow-moving bike, vulnerable to tipping over in the wind.

Just before he visited the White House in February 2004, Chancellor Schroeder expressed concerns about exchange rate disturbances and implied that these threats would be reduced if US domestic sectors radically increased their financial savings rates (that is they reduced consumption and investment relative to income). There is no doubt that such adjustment would be needed to get the economy back into balance, but they would have to be accompanied by a very large dollar depreciation if the US economy were not to be crushed by them, not something that Chancellor Schroeder wanted at all.

Large currency blocs, by their very nature, create their own problems for the international economy. It is true that economies with relatively small external exposure can be quite relaxed about the external value of the currency for much of the time, but if the domestic components of such economies become unbalanced and if recession is to be avoided, it requires a much larger depreciation of the currency to put that right than is the case for economies with larger external exposure. This applies to economies big and small, but the overall impact is obviously much greater when it is a large currency bloc like America.

America is here to stay, and the political union underlying the dollar-based monetary union is a robust and benign one. There is no question of the USA being broken up, but from the perspective of overall international stability it would be better if it were associated with a system of many currencies rather than two or three large blocs. The creation of unions such as EMU or a hypothetical Asian currency union or a pan-American monetary union, would be extremely damaging to the world in purely economic terms, let alone raising other possible sources of conflict that might be engendered by such blocs.

Assume for the moment that the economies within the EU each had robust monetary and fiscal frameworks focused on their respective domestic needs and their currencies were free to appreciate and depreciate against each other. Of course if it is felt that countries in Euroland, with the obvious exception of Germany, are incapable of establishing such a framework on their own, it may be a reason for having an external one imposed, but that is a massive indictment of their political systems and not an argument for Britain entering, since it has put together such a structure. However, assume such a framework was in place for all the countries of the EU. And assume that their relative and absolute position was much as it was around the turn of the year 2000–2001, when the Fed started to cut interest rates. (Though in practice if such robust monetary and fiscal frameworks had been in place, the countries of Euroland, individually and collectively would have been economically much stronger.) What would have happened when the Fed cut US interest rates aggressively?

On the basis of past experience, including the ERM, money would have flowed out of dollars into EU currencies. When this happened in the past, the deutschmark tended to appreciate within the ERM, but this would probably not have been the case if the separate currencies had been free to float in 2000–2001, given the post-unification burdens still being felt by the German economy. The deutschmark might actually have depreciated against some other currencies, including the French franc, and that would have helped recovery in Europe's biggest economy. Either way, currency appreciation would have helped dampen fears about imported inflation and to offset the monetary tightening that it implied, central banks would have been encouraged/forced to cut interest rates. Some central banks would have cut more than others because domestic demand growth varied between countries. However, the overall effect would have been to foster strong domestic demand in Europe that would have sustained the cyclical recovery already underway, reducing unemployment in the EU and helping the USA to adjust at the same time – in short, a better outlook for everyone. Unfortunately, that did not and could not happen because EMU did exist and this has helped create conditions in which the corrections to the international economy and its currencies were likely to be more dramatic and volatile than would otherwise have been the case.

Some potentially very difficult times lie ahead for the world's economies and the ride may get bumpy for Britain. Good times or bad, the lesson remains the same: the more benign the international environment, the better Britain can take advantage if the Bank of England can set interest rates to meet the needs of the British economy and sterling is free to appreciate and depreciate. The more volatile the international environment, the more important it is that Britain's monetary policy is geared to domestic needs too. In the next decade, it may be difficult to match the economic performance of the one that has just passed. But the more volatile the world environment, the more important that the pound be free to float. It is rather like being in the middle of a seesaw. The more volatile the swings between dollar and the euro, the more sterling's overall stability is enhanced by not being tied to either and the better the chances of navigating the rough weather that may be ahead.

CHAPTER TEN

Wrong Time, Wrong Rate

The ERM Experience

When he announced the Government's assessment of the five economic tests for joining Economic and Monetary Union in June 2003, Gordon Brown said there was to be 'no repeat of the experience of the ERM when Britain joined at the wrong rate and the wrong time'. 'We joined at the wrong time, at the wrong rate' is a line that has been trotted out dozens of times by many people to explain away the shambles associated with British membership of the ERM. All this raises an important question, if this was the wrong time and the wrong rate, when was the right time and what was the right rate? Geoffrey Howe and Nigel Lawson thought the pound should have entered the Exchange Rate Mechanism in 1985 and so did Tony Blair. What would have happened if Britain had joined in 1985? And what implication, if any, does sterling's brief period in the ERM have for the right rate for the pound's entry to its successor, EMU?

The ERM was designed to limit fluctuations in the bilateral exchange rates of those currencies participating in the system. The deutschmark soon became the effective 'anchor' to the system (see Chapter 4), imposing 'discipline' on the others, and any realignment of parities between currencies could only be carried out by agreement, and only under certain circumstances, broadly speaking when a country had become 'uncompetitive'.

In 1985, Nigel Lawson and Geoffrey Howe failed to persuade Margaret Thatcher to take Britain into the ERM (see Chapter 5) and, for Lawson, 'an historic opportunity had been lost, when the time really had been right.'

Subsequently, many others, including Geoffrey Howe, have endorsed Lawson's judgement on the significance of the decision to stay out of the ERM in 1985. And Tony Blair shared this view. In the summer of 1999, he addressed the pro-euro organisation 'Britain in Europe' and said, 'I tend to the Geoffrey Howe view that had we joined [the ERM] far earlier, the whole pattern of the economy in the late 1980s, and the boom and bust, might have been different. When we did join, however, we joined at the wrong time and the wrong rate.' When I questioned the Prime Minister about this section of the speech, he made it clear that he did think that Britain should have entered the ERM in 1985, but in reality it was just one of the nostrums that was repeated on pro-EMU platforms without much grasp of its implications. In a brief note, shortly after the speech, I set out why this argument didn't really hold water and, after reading it at Chequers over a weekend, Tony replied that he got the point. But he didn't and doesn't.

How do the assertions that Britain should have joined the ERM in 1985 stand up? It is worth recalling the background: in 1985 British economy was certainly recovering from the 1980–1981 recession, but it was a long haul.

Between 1980 and 1985, the dollar had been very strong, rising about eighty per cent against the deutschmark and at its peak, in February 1985, had come close to parity with the pound ($1.04). In the latter part of 1985, the dollar entered a period of weakness and through the year sterling recovered against all major currencies. In the early months of 1985, sterling was trading against the deutschmark (DM) at DM3.60 and was about a little over DM3.70 towards the end of the year. This was the rate at which Lawson wanted to take sterling into the ERM.

Oil prices declined through the latter part of 1985, but in 1986 this became a free fall, from about $25 a barrel at the beginning of the year to $10 at the end. Lower oil prices helped reduce inflation and the retail price index (RPI) fell from over five per cent at the beginning of 1985 to 2.5 per cent in the middle of the following year. The effect on the British economy of the fall in oil prices was different to that in most other industrialised countries. Lower oil prices raised profits and real incomes of households. People could spend more, taking up the supply of goods and services that improved profitability made possible. For Britain, the beneficial impact was dented because as an exporter of oil the fall in oil prices produced a partially offsetting reduction in national income and this lessened the scope for increased domestic spending. So if potential domestic output in the non-oil sector was not to be curtailed it meant diverting external demand to British goods. And the way to do that was a real depreciation of sterling, in other words a fall in the level of British costs and prices relative to foreign goods and prices. This can be done either though depreciation of the nominal exchange rate or by disinflation, depressing the rate of increase of costs and prices below the rate of increase in other countries. The second is slow and painful at the best of times, but in 1986 it would have been particularly difficult since inflation in industrial countries was already low and was being further reduced by the fall in oil prices.

Since Britain did not enter the ERM in 1985, sterling continued to float and between October 1985 and October 1986 the pound fell over twenty per cent against the deutschmark and sixteen per cent in trade-weighted terms. The economy continued growing, but unemployment didn't start to fall until October 1986. If sterling had been at a fixed rate within the ERM the real depreciation would still have been necessary, but the alternative route of disinflation would have been forced on the economy. Interest rates would have had to go up dramatically. If policy had aimed to hold sterling at DM3.45, where it was in the middle of 1986, let alone the DM3.70 that Lawson thought right in November of the previous year, or, as some commentators suggested, had policy been concerned to get British inflation down to German levels, where it actually fell in 1986, it would have required a sharp rise in UK interest rates possibly by as much as seven or eight per cent (they remained above ten per cent for the whole of 1986 as it was). Output and employment would have been crushed. There would have been no recovery.

Of course, the recovery that did subsequently take place got out of hand. But the reason for this was the attempt to prevent a rise in the exchange rate. In the latter 1980s, a policy of shadowing the deutschmark was adopted by the Chancellor, Nigel Lawson, with the aim of keeping the pound somewhere between DM2.90 and DM3.00, and this policy was based on the view that as Germany had a good track record on inflation, tying sterling to the deutschmark as a sort of 'shadow member' of the ERM would mean that Britain's own inflation would be brought into line with Germany. I recall a conversation at the time with Sir Peter Middleton, Permanent Secretary at the Treasury, who had come to a lunch at Barclays de Zoete Wedd (BZW), where I was working. I had known Peter for many years – he had been Denis Healey's press secretary – and he took the view, apparently in all seriousness, that it did not matter at what rate sterling was linked to the deutschmark, what mattered was that such a link was in place. There was no recognition that this made it impossible to set interest rates at appropriate levels for the domestic economy or the consequences that would follow.

The policy of shadowing the deutschmark was a disaster, particularly in the wake of the favourable supply-side reforms to labour and product markets during the first half of the 1980s. By 1987, these were becoming apparent and the rise in anticipated rates of return was generating a rapid rise in investment expenditure by business and households. The implications of such developments were spelt out in Chapter 7. There is a rise in the equilibrium real rate of interest – the rate of interest that keeps the economy in some sort of overall balance. In order for the anticipated real rate of interest in Britain to be above the world rate it is necessary for investors to anticipate a fall in the exchange rate, and for this to happen it must have risen first to levels from which it is expected to decline. The correct response is to raise short-term interest rates and allow the currency to appreciate.

In pursuit of a 'stable' exchange rate, Lawson did the opposite. As a consequence there was subsequently much greater instability in output, inflation and jobs, and membership of the single currency presents the same choice. In 1987 sterling was under upward pressure, as investors sought the higher rates of return anticipated from sterling assets. The strength of demand in the British economy should have elicited higher interest rates from 1987 onwards. They were edged up in August, but then cut. First in October 1987 (when there was some justification after the stock-market crash, although they should have been reversed quickly) and then again in February and May 1988, at the same time as heavy intervention on the foreign exchange markets to curb the rise in sterling. Shortly after, evidence of inflationary pressure became all too obvious. The upshot of trying to keep the pound stable in 1987 and 1988 was an unsustainable inflationary boom. There was a belated decision to uncap the pound in the spring of 1988 but the damage had been done. Inflation was out of control. The increase in the retail price index shot up to almost eleven per cent in late 1990.

Inflation at those levels requires draconian monetary tightening and takes a long time to squeeze out of the economy. So that although the demand boom had already peaked by autumn 1989 it was impossible to start easing monetary policy by cutting interest rates and allowing sterling to start drifting down. On the contrary, as both international investors and domestic businesses and households lost confidence, interest rates were raised in an attempt to restore 'credibility' and get to grips with inflation. Interest rates peaked at fifteen per cent in October 1989, where they remained for a year. The initial failure to allow sterling to appreciate meant that the subsequent inflationary surge could only be brought under control by recession.

Mistakes over monetary policy were compounded by at least two errors of fiscal policy. First, the stimulatory impact of privatisation 'giveaways' was probably underestimated. Secondly, the decision to announce in the 1988 budget that mortgage tax relief for couples would end four months later was not sensible, though Lawson says that the Inland Revenue advised him it could not be done sooner. Nonetheless, in the intervening four months there was inevitably a mortgage bonanza that further inflamed a very hot housing market.

There were also significant tax cuts in the budgets of 1987 and 1988. Some see this as the reason for the subsequent boom and bust in the late 1980s and early 1990s, but this is based on a misunderstanding. It probably was not very sensible to cut taxes in the 1987 and 1988 budgets, but there was no inherent reason that this relaxation of fiscal policy would lead to the boom and thus to the bust in the way it did. The reason this occurred was that the decision to 'cap' sterling stopped monetary policy operating properly and in particular prevented the exchange rate functioning in the way that it should and which would have offset fiscal policy 'mistakes' wrecking the economy. Furthermore, if monetary policy and the exchange rate had been allowed to work – so avoiding boom and bust – it is less than obvious that the tax cuts were an error.

At a speech to the IMF in 1988 in West Berlin, Lawson lectured the world on Britain's economic miracle. In particular he argued that the growing current account deficit, which was causing concern to some commentators, didn't matter since it reflected private-sector decisions and flows and hence would make a market adjustment in due time. However, the market adjustment could only occur if there was a domestically oriented monetary policy in place, which meant allowing the exchange rate to float. What Lawson did was to stoke up the domestic economy while neutering the effectiveness of monetary policy.

The rise and fall in the real exchange rate is a necessary feature of economic adjustment and allowing the nominal rate to move up and down is the best way of achieving this. This is because it helps the process of adjustment by operating on both demand and supply. It is very important to keep this apparently obvious distinction in mind. It is not the increase in demand that creates inflation, but the way this interacts with supply. Of course a rise in domestic interest rates will curb some spending. However, the associated appreciation of sterling allows some of the demand to switch to foreign supply as a rising currency reduces foreign costs and prices relative to domestic ones. It thus dampens excess demand that might otherwise lead to excessive strains on resources that tighten labour markets and push up inflation. As investment projects are completed, demand falls back at the same time the potential output of the economy increases as new factories and plants start producing. When that happens, the right thing to do is to cut interest rates and allow the currency to depreciate. In this way, the adjustment to new supply-side conditions can take place without the boom and bust cycle in output, employment and inflation. Total demand – and thus output and jobs – is maintained at high levels, but the appreciation and depreciation of the currency alters the balance between its domestic and external components.

This is in stark contrast to the alternative of tightening fiscal policy by raising tax or cutting expenditure. This works by curbing demand and output (supply) and thus ultimately the economy's future potential growth. Inflation will certainly be kept under control, but only at the cost of lost output as well as the spirit of optimism that is the essential ingredient for successful market economies. It is important to be clear about what using fiscal policy in this way means. It is not just allowing the 'automatic stabilisers' to work, that is to say, allowing the budget deficit to move up and down with the economic cycle while remaining broadly in balance over the cycle. If the exchange rate is fixed, the fiscal policy will have to be an active one, as the Treasury's assessment of EMU in 2003 made clear, and it is a throwback to demand management, a blunt instrument with huge lags between implementation and effect and very difficult, particularly if expenditure is used, to reverse. Furthermore, the more dynamic the economy, the more draconian will have to be the fiscal hammer if the optimism created by rises in anticipated rates of return are to be kept under control. That is what is on offer within a single currency.

Those who point the finger at fiscal expansion in the late 1980s miss the point. This did increase demand, but capping the exchange rate meant that there was no mechanism either to shift some of that demand to external markets or to help add to the potential supply of the British economy. In those circumstances, of course, domestic demand caused a major domestic inflation problem, but the error was one of monetary policy.

A recession is virtually the only way to bring an inflationary boom back under control. Membership of the ERM ensured that in 1990–1991 this became a slump, and at least in terms of household spending, the deepest recession since the 1930s. When John Major took sterling into ERM on 8 October 1990, the economy had just gone off the edge of the cliff. Unemployment was rising sharply, the current account was in large deficit, prices were rising at over ten per cent a year, and interest rates, cut at the point of entry, were fourteen per cent. Over the next two years unemployment rose, production fell and thousands of jobs disappeared. By the time Britain was booted out of the ERM, inflation was back down to about 3.6 per cent, roughly where it had been before Lawson lost control of the economy, and the public finances were in a shambles.

Many commentators suggest that the rate that sterling entered in October 1990 was the real cause of subsequent problems within the ERM and an explanation of sterling's exit a couple of years later. The implication being that the pound should have entered at a lower level than the central rate of DM2.95 (that was in fact the rate the pound was trading at the time). They point to the fact that the level was decided without consultation with other member states and that the Bundesbank thought the rate too high. Both are true but beside the point.

In 1985, Nigel Lawson wanted to take sterling into the ERM at a central rate of DM3.70. In his memoirs,[1] he says that the fall in oil prices the following year would have justified a realignment of the pound. He suggests that sterling would have participated in the general realignment that took place within the ERM in April 1986, to something closer to DM3.50. This retrospective view exposes some important issues that have to be addressed by anyone thinking of supporting entry to EMU.

First, Lawson, who was against EMU but who certainly believed in the disciplines of the ERM, could not possibly have anticipated the opportunity or the need for the pound to depreciate if he had been successful in taking it into the ERM at DM3.70. No more can any government taking the pound into EMU anticipate the need to depreciate (or for that matter appreciate). The opportunity of course does not does not arise with a single currency.

Secondly, the reasons for the necessary depreciation that Lawson identified were not brought about by any policy failing in Britain, but by changes in the international economy that affected this country differently to others. It is very doubtful in practice whether sterling would have been allowed to devalue within months of entering the ERM. But in any case realignments within the system were not made in response to genuine changes in economic circumstances. Within the ERM, realignments were only permitted to restore 'competitiveness'. In EMU, necessary realignments, whether on grounds of 'competitiveness' or changed circumstances, are impossible.

Thirdly, even had sterling been in the ERM and devalued in 1986, it would have been necessary shortly afterwards to revalue the pound because of the rise in rates of return and the incipient investment boom that were induced by the supply side reforms of the 1980s. Again, in practice this would not have been possible in the ERM, since no currency was permitted to revalue against the deutschmark. More importantly in the context of EMU, neither the depreciation nor the appreciation would have been possible, but the need for both illustrates how swiftly the appropriate level for a currency can alter.

In his memoirs,[2] Lawson says:

> I could not help noticing that those who castigated John Major for having joined at an excessively high rate of DM2.95 to the pound were the same as those who had earlier castigated me for having shadowed the deutschmark at the excessively low rate of DM3.00 to the pound... there is no way that it can seriously be maintained both that DM3.00 was too low in 1988 and DM2.95 significantly too high in 1990.

What this fails to recognise is what those who are preoccupied with the rate of entry to EMU fail to recognise, namely that it is the very fact that the appropriate real exchange rate can move very significantly that causes economic difficulties within fixed exchange rate systems, since within such systems the only way the real exchange rate can adjust is through relative inflation and deflation. The alternative is that the real exchange rate adjusts through movements in the nominal exchange rate. There is no permanently correct rate for the currency even if at the moment of entry the rate is in some sense 'right'.

Without the depreciation of sterling through 1986, there would have been no recovery at all, or at best a very anaemic one, from the recession of the early 1980s. Throughout 1986 and 1987, the perceived benefits of earlier supply-side reforms were reflected in a rise in rates of return and surging investment and at the time DM3.00 was too low to prevent overheating and inflation. By the summer of 1990, it is possible that something around DM2.95 was the 'right' rate but, if it was, it was clearly too high for the period of sharp recession that was just beginning.

Once the decision to enter the ERM had been made, the authorities did everything they could to make its conditions less onerous, cutting interest rates at every opportunity, from fifteen per cent to fourteen per cent immediately before entry and reducing them to ten per cent by May 1992. But this was not enough. Not surprisingly, given the parlous state of the British economy, sterling became bogged down close to the floor of the allowable bands of the ERM and this meant that, as in the single currency, interest rates could not be set at levels appropriate for the British economy. The loss of competitiveness in the boom years had been inevitable, but now had to be unwound. Domestic demand was depressed, over and beyond the natural cyclical down-phase after earlier exuberance, by falling house prices, high interest rates, rising unemployment, banking sector problems and a generalised loss of confidence in the Government's ability to manage the economy.

There could be no durable recovery unless competitiveness improved, boosting exports relative to imports. Within the ERM (or EMU), this would mean that British price and wage increases would have had to be forced down by deflation below those in competitor countries before net exports could even start slowly to fill the gap left by depressed domestic demand.

The ERM brought deficit financing back with a vengeance as the Treasury sought to offset the monetary squeeze (net borrowing was 7.4 per cent of GDP in 1992–1993 and 7.8 per cent in 1993–1994). In a state of panic ahead of the inevitable election, sometime before June 1992, the Government increased public spending significantly: in the first two years of John Major's Government, there was a real-terms increase in public spending of over five per cent a year. It is this spending boom that provided the 'evidence' for those who claim that economic recovery was underway before the exit from the ERM. It was nothing of the sort, but merely a rasping gasp of an economy on the verge of breakdown.

If Britain had stayed in the ERM, its public finances would have gone the same way as other countries – Italy, Sweden, Belgium and Finland – in which exchange rate 'discipline' had led to fiscal deterioration on a grand scale, and the same was already happening within the single currency by the end of 2003. As it was, Britain was pushed out of the ERM and recovered the freedom to run an independent monetary policy in time to avoid fiscal catastrophe.

The easing of monetary policy and the economic recovery after exit from ERM in September 1992 meant that steps could be taken to restore the public finances. These steps were inevitably painful in political terms and the Conservatives were very badly damaged. But the right measures could at least be taken, as they would have had to be taken at some stage if financial and economic chaos were to be avoided. But only the freedom to decide monetary policy on domestic criteria made it possible to take decisions in conditions of economic growth, or at least ones that provided some prospect of growth, instead of catastrophic slump. Both sharply lower interest rates and a sharply lower pound were needed. Expenditure was cut and taxes raised and Norman Lamont put in place a new monetary framework with considerable speed and ingenuity. He introduced a target range for inflation, and interest rates were to be decided on domestic criteria. It was not perfect, but it provided a stepping-stone on the way to changes introduced by the Labour Government in 1997.

From September 1992 and throughout 1993 there were successive cuts in interest rates and sterling depreciated. Interest rates fell below Germany's. This was necessary for recovery and, whatever sterling's rate, entry to the ERM would have been impossible with the deutschmark as the anchor for the system (and impossible within EMU if the ECB in Frankfurt set interest rates at an inappropriate level). By the early spring of 1993, the markets believed that both interest rates and sterling had reached levels appropriate for the Government's aims of economic recovery, necessary budgetary retrenchment and stabilising inflation in the official one to four per cent range. During the 1990s, recovery became firmly established yet inflation continued to fall into the middle of the target range.

The assertions of Tony Blair (and Geoffrey Howe and Nigel Lawson) set out at the beginning of this chapter do not stand scrutiny. Earlier entry to the ERM would certainly have changed the pattern of the economy, but not for the better. And the disaster created by the later entry had little to do with the rate. Before anyone thinks of supporting entry to the single currency they should take heed from experience of what happens when the pound is prevented from moving up and down appropriately, not in theory but in practice.

CHAPTER ELEVEN

To Be or Not To Be

Should Britain Enter EMU?

Proponents of the single currency never knowingly undersell its potential economic benefits. Entry to EMU would give Britain more real sovereignty over its affairs, if the pound is given up only the form of sovereignty is lost. The single currency would provide macroeconomic stability to replace the volatility that has characterised British economic performance since the Second World War. This framework and the greater price transparency engendered by the euro would enable Britain to reap the more significant microeconomic benefits of EMU that can be summarised in the phrase 'lower costs, less risk and more competition'. EMU reinforces the single market and fosters the growth of trade and investment and entry would result in faster rates of economic growth, higher productivity and living standards. Inside EMU, it is claimed that Britain would be better able to withstand any turbulence in the international economy as well as increasing its influence on economic policy-making in Euroland and on the wider stage. These formidable claims were set out in Chapter 6. How do they stand up in the light of subsequent chapters and the arguments put forward in the Treasury's assessment in June 2003?

For many of those who want to take Britain into EMU, the possibility of economic sovereignty for a country like Britain is dismissed as an anachronistic legacy of a past age. We are either told that the loss of sovereignty involved in the single currency is no greater than, say, being a member of NATO, it is merely being 'pooled' for the greater good, or that economic sovereignty is a mirage in the 'globalised' economy. The first point is simply factually incorrect: the NATO treaty gives Britain and other members the option of leaving at anytime after providing twelve months notice.[1] EMU is forever. The second argument is based on the notion that the integration of the international economy means that individual governments have less and less influence on economic outcomes, that economic sovereignty no longer exists.

Economic sovereignty has never been absolute, but it remains real. The integration of the world economy increases rather than diminishes the role of floating exchange rates for an economy the size of Britain. Critics dismiss having floating exchange rates as 'the right to devalue'. It is not. It is freedom for the currency to appreciate and depreciate at appropriate stages in the business cycle, benefiting output, jobs and living standards.

The economic argument for keeping the pound is not based on sentiment or tradition or comfort in seeing the sovereign's profile on our money. In fact, the 'Queen's head' has only been on banknotes since 1960 and keeping it there is no part of the argument. The economic case for retaining a separate currency is simple: overall economic stability will be increased and employment and output growth will be higher if the Bank of England can set interest rates on domestic criteria. That requires the pound to be free to move up and down and is a feature of national economic sovereignty that is real not form.

In Britain, there has always been a certain preoccupation with the 'right' rate to enter exchange rate regimes like the ERM or EMU. Tony Blair took the view that when Britain entered the ERM in 1990 the entry rate of DM2.95 was too high. (DM2.95 is equivalent to 1.50 euro to the pound or, put the other way round, a euro would be worth 66 pence.) But he supported the argument of Lawson and Howe that the British economy would have benefited by entry in 1985. Yet in 1985 Nigel Lawson and Geoffrey Howe were recommending the pound entering the ERM at a rate of DM3.70 (1.89 euro or 53 pence). Numerous suggestions have been made since about the right rate, and the Government's assessment of EMU in June 2003 pointed out that in recent years estimates of equilibrium exchange rates have ranged from 1.15 to over 1.60 euro (or DM2.25–3.13). The relevant background paper from the Treasury examined other studies that put the appropriate euro rate against sterling between 1.175 and 1.33 (or DM2.30–2.60 in old money), concluding that the right rate of entry for sterling was 1.37 euro to the pound, which is equivalent to DM2.68.

Much of this and similar studies on the right rate are accompanied by a variety of sophisticated econometric wizardry and almost all of it misses the point: the appropriate real exchange rate can move very significantly over quite short periods of time, certainly over a couple of years or so. This means that there is no such thing as the right exchange rate to join EMU. The rate that is right today may not be right tomorrow and the rate that may be right tomorrow may not be right today. Yet the whole point of the euro is that a currency is fixed in perpetuity. If the nominal exchange rate can't move up and down, the necessary adjustment in the real exchange rate will be via relative inflation and deflation. It was one of the extraordinary features in the background papers assessment in 2003 that it was implied that it was immaterial whether the real exchange rate adjusted through relative inflation/deflation or through appreciation/depreciation of the nominal exchange rate.

At least the economic case for British entry now has to be made and this was not always the case. For a long time the argument for an external anchor, whether the ERM or EMU, reflected a view that Britain was an economic 'basket case' and incapable of managing its own affairs, and advocates of entry to EMU still put a lot of weight on Britain's past economic failings. Their memories are long, but a bit selective.

Between the end of the Korean War and the commodity price explosion during the early 1970s, the world economy enjoyed a 'golden age' of unparalleled economic prosperity. Britain participated in this, GDP growth averaged about just under three per cent and living standards rose, but they fell behind those in both Germany and France where economic growth was much stronger. Indeed, almost every other European country except Britain enjoyed a vigorous spurt of economic growth at some stage during this period.

Euro-enthusiasts point to this as the time when it all started to go wrong for Britain. In fact there are some quite straightforward factors that at least partially explain Britain's relatively poor economic performance between the early 1950s and 1970s. For example, Germany, France and Italy (a latecomer to industrialisation) enjoyed much greater scope for 'reconstruction growth' than did Britain and all had much bigger reservoirs of low-productivity workers in agriculture and self-employment to redeploy into modern industry. To that extent, at least part of Britain's relative decline was 'inevitable'. This is by no means the whole story and there were some obvious weaknesses that were not tackled, but this has no relevance to a decision on EMU membership now: Britain and the international economy have both changed enormously since 1950–1973.

Euro-enthusiasts say that late entry to the EEC deprived Britain of the benefits from the expansion of intra-European trade. These were substantial, but the late entry to the EEC was not a factor in Britain's failings at the time and in the 1950s and 1960s most of Europe's biggest economies grew by focusing on domestic rather than export markets. Britain's trade patterns were already shifting towards its European neighbours before entry to the EEC and, by the time Britain entered in 1973, France and Germany had exhausted most of the structural gains from switching resources out of agriculture. Against a deteriorating international economic background, Britain's growth rate slowed in the 1970s, but it did so by rather less than its main European competitors. Nevertheless, this was certainly not a good time for the British economy. The 1970s brought to a head many of the economic failings that had been brewing since the end of the Second World War, culminating in rampant inflation, recourse to the IMF, industrial disputes and the 'winter of discontent'. During the 1980s, some important changes took place that ultimately improved the performance of Britain's economy. It is not necessary to be an uncritical enthusiast for Mrs Thatcher's stewardship of Britain or to pretend that errors were not made. But no objective critic can deny that the supply-side reforms, particularly to labour and product markets, and other measures to encourage enterprise and wealth creation, brought about a significant improvement in Britain's underlying economic performance, though the full significance of this only became clear in the 1990s. In part this was because such policies always take time to take effect, but also because of monetary policy errors identified in the previous chapter. During the Thatcher and Major administrations, output, inflation and interest rates were very volatile with two deep recessions that sandwiched a boom in between, largely created by subjugating domestic policy objectives to external disciplines, initially through shadowing the deutschmark and latterly by entering the ERM.

The problem for Britain at the time was that it did not have a coherent domestic framework for monetary policy. Initially, during the Thatcher administration, the growth of money supply was targeted, but as this policy unravelled an external 'anchor' was favoured. As a result, macroeconomic policy went off the rails in the latter 1980s, temporarily burying the supply-side improvements, and led to a rollercoaster ride that established 'boom and bust' as a mantra in the current political lexicon. However, one consequence of the ERM blowing apart was that Britain developed a coherent framework for setting monetary policy. The first steps were taken by Norman Lamont, when Chancellor, and were completed by the Labour Government in 1997, when the Bank of England was made independent.

Even if the selective view of history put forward by euro-enthusiasts were accepted – that Britain's economic performance was abysmal, absolutely and relatively, in the twenty years before 1973 and in the twenty years after that its economy was more volatile than any other in Europe – it is backward looking and should now have no part in any decision on EMU. Bad policies will always lead to trouble and these are themselves much more likely without a clear monetary framework. No external anchor is an adequate substitute for a coherent domestic framework for monetary policy and, for the first time, Britain now has one. This does not mean that everything will run smoothly, economics – domestic or international – is not like that, nor does it guarantee that governments will not make mistakes, but it does provide as good a platform as any to foster the overall economic stability that everyone desires.

Proponents of the euro argue that short-term interest rates would be lower inside EMU and so far that would have been true, but interest rates can be too low as well as too high. It was inappropriately low interest rates in pursuit of an exchange rate target that set off the 'Lawson boom' in the latter 1980s. If Britain had been in EMU from the start, similar problems would have arisen, as was freely acknowledged in the Government's assessment in 2003.

When it started in January 1999, the euro was worth $1.16 and, despite the occasional rally, weakened steadily for the best part of three years: in February 2002, the euro was worth eighty-four US cents. And the euro was also soft against sterling, worth seventy pence in January 1999 but down to just over sixty pence three years later. If the pound had been in EMU at the beginning, it would have been much weaker against the US dollar, with implications for raw material prices. The weakness of the pound would have represented a significant easing of monetary policy in Britain. Short-term interest rates would also have been lower: the ECB set interest rates lower than has the Bank of England. For example, inside EMU interest rates in Britain would have been 2.5–3.0 per cent for the whole of 1999, half the level judged appropriate by the Bank of England.

Inside the single currency, Britain's economy would have experienced another raging boom on the way to the inevitable bust. Alternatively, fiscal policy would have been tightened – taxes up or expenditure cut – to offset monetary loosening entailed in EMU entry. Leaving aside the political problems that this would have caused or the need to improve the country's infrastructure and public services, it would have resulted in greater loss of output and jobs for the economy as a whole. This is not to say that policy in Britain hadn't any problems during the first years of EMU, and one concern was the so-called 'imbalances' or 'two-speed' economy, but most of these difficulties were created by the weakness of the euro. In Britain, the alternative to a two-speed economy would have been a one-speed economy growing at a slower pace.

In 1997, the Bank of England was given a clear mandate, to keep inflation around 2.5 per cent. To achieve this, total aggregate demand needs to move broadly in line with output or supply potential. Final demand is the combination of domestic and external (exports) demand. The weakness of the euro, or sterling's bilateral strength against the euro, dampened external demand and from late 2000 this was weakened further by the slowdown in Euroland and the USA. There is not much that can be done directly to affect the various external influences on the British economy. But policy can attempt to offset their effects, by encouraging private sector demand in order to keep overall demand in line with potential supply. In broad terms that is what happened. Of course this had its risks too, since it involved accepting a growing imbalance between the internationally exposed and domestically oriented sectors, but the alternative would have been to tolerate lower overall demand and output, with consequences for employment and incomes.

In an ideal world, it might be desirable to share the burden more evenly between the domestic and external sectors. In the early years of the euro it would have been better for Britain if the pound had been a bit lower against the euro and interest rates a bit higher, leaving the overall stance of monetary policy unchanged. But that was not an option. Within EMU, of course, both the currency and interest rates would have been much lower, but as noted earlier this would have merely reopened the risk of another boom, unless fiscal policy had been tightened aggressively. It did not require membership of EMU to get sterling lower. The Bank of England could have cut interest rates and 'talked' the pound down without any difficulty if it had been thought a sensible thing to do. But it wasn't for the very obvious reason that it would have increased domestic and external demand putting strain on supply capacity and in the end higher prices and greater instability. Of course, the 'imbalances' that were created couldn't go on forever. When external demand strengthened because sterling fell or domestic demand picked up in the economies of our trading partners, the rate of domestic demand would need to reduce to keep overall demand in line with potential supply. Whether this adjustment took place smoothly or otherwise would depend on the circumstances and the policies being pursued at the time, but the Bank of England was certainly alert to the potential dangers. And again, the alternative course of preventing such imbalances occurring in the first place could only have been achieved with considerable loss of output and jobs.

The weakness of manufacturing alongside continuing growth in the service sector was a crude reflection of these imbalances and it was sometimes argued that manufacturing in particular would have benefited from Britain entering the single currency. British manufacturing did go through very difficult times after the start of the euro, although experiences differed between sectors and conditions were bad for manufacturing across most of the world throughout 2001 and 2002. However, being part of the euro would not have been an undiluted bonanza for manufacturing. Take Rover, the car manufacturer based in the West Midlands, as an illustration of a wider point. Rover suffered from a variety of problems that went well beyond the level of sterling, including the age of some of its sites (my grandfather worked on the production line at the Longbridge plant in 1916, albeit making military vehicles rather than cars). Nonetheless, when BMW, which had bought Rover in 1994, decided to sell the company in 2000, the strength of sterling was cited as a factor by some commentators. In the latter 1990s, a lower-value pound would have helped the export of Rover cars and improved the relative profitability of cars made in Britain. However, if membership of EMU had forced the British Government to tighten fiscal policy to avoid a boom and bust cycle, this would have inevitably hit the wider West Midlands and British economy and the domestic market for cars that was just as important for the company as the overseas market.

It may seem unfair that the burden of adjustment appears to fall disproportionately on the traded sector (including goods and services, not just manufacturing), but in a crude sense there are only two sectors: the domestic and external. There is no channel other than the external sector to release excessive pressure that builds up from time to time in the domestic economy. About fifteen per cent of UK output is exported to Euroland. The rest goes elsewhere or is not traded at all. Permitting the exchange rate to move up and down allows supply and demand to adjust with less disruption to overall output, employment and inflation. The alternative is to knock the domestic economy on the head, hard.

By the middle of 2004, the British economy had had more than a decade of sustained economic growth since sterling left the ERM. There had been nearly fifty consecutive quarters of GDP growth, the longest period of economic growth for fifty years, averaging just above 2.5 per cent a year (compared with less than 2.0 per cent in France and about 1.25 per cent in Germany) with inflation around 2.5 per cent and within a very narrow range. If that is not stability, it is difficult to know what is. However, nothing goes on for ever and one of the factors influencing the absolute performance of the British economy in the decade after 1992 was the generally benign international environment particularly the strong demand from America and of course this was true for the economies of Euroland too. In the wake of the US slowdown in 2001 and subsequent turmoil on the stock markets, the international economy became more difficult.

Against that background, it was inevitable that the economy slowed in Britain, but it performed relatively well compared to the dire state of many of those in Euroland. Throughout the course of 2003, prospects for the American economy improved, but the outlook beyond 2004 was very uncertain (for the reasons set out in Chapter 9) and it may become more difficult in Britain to maintain the absolute levels of output growth that were achieved in the last decade or so. However, if the Bank of England can set interest rates on the basis of judgements about the domestic economy and the pound is free to float, Britain should be able to weather any economic and financial storms with less damage than within EMU.

Proponents of EMU argue that the loss of exchange rate flexibility can be made up in other ways and two particular options are put forward: increased flexibility, particularly in labour markets, or a more activist fiscal policy. These issues were examined in the background papers to the Government's own assessment in 2003, but neither of these two purported alternatives adequately compensate for the loss of monetary sovereignty inside EMU.

It must always be desirable that labour and product markets function efficiently and more flexibility is usually viewed as cushioning a country from an 'asymmetric shock', but it can also be the cause of one. Measures that increase flexibility within a particular country, including improvements in the functioning of labour markets, increase the rates of return on investment and this is itself a form of asymmetric shock that will result in an appreciation of the equilibrium real exchange rate. If the economy in question is to adjust smoothly to this shock the nominal exchange rate needs to appreciate. Thus more flexibility in a single economy makes it more, not less, necessary that its currency can appreciate and depreciate. In EMU this is not possible, so the adjustment in the real exchange rate has to be via inflation or deflation.

Nor is fiscal policy a substitute for monetary policy: it works more slowly, is far harder to reverse and most importantly, as noted in the previous chapter, does not have the same impact on the economy. None of these failings were adequately addressed in the background papers published by the Treasury in 2003 let alone the Government's own assessment of EMU. It is true that when an economy is suffering from inadequate demand and there is spare capacity, fiscal policy – cutting taxes or increasing expenditure – can help put things right. But once supply is close to full capacity problems arise because further increases in demand come up against temporarily constrained supply, creating a potential problem of inflation. To head off this threat fiscal policy must be tightened, but it only curbs inflation by cutting demand and output.

Monetary policy works in a different way. When there is excess capacity, a cut in interest rates will boost spending by households and business, but the effect of a cut in interest rates is enhanced by the associated fall in the currency that channels external demand to the benefit of domestic output (exports rise). When output is close to capacity a rise in interest rates will curb some demand, but it is the associated appreciation of the currency that diverts other excess demand abroad to overseas supply (imports increase). This allows time for domestic supply to be installed and when this has been completed interest rates can be cut and the cycle continues. Fiscal policy 'works' by operating mainly on demand and thus output. Monetary policy operates on both supply and demand and gives a much better chance that overall output will be sustained at high levels. It does this because the exchange rate is free to appreciate and depreciate.

The importance attached to allowing a national currency to appreciate and depreciate is not based on a naive assumption about foreign exchange markets: they can and do overshoot (see Chapter 7). However, it is important to be clear about the causes and draw the right conclusions. Prior attempts at fixing exchange rates can cause subsequent exchange rate overshooting. When a managed exchange rate is combined with domestic policies that are clearly unsustainable, in the sense that they are incompatible with combining any semblance of internal and external balance, it makes it even more likely that currencies will eventually overshoot. In addition, particular developments within foreign-exchange markets from time to time reduce their efficiency and cause currencies to move a long way from fundamental value. The various reasons causing currency volatility are rarely considered by proponents of EMU. Indeed there is almost a presumption that any currency fluctuation is, by its very nature, harmful. However, the appreciation and depreciation of the nominal exchange rate helps smooth the normal business cycle and is vital for any country embarking on economic reform. To that extent, fluctuations in exchange rates enhance not diminish the prospects for overall economic stability. Beyond that, the way to reduce undesirable volatility is not to impose a single currency, but to pursue sensible and sustainable policies at home and to try to remedy any other factors distorting efficiency in the foreign exchange markets.

But EMU would not even provide currency stability for Britain. It would eliminate exchange rate risk and volatility with other members of EMU, but by the same token it must also increase the degree of risk and potential volatility against the dollar. This danger was accepted in the Treasury's background paper to the Government's assessment in 2003,[2] but it argued that this was dependent on the recent volatility of the dollar against the euro continuing. However, the introduction of a new currency bloc is bound to increase the likelihood of currency volatility. The reason being, as noted in Chapter 9, that when a large, relatively closed economy becomes unbalanced, if recession is to be avoided, it requires larger adjustment in its exchange rate than is needed in smaller and more open economies to put things right. And the rate between the pound and dollar still matters to Britain. Goods exports make up the largest share of the current account and more than half of Britain's exports of goods go to Euroland (though this is still less than fifteen per cent of total output) but this is not all that matters. Trade in services is also potentially sensitive to the exchange rate and here Europe is less important for the UK, accounting for about thirty per cent of UK credits and over forty per cent of UK debits. Roughly the same applies to investment income, Euroland's share of UK credits is about thirty-five per cent and a bit less on the debit side.

Investment income is different from goods and services in that when the pound rises, Britain's investment income from abroad cannot become uncompetitive in the way that exports of goods and services may. But investment income is not immune to exchange rate movements. A stronger pound will reduce the sterling value of investment income paid abroad, while not affecting at all the sterling value of investment income paid out to foreigners who have invested in the UK. Accordingly, the exchange rate impact on 'investment income' is in the same direction as the impact on the 'trade in goods and services' and the profitability of foreign investment is affected by movements in exchange rates. Proponents of entry argue that staying out of EMU will damage inward foreign direct investment (FDI) and this will be addressed later, but it is illogical to advance this point while simultaneously excluding the implications of EMU for the income flows that result from investment.[3]

There is a more fundamental point beyond the exact shares of Britain's trade with Europe and the USA or what sorts of trade should be counted (in goods, in goods and services, or in all cross-border transactions including foreign investment and earnings on them). Exchange rate risk can be considered a sort of tax on exchanging transactions involving different currencies,[4] so the broadest definition of trade should be used for the trade affected by this tax. Most of the world outside Europe either uses the dollar or is tied to it in some formal or informal way. Britain trades and invests roughly half with the euro and half with the much larger dollar area. The euro-dollar rate has been highly variable for a long time (using the deutschmark-dollar rate as a proxy before January 1999) so joining the single currency would increase Britain's exchange rate risk against the dollar. Outside EMU, sterling's overall stability is enhanced since it is free to float between the two main 'blocs' rather than tie itself to one and increase its volatility against the other.

Another purported benefit of membership of EMU is the greater price transparency induced by the euro: with everything priced in euro, differences in prices across countries will be exposed. This will benefit consumers in lower prices and put pressure on businesses to cut costs and restructure to become more efficient. Clearly there are many factors at work in the international economy increasing competition, but the specific impact of the euro on the competitive environment and prices, particularly retail prices, is more problematic and so the microeconomic gains claimed for the single currency are that much reduced. However, before looking at the implications of this, it is worth exploring the macroeconomic implications of price transparency, assuming for the moment that it did work in the way anticipated by enthusiasts for the single currency.

If the euro were to work in the manner claimed, the price levels in different countries in Euroland would converge, and the bigger the impact of the euro's transparency, the more quickly the effect would be observed. Assuming that there is no outright price deflation so that price levels will not actually fall, effective price transparency would mean that the rate of change of prices (the rate of inflation) in low price-level (poorer) countries would be faster than in high price-level countries. However, with the ECB setting one interest rate for Euroland, the differential rates of inflation produced by price transparency means that real interest rates (interest rates adjusted for inflation) will differ across countries. In particular, countries that have faster rates of inflation will have lower real interest rates than the countries with higher price levels. This will reinforce further the tendency for EMU to exaggerate the volatility of the economic cycle: for some countries real interest rates are too low in the upswing and too high in the downswing. This, it should be emphasised, is additional to the higher inflation rates that might be thought normal for less developed countries catching up their wealthier neighbours, the so-called Balassa-Samuelson effect explained in Chapter 8. So if price transparency works in the way that euro-enthusiasts expect it to work, it will be at the cost of greater economic instability of output and inflation. But will the euro bring about price transparency in the way suggested?

Even with separate national currencies, it has always been relatively easy for people living close to national frontiers to compare the prices of goods and to travel short distances to take advantage of any marked differences. It is reasonable to assume that a single currency will accentuate this affect, but it is less clear how far it will spread beyond border regions. And, with the exception of the border between the Republic of Ireland and Northern Ireland, it has little relevance to Britain's decision to enter EMU since it has no border with the rest of Euroland. Nonetheless, some proponents of EMU think the effect will be very large and quote studies on the impact of the border between the USA and Canada. These show that prices for the same product differed substantially across the borders of the two countries and that it was only huge distances within the USA and Canada that created equivalent differences of prices within each country. This, it is suggested, illustrates that borders introduce substantial hurdles to traders despite the lack of trade barriers and a (mainly) common language. The implication is that a single currency will remove these border-induced differences and since Europe has many more borders than the USA and Canada it has that much more to gain from a single currency. The argument is bizarre. Separate currencies are not the only factor defining a national border. There are cultural and political barriers too. And the fact that there appears to be marked price differences across the US-Canada border despite small linguistic and cultural differences, at least compared with much of Europe, is telling us something too. There are frontier areas in Europe where history has blurred some of these differences, but generally cultural, linguistic and political differences remain important, and it is hard to see how the mere existence of a single currency will reduce these or their effect in segmenting markets in Euroland.

The argument for the benefits of transparency from EMU is naive. Even before the introduction of the euro, it didn't take a genius to compare the prices across Europe by dividing by the appropriate exchange rate: people did it on holiday all the time, and the internet is making it possible for more and more people to make such comparisons on a wider range of products and services. However, the internet is not available to all and there are many factors that constrain cross-border purchases by consumers in Euroland and elsewhere in the world. The interesting thing is how many price discrepancies are due to sheer ignorance and inertia or arise from long-standing factors that make them unlikely to yield to the euro. And there is plenty of evidence that disparities in price levels in various cities can differ quite sharply even within the same monetary area. For example, one recent survey showed that prices in Frankfurt were eight per cent higher than in Berlin and prices in Houston were twenty-six per cent higher than in New York, and somewhat less than Los Angeles.[5] This merely confirms what anyone who travels around a country knows from experience and suggests that price differences will not change much despite the greater transparency induced by the euro.

There is a saying in the USA: 'All politics are local.' Much the same is true of prices. Even within individual cities, prices vary for haircuts and much more besides. It's expensive in rich parts of a city and cheap in the poorer parts. The implications of this are that price divergences are here to stay and the euro will not do very much to change that and in general terms this was the conclusion reached in 2003 in the Treasury's background papers. Price convergence in EMU will be slow and where there is some evidence that it is taking place, for example between France and Germany, it is continuing trends that were in place before the euro. But, to the extent that price convergence is slower than argued by proponents of EMU so too is the potential beneficial impact on competition and efficiency. Over time, there is certainly a tendency for prices to converge, though the increasing share of services in GDP means that more price differences can be expected, but any pressure here will not come from the euro. It will come from competition and functioning markets (provided they are allowed to operate), but when the process has been completed Euroland will resemble the USA, where large divergences continue to exist a century after the introduction of free trade and common money.

One of the boldest claims of its proponents is that EMU will boost trade. In his statement to the House of Commons on 9 June 2003, Gordon Brown declared:

> Our assessment makes clear that, with the advent of the single currency, trade within the euro area has already expanded and that, with Britain in the euro, British trade with the euro area could increase substantially – perhaps to the extent of fifty per cent over thirty years.

This was somewhat disingenuous in that the Treasury's background paper made clear that any trade gain:

> is clearly dependent on the substantial convergence of the UK with the euro area economy. Joining the single currency in the absence of durable convergence would lead to greater economic instability, with harmful consequences for trade and investment.[6]

There is no controversy that when full economic convergence exists there will be trade gains from a single currency. But without convergence there may be none, and the degree of convergence required to reap these trade benefits goes much further than that set out in the Government's five economic tests.

Most areas covered by a single currency also have free trade within their boundaries, but this is not surprising since, outside Euroland, most of them are also countries. On the other hand, the existence of separate currencies has very often been associated with trade barriers of one sort or another. These have been reduced in a series of trade 'rounds' and there has been a massive expansion of international trade in the past fifty years, but it remains well short of a genuinely single world market. But the obstacles to this are nothing to do with currencies (a single world currency!) but to a myriad of other factors, including the reluctance to remove tariff and non-tariff barriers to trade. It was the removal of some of these that led to the surge in intra-European trade after the Treaty of Rome, and the absence of a single currency provided no obstacle to this expansion. It is also clear that a truly single market involving several nations can exist and be beneficial without inevitably requiring a single currency. Nobody expects the creation of a single currency as a consequence of the North America Free Trade Area (NAFTA). A single market does not need a single currency.

Trade and growth go together, but the relationship works both ways: economic growth is stimulated by the promotion of trade but stronger economic growth and higher incomes lead to an increase in the volume of trade. And this is one of the reasons why there is no great mystery to the acceleration in the growth of intra-Euroland trade between 1998 and 2001 that proponents of entry highlighted as evidence that Britain was suffering by being out of EMU. These were three years when, as noted in Chapter 8, the whole of Euroland including Germany enjoyed a belated and short-lived cyclical recovery and Britain was experiencing a couple of years of more modest growth having grown more strongly than Germany and France for the previous five. And, as the Treasury's background papers point out, extra-EU trade has grown faster than intra-EU trade since the start of EMU so that any decline in Britain's share of intra-EU trade in this period is in itself neither worrying nor surprising.[7]

But proponents argue that being part of EMU will itself lead to an increase in trade and thus economic growth, primarily through the reduction in transaction costs, greater transparency in prices that should reinforce the single markets and the reduction in exchange rate uncertainty. EMU does reduce transaction costs but everyone accepts that this is a relatively insignificant part of the case for membership. As noted earlier, any tendency for the single currency to bring about price convergence is liable to be slow and appears merely to confirm previous trends rather than producing a distinctive change in behaviour. And enthusiasts for the euro arguing that the growth of trade is impeded by fluctuations in a currency have to face the awkward fact that membership of EMU would increase the instability of the pound-dollar rate, which is still important to Britain. However, in the aggregate there is very little evidence that exchange rate fluctuations affect the growth of trade. Although of course from the point of view of an individual firm exporting a large proportion of its output to the EU, EMU might provide a welcome increase in stability, though that too might be offset by the greater instability and slower growth that EMU imposes on Euroland as a whole.

To quote from the Treasury's background paper on the subject: 'Despite the existence of a large body of research, no firm conclusion can be reached as to the size of the impact of currency volatility on trade. In fact, there are even doubts that any negative relationship exists at all.' Trade has risen continuously since the 1960s, yet exchange rates have gone through periods of greater and lesser volatility. Nonetheless, proponents of EMU have continued to put forward particular claims for the trade-inducing benefits of monetary union, and two studies in particular are often quoted.

The first study suggested that members of currency unions trade over three times more with each other than do non-currency union countries.[8] However, many of the currency unions used in the sample were small, dependent territories – including the Vatican, Tuvalu and the Pitcairn Islands – with large, 'mother' countries. There is no way of distinguishing the effect of close ties of dependency on trade patterns from that of monetary union itself. Even the author of the study admitted that his findings shed little light on EMU: 'Any extrapolation of my results to EMU may be inappropriate since most currency union observations are for countries unlike those inside Euroland.' Subsequent research has attempted to deal with the problems identified in the original study; many of these have shown smaller though significant benefits. However, as the Treasury's background paper suggests, 'Most cross-country studies have been susceptible to the criticism that the results may not be applicable to the case of currency unions among larger, richer economies.'

The second study in 1995 focused on Canada's trade with the USA.[9] It showed that in spite of a free market with the USA, Canada traded much less with the USA than it did within its own borders, even in contiguous states. This was not very surprising given the history of the two countries: both the USA and Canada expanded east to west and transport links reflected this too. Furthermore, tariffs were only eliminated in 1998, after the study was published, and as free trade was completed Canada's total trade with the USA increased dramatically. Nonetheless, the study concluded that Canadian provinces traded around twenty times more with each other than with US states of similar size and proximity. The implication was that were Canada to have monetary union with the USA, trade would be much higher. But the study claimed nothing of the sort. It asserted merely that 'the existence of a border' reduces trade. Canada, being a different country, has a variety of institutions that between them change the incentive to trade, these being summarised in 'the border'. One of them is plainly the separate currency, but only one of them. Canadians do not want to be in a monetary union with the USA. Canada takes the view that its economy is best served by keeping its monetary independence. If there were to be a monetary union with the USA, institutional differences would be removed, and this would lead to a Canadian province on one side of the US border being essentially like a US state on the other side. Regulatory arrangements, legal procedures and the rest would be the same, there would be no customs posts or different forms to fill in and so on. 'The border' would have gone, but this would not just be a matter of separate currencies, Canada would have gone too, at least as an independent country.

Among its supporters, there is a notion that a single currency is necessary for the completion of the single market. This view, encapsulated in *One Market, One Money*, published by the EU Commission in October 1990, has a superficial appeal, but is wrong. Indeed the single currency will actually hinder the emergence of a single market in the EU, at least one that is competitive and dynamic. There are conditions in which a single market and a single currency reinforce each other. However, they do not apply in Euroland and involve a degree of economic and political convergence that goes well beyond the Blair Government's five tests. Euro-enthusiasts persist with the argument, but this stems from a particular view as to what characterises a single market, and one that is very different from that generally understood in Britain and other so-called Anglo-Saxon economies.

Economic liberals have a clear notion of what would constitute a single market in the EU. It would be in place when labour, goods, services and capital can flow as freely between EU countries as they can do within any one of them. Policy is therefore directed at removing non-tariff barriers that prevent this happening, and taking steps to ensure that markets for labour, products and capital work efficiently. People differ in their enthusiasm for this within Anglo-Saxon economies and getting to an approximation of the 'ideal' will take time to complete, but in principle the destination and its framework is clear and requires very limited common standards or 'harmonisation' to make it work.

It is less clear whether the various measures to remove non-tariff barriers to a single market in the EU would increase the rate of return in any particular country, for example by permitting economies of scale and reductions in costs, or reduce it, by reducing barriers to competition. The safest bet is that, as the single market develops, different countries, depending on their initial economic structures, will experience different movements in rates of return. As a result, real rates of interest would need to diverge temporarily while differential rates of return disturbances work themselves out. The implications of this were set out in detail in Chapter 7. The basic point is that in a world of free capital movements, temporary divergences among countries in the real rate of interest would be possible only if there were expected movements in the real exchange rate and the best way of accommodating that is by allowing nominal exchange rates to appreciate and depreciate. Without that, there will be unnecessary volatility in the economic cycle or, at an extreme, boom and bust, and these are injurious to supply-side improvements. A dynamic view of the EU single market in which non-trade barriers are removed therefore requires the freedom for currencies to appreciate and depreciate.

However, there is another view as to what constitutes a single market that prevails in much of continental Europe, where there is widespread suspicion, if not hostility, to market liberalisation or flexibility. The alternative model was set up and consolidated in the decades after the Second World War, when a great deal of importance was attached to 'social solidarity'. The result has been termed the 'European social model', or 'Rhenish capitalism', and this was apparently successful for several decades, but this was when private-sector capital flows were few. This essentially corporatist European social model is less well suited to the modern world, and it puts much emphasis on establishing what is called a 'level playing field'. From this perspective, the route to a single market is by the establishment of a framework of pan-EU standards, both economic and social, within which business, labour and capital operate.

A single currency is part of this framework. Currency movements are not seen as helping countries to adjust to changing circumstances, but as sources of instability or unfair competition. What tends to happen in practice in Europe is that governments try to resist rules and regulations, standards of behaviour and even rates of tax that undermine their own competitive position. This leads to compromises that penalise the most competitive aspects of individual economies within EMU, and it brings down the collective performance in the process. This approach is reminiscent of that in the 1950s and 1960s, when US multinationals set up in Europe and some American labour unions tried to insist on pay and conditions for European workers on a par with those in the USA. It sounded fair, but was designed to prevent countries in Europe competing on one of the few bases that were available at the time, lower labour costs. Within Europe, the concept of a 'level playing field' sounds common sense and fair too, but in practice it stifles competition and prevents markets working properly or adjusting as smoothly as might otherwise be the case. And properly functioning markets offer the best opportunity for outsiders, whether the unemployed or new companies, to get on the inside. The effect of an ever-widening level playing field can be compared to smoothing a roll of carpet across a room: the more that humps and undulations are removed across the floor, the bigger will be the final fold in the carpet as it hits the edge of the wall. In a market economy, the fewer the channels for competition and prices to allocate resources, the bigger the final distortion. In much of Europe, malfunctioning markets are reflected in very high levels of unemployment. When competition and markets are functioning properly there will be a tendency for some convergence of labour standards, tax and a raft of other features that may otherwise remain distinctive between countries. However, a prior imposition of a so-called level playing field actually prevents markets operating efficiently, delaying the completion of a genuinely single market. There is a huge difference between a level playing field emerging as a result of competition working through properly functioning markets and being imposed in advance to reduce the implications of competition.

The contrasts between the so-called Anglo-Saxon and European social models have been presented in stark terms in the paragraphs above. In practice, the British economy (or that of the USA) is far from being an experiment in laissez-faire; liberal markets are circumscribed by all manner of social and labour legislation. And within continental Europe there is no single pattern. Nonetheless, the underlying difference in attitude and perspective between the two models is clear enough and explains much of the exasperation in Britain with the painfully slow progress in establishing a genuine and functioning single market.

The slow progress in completing the single market is bad enough, but there is a more fundamental point. The single currency is only compatible with a view of a single market that is close to the caricature of the European social model. The more continental economies come in practice to resemble 'Anglo-Saxon' economies, the less suitable becomes the single currency. Fixed exchange rates or a single currency are a natural corollary of a static and defensive view of what constitutes a single market. A single currency has no part in a dynamic single market since exchange rates need to be free to appreciate and depreciate to absorb the shocks that are inherent parts of a dynamic economy in a world where capital flows to the highest rates of return. Of course, the countries of Europe have different political and economic cultures and it should be no business of Britain or any country to tell others what they must do. The problem is that when the single market and the single currency are combined it creates a framework that can only 'work' by stifling the potential dynamism of all its participants individually and collectively. If an individual country embarks on policies to raise rates of return on investment, as in the case of Ireland in the late 1990s, it will be burdened with inappropriate monetary policy. The more dynamic such an economy becomes and the more significant the real exchange rate appreciation, then the greater the danger of boom and bust. Outside EMU, a country can pursue policies to raise rates of return and productivity growth secure in the knowledge that monetary policy can be set appropriately. In Europe, the combination of single market and single currency either leads to more instability or to stability that is attained only at the expense of economic dynamism – the stability of a stagnant pond – what it can't deliver is an economically dynamic continental economy and overall economic stability. The structure of EMU means that in economic terms it must remain essentially corporatist and un-dynamic to 'work'.

Britain now has a macroeconomic framework that is robust and goes a long way to providing the overall stability that is essential for investment. Beyond that, many things will affect the environment for business. These include the quality of the labour force, the burdens of regulation and red tape, the levels and incidence of tax and many other factors too, including a political and economic culture that supports an environment in which it is good to do business. This can be affected by government policies, for good or ill but, outside EMU, macroeconomic policy can at least provide support for the former and limit the damage of the latter. The business environment in Britain may be made less attractive by various directives and legislation that result from being in the EU, but that is analytically separate from the impact on business and investment of a decision on entering the single currency. Business will only invest if it expects to earn rates of return that are attractive, but if there is a rise in the rate of return, the real rate of interest needs to rise and this requires the nominal exchange rate to adjust if overall economic stability is to be maintained. This is not possible within EMU so that it is hard to argue convincingly that the single currency will encourage investment let alone economic dynamism.

If one element in investment decisions is the anticipated rate of return, the other is the real cost of capital, which is the nominal cost adjusted for anticipated inflation. One of the purported benefits of EMU is that the cost of capital will be lower for British companies. When companies want to raise external finance they can do so either by issuing debt (corporate bonds) or equity (stocks and shares) and the cost of capital can be broken down into the risk-free rate of return and a market-risk premium. The risk-free rate of return is essentially the rate of return that can be earned by investing in government bonds. Governments don't go bust (at least not those in industrialised countries with sustainable levels of debt) and government bonds serve as the benchmark for setting the price of corporate bonds (companies do sometimes go bust). The second component, the market-risk premium, is determined by the size and efficiency of the markets (larger and more liquid markets reduce the risk premium) and the credit risk associated with a particular company. The argument that membership of EMU will make it easier and cheaper for companies to raise debt finance has three main strands. First, it was suggested that membership of EMU would result in lower short-term interest rates that in effect act as the anchor point for longer-term bonds which normally have higher yields to reflect the greater risk of their longer maturity. Secondly, inside EMU, there would be a reduction of inflationary expectations in Britain and this would reduce the yield on UK government bonds or 'gilts'. Finally, the euro would open up a larger pool of potential investors and thus reduce the cost to companies of issuing corporate bonds or equities.

It cannot be assumed that low short-term interest rates and bond yields are signs of an economy in good order: they may reflect the opposite. For example, prolonged recession in the 1990s saw the Bank of Japan (BOJ) set short-term interest rates at zero and yields on ten-year Japanese government bonds (JGB) traded below 0.5 per cent. The important thing is that a central bank is in a position to set short-term interest rates at a level that is appropriate for the economy in question. Nonetheless, it is obviously desirable that at any particular time short and long-term interest rates are as low as is consistent with that framework.

That is what has happened in Britain since the Bank of England was given independence and some of the arguments put forward by supporters of EMU are out of date. In the past few years short-term interest rates have been lower than at any time for forty years. They have been a bit higher than those set by the ECB, but the level was set to meet Britain's needs and over the period its inflation has been on a par with France and Germany and its GDP growth rates superior. The markets responded to Bank of England independence with a sharp reduction in long-term interest rates, and since then the yield on ten-year 'gilts' has periodically dipped below the yield on German bonds ('bunds') that set the benchmark for yield on bonds in Euroland, and the 'spread' between the two has been very narrow by historical standards. Despite this, long-term interest rates in Britain have tended to be a bit higher than Germany, though lower than some other participants in EMU, and it is against these that companies price their new issuance. On this basis it means that for two 'identical' companies – with the same credit rating and so on – it would have been marginally more expensive to raise money in Britain than in Germany. But very long (thirty-year) gilt yields were below the equivalent duration German bunds and in any case a British company may choose to raise money in euro or dollars rather than sterling and there are other costs associated with issuance that need to be taken into account and which reduce the cost of raising capital in London. Furthermore, as we have seen, there are structural flaws in EMU that lead not only to greater volatility in output and inflation, but also to a likely deterioration in the public finances. As these become apparent there is absolutely no reason why, provided Britain stays out of EMU, the yield on 'gilts' should not be below that of euro-denominated debt, like Swiss bonds, thus helping to reduce the cost of capital below that in Euroland. And this is reflected in market expectations, as the Treasury's assessment in 2003 suggested:

> UK forward interest rates on government bonds are lower than euro area rates from about five years in the future onwards. This suggests that the market does not expect the euro area to have lower interest rates than the UK in the medium to long term.

It is correct, as one of the Treasury's background papers suggested that: 'One of the most significant potential benefits from EMU comes from the creation of a deep and broad capital market across the euro area.'[10] When national capital markets are segmented, each country's investors have to bear the full risk of a country's economic activity. Integrated markets allow diversification and as some of the credit risk of domestic and foreign asset is likely to offset each other, investors can hold an international portfolio that has the same expected returns as previously but with lower risk. Therefore investors will demand lower risk premium from firms when they are able to diversify.

As anticipated, the corporate bond market in Euroland became very large after the launch of the euro. In its first couple of years, the issuance of euro-denominated corporate bonds exceeded those denominated in dollars and a great deal of this business was done through London. Because issuers were able to tap a larger pool of savers, the size of euro issues tended to be higher than those denominated in sterling. Equity issuance in the euro area rose sharply in 1999 and 2000 compared to the pre-euro period but, as the Treasury's background paper suggested, factors aside from the euro explain this increase. Until 2000, the value of European equity markets was rising sharply, mirroring those in the USA, and this encouraged equity issuance. In addition, a substantial proportion of new issuance was in the technology and telecommunications sectors, propelled by rapid growth in these areas across the world. Afterwards, equity markets in Euroland, the USA and the UK fell, especially in telecoms and technology sectors, making it all the more difficult to isolate any effect from the start of EMU. In any case, as the Treasury background paper explained, 'UK firms can access this market whether or not the UK enters EMU.'

It should now be clear that most of the supposed gains of entering EMU, identified in Chapter 6, are less than claimed or non-existent, but what of the purported costs of staying out? Two specific ones are usually put forward: that Britain will lose inward investment and that the City of London's position as a financial centre will be jeopardised.

The UK has the second-largest stock of foreign direct investment (FDI) in the world. Only the USA has more. And a big difference from other countries in the EU is the UK's share of US investment, and consequently higher share of non-EU FDI. Britain's inward and outward investment is overwhelmingly with countries outside the EU. Britain has been the dominant country in Europe as a location for inward investment for at least a quarter of a century, receiving more inward investment than do France and Germany combined. However, in June 2003 the EU Commission published a report that the UK's share of foreign investment from outside the EU had fallen from forty-eight per cent of the total in 1998, the year before the creation of the euro, to twenty-five per cent in 2001. This was used by euro-enthusiasts as evidence of the damaging effect of staying out, but this does not really stand up. FDI figures can fluctuate by large amounts over short periods and in any case the figures reflected conditions that went well beyond Britain or EMU. According to the Treasury's background paper, global FDI flows rose almost ten times between 1991 and 2000, to $1.5 trillion a year.[11] This was a time of unprecedented mergers and acquisitions and these activities accounted for about three quarters of global investment flows in 2000. And individual deals were a significant contributor to volatility.

For example, the decline in the UK's share of FDI flows reflected Vodafone's acquisition of Mannesmann in 2000, an extremely large deal that boosted Germany's share of EU FDI. In 2001, world investment flows fell by fifty per cent and inward investment flows fell by fifty-four per cent in the UK, fifty-nine per cent in the USA, eighty-four per cent in Germany and sixty per cent in the EU as a whole. Later survey data suggested that Britain had regained its pole position for investment projects coming into Europe.[12] As the assessment in 2003 pointed out: 'The stability of the macroeconomic environment affects FDI in the same way that it affects overall business investment.' Britain is the most attractive site in Europe for foreign direct investment for the same reasons that most British direct investment goes to parts of the world other than Europe: relative to the rest of Europe, Britain has provided a market friendly, outward-looking, non-protectionist, politically stable environment. Compared to the rest of the world, Europe looks corporatist, inflexible, protectionist and inward looking. And since the single market and the single currency cannot coexist with any degree of economic dynamism, outside EMU the relative attraction of Britain as a recipient of inward investment is liable to increase if it stays out.

Some individual investment projects might be diverted from Britain if it stayed out of the single currency, but this cannot be very significant. Given the state of public opinion and the obvious economic problems about entry, there cannot be many decisions to invest in Britain taken on the assumption that it is imminent. Any threat to the attractiveness of Britain as a place to invest does not come from staying out of EMU. It can be undermined (as well as enhanced) if the Government itself introduces measures inimical to business or, more likely (and less easily reversed) from regulations and directives from the EU. These are very often introduced in the name of the 'single market' but which in practice prevent markets and competition working effectively for the reason explained earlier in the chapter, and since some of these directives can be imposed by qualified majority voting (QMV), Britain's vulnerability on this score has increased. However, staying outside EMU with the pound free to appreciate and depreciate, can at least help reduce the effects of other economically damaging EU directives and regulations that might be introduced and thus help the overall economic performance of Britain.

Financial services are one of Britain's most important industries and the City of London alone accounts for about six per cent of GDP, employs nearly one million people and earns about £20 billion overseas for the UK each year. But London's predominance is quite recent. In the mid 1980s, the so-called Big Bang modernised financial markets and practices so that London could challenge for world financial leadership for the first time since 1914. The City is an international market that is based in London and its position cannot be taken for granted, but any threat does not come from the euro. London is a successful financial centre because it provides the right environment for the markets it hosts, and as a global financial centre it is vital that London is able to compete with New York and other global centres. To do that, it needs to remain innovative and appropriately regulated. As long as this is the case London's predominance and the contribution of financial services to the British economy will continue; if conditions deteriorate so will London's position.[13]

Whether or not Britain joins, the City of London will lose some business as a result of EMU. Some of it will (if it has not done so already) simply vanish, and some will go to its continental rivals. This is because EMU eliminates some markets, while at the same time creating new ones. For example, the decision to replace individual national currencies by the euro meant the end of some foreign-exchange business, though the City's dependency on this was relatively small with Frankfurt and Paris being hit harder, and London is still the dominant foreign-exchange market in the world. One effect of the creation of a single capital market in EMU may mean that continental businesses rely less than they have in the past on bank finance so that many new companies will appear on continental exchanges. The value of listed companies in Germany is very much lower in relation to GDP than is the case in Britain and the USA, so there is in principle much greater scope for the capitalisation of the Frankfurt stock exchange to grow in coming years as new markets open up and the same is potentially true for France and Italy. This process could create new investment banking business on the continent regardless of Britain's position on EMU since many of the companies coming to market will be local in character: small and medium-sized enterprises wanting to list on a familiar local exchange, not aiming for global exchanges.

It is sometimes suggested that the way in which trading in 'Bund futures' switched from London to Frankfurt is a harbinger of what will happen if Britain stays out of EMU. This is not the case. For much of the 1990s, London and Frankfurt vied for supremacy in the market for derivatives based on the Bund, the German government bond. In London, derivatives were traded in open outcry pits at the London International Futures and Options Exchange (Liffe). In Frankfurt, they were traded on electronic screen-based systems run by the Deutsche Terminborse (DTB). London began with the lion's share but in early 1998 volumes traded in Frankfurt began to creep up until they overtook London, at which point virtually all of the trading suddenly switched to Frankfurt. The reason was that Frankfurt's screen-based market was much cheaper and more efficient than London's open outcry market.

Although the switch was seen as a 'victory' for Frankfurt, nothing much changed on the ground. The people who traded the Bund futures remained in London, and simply put their orders through a computer in Frankfurt. Frankfurt gained because it won a symbolic victory and now collects the transaction fees for the trades, but London also won because it proved that the City was the place where banks and traders actually wanted to be, so that the British economy still benefited from broking commissions and the tax on incomes of City-based traders, which are much more valuable than transaction fees. Furthermore, if the Bund contract could switch that easily, at some stage it may move on from Frankfurt to whichever centre develops even cheaper and smarter technology. Just because Germany issues Bunds, it has no preemptive right to run the market in Bund derivatives. This switch from London to Frankfurt had nothing to do with the euro. It was entirely a matter of market efficiency and the lesson for the City is not that Britain needs to join EMU but that it must be quicker to adapt to new technology. Nonetheless, the switch does illustrate some important features that have wider relevance.

First, markets are now becoming increasingly 'dematerialised'. Trading in central market places such as stock exchanges is being replaced by trading through screens. This has been true for a long time for the markets in foreign exchange and Eurobonds, but it has spread to other markets. This means that there is a distinction between markets and trading communities that did not exist in the past when traders had to be physically present in markets.

Secondly, in modern electronic markets, liquidity cannot be split between two centres, particularly when they are in the same time zone. Business will gravitate towards the biggest and most efficient market. In Europe this means that the major traded instruments (big equity stocks, government bonds, foreign exchange and their derivatives) are all likely to end up with their single focal point and London has more of these markets than anyone else.

In this world a financial centre is not defined by the presence of physical markets or even the proximity of governments or central banks that issue the currencies and set the interest rates that are traded in the markets. If they did, the dollar market would never have got going in London. Much more important in determining where business is done is the trading environment and that means good infrastructure, a hospitable regulatory regime and plentiful supplies of professional skills. It is this that has made London overwhelmingly the predominant financial centre in Europe, in or out of EMU. This is not to ignore the threats to the City. London's new rivals should not be underestimated and they are actively supported in their challenge to London by a political culture that supports national champions. Governments across Europe, particularly in Germany and France, are prepared to use political pressures on domestic banks and institutions to support strategic political objectives, one of which is certainly to relocate business and undermine London. This can be counter-productive, but cannot be ignored. Again, however, this threat is nothing to do with being in or out of EMU. Apart from potential complacency, the threat to London and Britain's dominance in financial services stems from the particular notion as to what constitutes a single market, which was examined earlier. Many policymakers in continental Europe continue to view financial markets with suspicion or worse and there is little understanding of their function and how they work.

There are many factors behind the strength of London, but the regulatory environment is one of the most important. The nature of this environment in London has generally exhibited three characteristics. First, regulation can be changed very quickly when needed. Secondly, regulation is generally proportional, that is to say some activities require a lighter touch than others, for example retail markets involving consumers will be treated differently from wholesale markets where the participants are professionals. Thirdly, those regulating London have been prepared to be more stringent than other markets if this makes the overall market more efficient and transparent. For example, in the German stock market, off-market trading does not have to be disclosed. This allows preferential treatment to be given to some clients. In London it has to be disclosed and this increases overall confidence in the market.

All three aspects are potentially undermined by the current perception of a single market in Euroland. With several countries involved, regulations are almost bound to involve legislation so that making changes will be more cumbersome and time consuming. Proportionality is made more difficult since in a number of Euroland countries different rules are open to challenge in constitutional courts where regulators often lose out. Finally, differential standards are seen as incompatible with a single market in principle, and others in the EU see London's obvious attractiveness as a place to do business as 'cheating'.

These potential threats from the single market are real, but are not reduced by being in EMU and can only be averted if British governments show themselves ready to attach as much importance to financial services as Germany have to industry or France to agriculture, but with one very important difference: the aim is not to protect financial services but to sustain the competitive market environment that is essential for financial services to flourish. The Treasury's assessment in 2003 was remarkably clear on this point:

> Experience to date suggests that cultural differences have been the usual motivating factor behind member states positions on financial services dossiers. Britain's decision on EMU is unlikely to shift such deeply held positions. If the UK were inside the euro area, there would therefore be likely to be little additional benefit to the prospect of achieving the UK's regulatory objectives – it could be argued that pressure to confirm to the rules of the euro area 'club' might even lead to worse outcomes.

Britain has no interest in protecting inefficient markets but it does have one in preserving an environment in which markets can operate efficiently. Again, this is not made easier by the fact that single-market decisions are made under QMV, but if France or Germany had the biggest and most efficient financial services industry in Europe, either would do whatever was necessary to ensure that it was not wantonly damaged. Nothing less is required of any British government and being in EMU does not make a jot of difference.

Proponents of the euro are certain that Britain's 'influence' will decline outside EMU, but it is unclear what, if anything, this amounts to. One argument is that by being out of EMU, Britain reduces its influence on the whole range of issues that preoccupy the EU. This is the notion that Britain (and presumably others) who are outside the single currency are not full members of the 'club' so cannot expect to be taken seriously. The wider and political aspects of influence will be addressed in Chapter 16, but what about the specific influence that is said to be associated with EMU?

If Britain joined EMU, it would be able to affect the monetary policy of Euroland, though put another way that means that other countries would be given a say in setting interest rates for Britain. Clearly, inside the single currency the size of the British economy would mean that its needs should carry some weight in the deliberations of the ECB, though probably less than Germany. But having a say in setting monetary policy for Euroland, which will not be appropriate for Britain unless by accident or coincidence for a particular moment, and cannot even be appropriate for Euroland as a whole, cannot outweigh the importance of being able to decide the appropriate policy for Britain. But this particular notion of influence exposes a wider flaw in the case being made for entering the single currency. Members of the ECB are not supposed to be representatives of their countries, but to take an objective view of needs across Euroland. No doubt some do this more assiduously than others, but if ECB members do act responsibly and make decisions on the basis of their assessment of the Euroland economy then the case for a British voice on the ECB is that much reduced. If Britain entered EMU the Governor of the Bank of England could not be seen as a representative of Britain on the ECB. On the other hand, if ECB council members do in some sense act as representatives of their countries, then it merely confirms the political nature of ECB decisions, strengthening the case for keeping well clear of it and sticking to our existing monetary framework. The Bank of England is given a remit by the Government, ultimately accountable to the electorate, but is otherwise free from politics when setting interest rates. And there is a further point that may arise in the future. With enlargement, the voting arrangements on the ECB will have to change and even the big countries may have to accept some degree of rotation, so if Britain joined EMU, it is perfectly conceivable that from time to time at some stage in the future decisions will be made on the level of interest rates that will apply to Britain without any 'representative' of Britain being directly involved. This would certainly be implied by the 2003 proposals for voting after enlargement put forward by the ECB itself.

Proponents of EMU emphasise the purported loss of influence occurring as a result of being excluded from discussions in the so-called 'euro group'.

This is made up of finance ministers of those countries that are in EMU and meets regularly and prior to meetings of the wider EU gathering of ministers in Ecofin. What is the nature of these discussions and what is the loss of influence in not being party to them?

The euro group is in its formative stages but greater 'coordination' is thought to be desirable. Coordination is a bit like motherhood and apple pie, few people are going to advocate uncoordinated policy, but it is much less clear what it amounts to in practice in the euro group. There is a range of issues that can usefully be discussed between all governments, but this is not confined to countries within Europe let alone Euroland, and Britain will be a participant in or out of EMU. Coordination within the euro group has to mean something more. There are two possibilities: coordination between members of Euroland, particularly about fiscal and structural (supply-side) policies, or coordination between the euro group and the ECB.

The Stability and Growth Pact (SGP) came under considerable strain during 2002–2004 and the possible remedies for this and their political implications will be addressed in Chapter 13. The euro group provided a forum to discuss the SGP, but Britain has been involved too as a member of Ecofin. However, participating or being excluded from a greater degree of fiscal coordination as part of the euro group is irrelevant to Britain as long as it stays outside the single currency and holds to its chosen fiscal framework rather than the SGP.

If greater fiscal policy coordination is to be part of a move towards more active demand management then Britain is well out of it since the record of activist fiscal policy is in the main one of dismal failure. In most cases, an attempt to use taxes or public spending to boost or restrain an economy operates with such long time lags that it becomes inappropriate or pro-cyclical when it takes effect. In any case, for reasons that were outlined earlier, fiscal policy is no substitute for monetary policy since it impacts on an economy in a very different way.

Perhaps Britain will miss out on the greater coordination of structural or supply-side policies? At several EU summits (Cardiff, Luxembourg, Lisbon), various 'processes' have been designed to encourage structural reform, but progress has been patchy and there is certainly no harm in discussing these issues. However, the remedies to most of the structural problems are already in the hands of individual governments. They don't need to coordinate anything, they just need to get on with the action, 'walking the walk rather than talking the talk'.

The other area where scope for improved coordination is envisaged is between the euro group and the ECB to get a better 'policy mix' between monetary policy (for which the ECB is responsible) and fiscal policy and supply-side policies (still in the hands of individual governments). For the sake of argument, assume (however improbably) that each country is convinced of the benefits of labour and product market reforms and fiscal restraint and moreover is prepared to implement the necessary policies to bring them about in their individual economies. For an economy to benefit fully from such measures, they need to be accompanied by appropriate monetary policy. This is not a particular problem for a country where monetary policy remains focused on the domestic economy. The government can be reasonably sure about the policy response of the central bank. In EMU, there is much greater uncertainty since the brief of the ECB is to focus on conditions across Euroland not in an individual country, so individual countries may be concerned that the initial cost of labour and product-market reforms or that fiscal consolidation will not be cushioned by an easing of monetary policy.

However, this is not something that need concern Britain outside the single currency and any influence it might acquire within EMU would be far outweighed by inability to keep both fiscal and monetary policy in tune with the domestic economy. In practice, such coordination between the euro group and the ECB would not have the desired effect since the level of interest rates set by the ECB would still not be appropriate for all countries. Furthermore, arguments for such coordination fail to take account of the economics involved in structural reform – reviewed in Chapter 8. Even if structural reforms were coordinated to ensure that every country proceeded at the same pace, which is very difficult to imagine in practice, it would still cause problems. The equilibrium rate of interest would only be the same for all countries if they were starting from the same base in terms of economic structure and productivity, which they are plainly not. The result is that even with coordination the inevitable adjustments in real exchange rates would take the form of differential rates of inflation between countries. It is simply ludicrous to suggest that Britain is losing influence by not being part of such discussions within the euro group.

But the euro, we are told, will come to rival the dollar and being part of this will give Britain a bigger voice in the world's financial arenas. It is difficult to know what this means: Britain has its own right to membership of international institutions such as the group of seven (G7) industrial countries and the IMF. The euro is a major currency bloc, but if it is to rival the dollar in a serious way it will have to generate the economic dynamism of the USA too. But for reasons spelt out earlier in this book there are structural features about EMU that prevent this happening. And it is one of the more curious features in discussions about EMU that those who appear most confident that Euroland and its currency will challenge the USA and the dollar are generally those most hostile to the economics that underpin both.

Some of those seeking to strengthen coordination within the euro group and increase its role and power do so with the aim of creating an 'economic government' to counter and eventually undermine the independence of the ECB and this is a particular obsession with the French. The political implications of this will be outlined in Chapter 13, but there is an economic objective too:

the political management of exchange rates. Proponents of the single currency point out that it is the US Treasury and not the Fed that decides 'dollar policy' in the USA. Article 111 of the Treaty of the European Union states that the ECB can be instructed by the Council of Ministers (in effect Ecofin) to implement an exchange rate target. This is a step that can only be initiated by the Commission or the ECB and would not be taken lightly, since it would expose the limits to the independence of the ECB, but it could happen and reflects a preoccupation of many EMU enthusiasts. They want not only to eliminate currency fluctuations within Euroland, but also to use this as a base for intervening in foreign exchange markets in an attempt to manage those as well. This will not work and is a bad idea anyway and Britain should not seek to be part of the attempt.

In the right circumstances, intervention by central banks in the foreign exchange markets can be an effective and useful way of dampening down currency movements, since policy-makers may have justified concerns about rate of change as much as the level of a currency. However, beyond that, central bank intervention, even when coordinated, generally only 'succeeds' in turning a currency when it is in line with market sentiment. The Plaza Agreement in September 1985 is sometimes put forward as an example of successful coordinated action, in that case to bring about a lower dollar. The dollar certainly did fall after Plaza, but the process had already been under way and in fact the rate of decline in the dollar in the six months after was broadly similar to that in the six months prior to the agreement. And apparently successful intervention can also wreak havoc on an economy. For example, the Louvre Accord in February 1987 was designed to put a floor under the dollar, but this resulted in Japan keeping interest rates much lower than appropriate for its economy and was one of the reasons that asset prices rose excessively before bursting with very damaging effects that still remained unresolved fifteen years later.

The attempt by some policy-makers in Europe to control currency movements, within Euroland and more broadly, is understandable. As noted earlier, the so-called European 'social model' was founded in a world in which exchange rates were fixed and private sector capital flows were limited. Most of Europe's political leaders are uncomfortable with the implications of vast amounts of private capital flowing around the world. There is no going back, but the excesses generated in the final phase of the long upswing in America during the 1990s led to a climate in which it might seem propitious to those seeking to consolidate their old model. Of course, the 'social model' was associated for quite some time with a period of very successful economic performance in Europe's economies, and this was accompanied by many of the features that are now said to explain Europe's poor performance, excessive regulation and tax, high levels of public spending and inflexible labour markets. But the long-term economic effects of these were partially hidden by the particular circumstances of post-war Europe, including the scope for catch-up with the

USA that provided huge potential to sustain fast rates of GDP growth. Since the mid 1970s, the European model has been much less successful and in the 1990s the contrast with the USA was stark.

Tony Blair and Gordon Brown both seemed to be aware of the drawback to Europe's economic and social model, though when they call for economic reform neither seem alert to the economic implications of this (rates of return on investment rise) and the debilitating effects of the single currency on the potential benefits from economic reform. This reflects a failure to grasp the degree of economic convergence that is required to make a single currency work in the absence of a political union. The loss of an independent monetary policy will create serious economic problems unless convergence goes very much further than either Tony Blair or Gordon Brown deem necessary.

The Blair Government's tests were first set out in October 1997 and were summarised as follows:

> Are business cycles and economic structures compatible so that we, and others could live comfortably with euro interest rates on a permanent basis?
> If problems emerge is there sufficient flexibility to deal with them?
> Would joining EMU create better conditions for firms making long-term decisions to invest in Britain?
> What impact would entry into EMU have on the competitive position of the UK's financial services industry, particularly the City's wholesale markets?
> In summary, will joining EMU promote higher growth, stability and lasting increase in jobs?

In June 2003, the Government came to the conclusion that, on its own definition, 'convergence' was incomplete so that the economic gains that it thought might flow from membership of EMU could not be delivered either – at least for the time being – and entry without convergence would be damaging to the British economy. The Government's assessment stated that macroeconomic stability is 'a prerequisite of successful economic reform'. However, there was a fundamental weakness at the heart of the eminently sensible desire to combine overall economic stability with economic dynamism: it can't be done with a single currency, at least not without a degree of convergence that goes much further than the Government's two most important tests.

As seen above, the first one of these suggests that business cycles and economic structures need to be 'compatible' if Britain is to live 'comfortably' with interest rates set by the ECB. 'Compatible' is hardly the same as 'fully convergent', and the assessment argued that, 'the convergence test does not require complete convergence at all times. That would be an impossible standard, and one not met in existing monetary unions.' But other successful monetary unions (for example, the USA, Australia or Great Britain) have a variety of political and cultural ties that do not apply in Euroland, but which hold them together as viable, if not necessarily optimal, currency unions (an important distinction that will be addressed in the next chapter). The second of the five tests was intended to cover any failures of the first. However, there were problems with the second test too: the need for more 'flexibility' to deal with insufficient convergence under the first test. In the assessment, there was much stress on the need for this flexibility to make up for the loss of exchange rate flexibility in riding out economic shocks of one sort or another.

Of course the need for this alternative source of flexibility was an explicit acknowledgement that allowing a currency to move up and down is an important tool for helping stabilise an economy, otherwise there would be no 'loss' to make up. As the Government's assessment stated, the 'removal of these adjustment mechanisms means that the remaining ones have to work harder'. But nowhere did the assessment recognise that measures that improve the supply-side performance of the economy are themselves very often forms of asymmetric shocks. Gordon Brown saw improvements in the flexibility of the British economy as one of the most important issues to be addressed if Britain is to be convergent with Euroland and he has made numerous speeches and written articles to that effect. It is very desirable that the British economy is flexible, but if the structure of the economy actually were to improve and become more 'flexible' there would be macroeconomic consequences that will be apparent to those who have been following the argument in this book. The anticipated rate of return on capital would go up. To maintain overall economic stability, interest rates would have to go up and sterling would have to appreciate to a level above the notional long-run equilibrium rate. That, in the logic of the economic tests, would mean reduced convergence and thus make entry, if judged on those tests, less likely. If successful supply-side reforms were made, it would take several years before the disturbances to the rate of return, to interest rates, to the growth of the capital stock and to the exchange rate had subsided again. And, of course, if 'successful' supply-side reform actually took place inside monetary union, it would provoke an uncontrollable boom and bust. For the reasons explained in Chapter 8, even if the political will existed, the single currency has made it more difficult for existing participants to embark upon economic reform. In a joint article, Gordon Brown and the finance ministers of Germany and France stated: 'We will continue with our two pronged approach – macroeconomic stability and growth, and structural reforms to release the strong underlying potential within our economies.'[14] Within EMU, this combination of stability and dynamism is next to impossible since individual countries have thrown away the most important policy tool to support economic reform and budgetary consolidation: an independent monetary policy focused on the requirements of the domestic economy. It is this that provides the necessary stability.

The assessment in 2003 looked to fiscal policy as a 'substitute for the loss of national monetary policy', though it acknowledged with commendable understatement that it was a blunt instrument – 'Discretionary fiscal policy is not without its problems.' As the relevant background paper observed:

> Simulations in econometric models assume policy-makers can implement fiscal policy in a timely and well-targeted manner. The experience of the UK in the 1950s and 1960s when stabilisation policy was primarily done through fiscal policy, and the experiences of other countries, illustrates the difficulties in operating an effective counter-cyclical discretionary fiscal policy in practice.[15]

After the assessment, various institutional changes were put forward by the Government to improve the effectiveness of fiscal policy were Britain to join EMU. However, these were wholly unconvincing and likely to be destabilising forces on the economy, and in any case missed the most important point. Fiscal policy provides no substitute for a domestically oriented monetary policy for reasons set out earlier: they operate in different ways and have very different effects on an economy.

The five tests were simply inadequate for the task for which they were designed, as some of those involved admitted to me in private, and not just because of the difficulties associated with the results needing to be 'clear and unambiguous'. This is perhaps not altogether surprising, since, as will seen in Chapter 15, the tests were constructed in response to newspaper stories that made it necessary to construct a rational basis for any decision by the Government. Any criticism about the coherence of the five tests is not to disparage the Treasury officials involved in the undertaking and sharing in Geoffrey Robinson's champagne on the completion of a hectic weekend's work. They were given the task by their political masters and they were never asked to evaluate the merits of a single currency and in this respect they mirror both the Werner Report and the Delors Report (see Chapter 4), both of which started from the assumption that economic and monetary union was a 'good thing'. When Gordon Brown announced the tests in October 1997, he said: 'The potential benefits of a successful single currency are obvious.' They are not, though the potential economic benefits from genuine economic convergence may be, but those drawing up the five tests were never asked to examine the degree of economic convergence that was necessary to make a single currency successful and sustainable in the absence of a political union. In October 1997, Gordon Brown said (and has repeated many times since) that, 'convergence must be capable of being sustained,' but this goes well beyond any need for convergent business cycles. The five tests miss the point. A single currency in Europe would be consistent with integration and economic convergence, with drawing the full advantage from capital liberalisation and with a successful single market only if asymmetric real shocks were of minimal importance. For this to happen, the process of levelling up productivity and income standards would have had to be completed – for the changes that trigger such levelling up are themselves asymmetric real shocks (as noted in Chapter 8 when considering the nature of economic reform in Europe and in Chapter 10 for Britain in the 1980s).

However, even that would not be enough. The whole 'economic culture' would have to become uniform across countries, to rule out the possibility of future divergence. The relative sizes of the public and private sectors, the degree of government regulation and subsidy, the role of corporatist institutions versus free markets, the scope and direction of social security systems, the cast of education – all these would have to be 'harmonised'. What is more, there would have to be complete certainty that no country in the monetary union could ever move away from this state of conformity in the future. These conditions amount, in effect, to the prior existence of a single government – complete political union. But, of course, if these conditions existed, exchange rates would be stable anyway, so there would be no need to invent a single currency for the minimal reduction in 'transaction' costs that even enthusiasts for EMU regard as insignificant.

PART FOUR

The Politics
of Europe

CHAPTER TWELVE

It's the Politics, Stupid

Other Monetary Unions

In June 1999, Professor Willem Buiter[1] wrote:

> For a rather small economy like Britain, which is quite open to
> international trade in goods and services, and very open to international
> financial flows, the cost benefit analysis of monetary union is simple.
> A national currency and independent national monetary policy are an
> expensive luxury, a costly way of expressing a preference for national
> sovereignty. The UK is not an optimal currency area. A superior
> alternative, UK membership in monetary union is available.

This was picked-up by some of the Prime Minister's policy advisers on Europe
in No. 10 and in the Cabinet Office, so I commented on the economic arguments
in a brief note for Tony's weekend 'red box'. The notion of an optimal or
optimum currency area (OCA) often features in the debate on EMU, so it is
worth spending a little time on the concept and its significance.

There is now a huge literature on what constitutes an optimum currency
area: that is to say the area that is best served in economic terms by sharing a
single currency. However, deciding whether an area is an 'optimum' currency
area is fundamentally less interesting or important than is assessing whether it
is a 'viable' one. This is a matter of politics.

All nation states, with the exception of those participating in EMU and very small ones (like Panama, Monaco, Liechtenstein and one or two others), have a single currency. Are they all really optimum currency areas? Is Britain an optimum currency area? Is Western Australia really part of an optimum currency area with Victoria or Alberta with Quebec? It is not clear and doesn't matter. What is clear is that a viable currency union is essentially a function of political cohesion and when that goes, so does the currency. When formerly federal states, such as the USSR, Yugoslavia or Czechoslovakia, broke up, the now-divided nation states rapidly introduced their own separate currencies.

Monetary unions can be either multinational or national. Some advocates of the single currency who think that it is possible to have a multinational monetary union without political union point to the Gold Standard as an example of a long-lasting monetary union that did not involve political integration, but the Gold Standard is not analogous to EMU, for several reasons.

First, although each country pegged its own national currency to gold, there was no single currency and each country could, and some did, adjust or revoke its peg. Moreover, central banks had various stratagems for retaining a considerable degree of independent national control over domestic monetary policies so there was no single monetary policy either.

Secondly, the Gold Standard was not a free-trade area, far less with any ambition to become a single market. If participant countries felt that their own domestic interests required it, they could adjust to external competitive pressures by changes in their tariffs and duties.

Thirdly, the Gold Standard existed in a period before governments were perceived to have the capacity or duty to use macroeconomic policies to maintain employment and living standards. Government spending was a small proportion of GDP and the use of fiscal policy (let alone fiscal transfers between regions) to cushion economic downturns was never envisaged.

Fourthly, wage/price flexibility was probably greater in the nineteenth than in the twentieth century but, more importantly, labour migration between members of the Gold Standard, especially from Europe to the Americas and Australasia was vastly greater before 1914 than is ever likely to be case within the EU.

Finally, although the Gold Standard may have become an article of faith in some of the central countries in the system (notably Britain), by the early twentieth century, many of the participants, particularly on the periphery, regarded continued membership as a matter of choice that depended on perceived national advantage – and this had the potential to change, it was not an irrevocable commitment. Each country decided independently. There was no international treaty.

In the event, the credibility and cooperation required to maintain the system were eroded by the political and economic consequences of the First World War. And although a gold standard was reinstated in two variants in the twentieth century (the inter-war gold standard, 1925–1937, and the Bretton Woods system, 1945–73), like Humpty Dumpty it could never be put together again after 1914.

There are two other multinational currency unions worth looking at.[3] The first of these was the Latin Monetary Union, which lasted for sixty years from 1865. In practice, this was a last-ditch attempt to shore up currencies based on bimetallism (gold and silver). The second was the Scandinavian Monetary Union that ran from 1873 to 1931, which represented a coordinated effort by participants to move from silver to gold as the base for the currency system.

The Latin Monetary Union involved France, Belgium, Switzerland and Italy and was joined a bit later by Greece and Romania. Soon after the inauguration of the union the gold price rose. This caused inevitable problems with a bimetallic monetary system so, in 1885, the union considered adopting a single gold standard. This was rejected since the cost of redeeming the silver coins in circulation, then intrinsically below its par value, was too expensive; but it was only this threat that held the union together. A new agreement was signed that stipulated that any country leaving the union would have to exchange the others' holdings of its silver coins into gold.

The union eventually broke up as a result of the First World War. The sharp increase in military expenditures left members no choice but to issue paper money and this remained in circulation after the end of hostilities. As paper money was not recognised as legal means of payment in any other than the issuing country, the union no longer had any practical effect and during the war silver coins had been melted or exported, so remaining coins were a small part of money supply. In 1925, Belgium announced its intention to leave and the others followed, but in practice this formalised a collapse that had occurred earlier.

Prior to the formation of the Scandinavian Monetary Union in 1873, Sweden, Norway and Denmark had had a long history of similar units of account and exchange of notes and coins between them and they were all on the silver standard. During the latter part of the nineteenth century, three factors combined to create a more formal union. First, all Scandinavian countries became convinced of the benefits from a currency based on gold, not least for the fact that both Britain and Germany were both on gold and these were the most important trading partners for the countries of Scandinavia. Secondly, the decimal system gained favour and, finally, the nationalistic sentiments running through Europe in the latter part of the nineteenth century took the form of 'Scandinavism' in Scandinavia – a social and political willingness to bring Nordic countries closer together in many areas.

The formation of the Scandinavian union saw the emergence of a new currency, the Swedish krona and this was specified in terms of gold and was to be equal in all three countries where the new gold coin was minted. Subsidiary coins were minted in silver and copper and, although there was no restriction on the amount that each country was allowed to mint, all were legal tender in the three countries.

No particular economic strains seem to have appeared in the union prior to the First World War, but with the outbreak of war Scandinavian notes were declared inconvertible to gold and at the same time, in order to prevent an out-flow of gold, the export of gold was prohibited. The growth of the money supply thereby ceased being tied to the price of gold and the basis for the exchange of Scandinavian notes at par was eliminated. By the end of the war, to all intents and purposes, the union had ended. Outstanding matters were dealt with in a supplementary agreement in 1924 that terminated the original union.

For various reasons, therefore, the multinational monetary unions broke under the strain of events. National monetary unions have fared rather better and the monetary unions of the USA, Italy and Germany (as well as Great Britain) all took place after political union had been established.

In the case of Italy, there is no room for debate. The forces for political integration were (and still are) weak, but unification was completed in 1861 and a new unified coinage system was introduced in 1862 based on the lira, though an effective single monetary authority was not established until later.

In Germany, there is some disagreement as to the most important step towards monetary union and its timing in relation to political union. Some point to the unification of the coinage in 1857 as a significant step on the way to monetary union, but most commentators now accept that, as in Italy, the most significant elements of monetary union in Germany came after the establishment of the new, unified German Reich in 1871. Unlike Italy, the forces of political integration – Prussian arms – were strong in Germany and political unification was followed by three major changes in the monetary system. These were the conversion of the currency standard from silver to gold, the introduction of the mark as the unit of account throughout the Reich in the Banking Acts of 1871 and 1873, and, finally and most importantly, the establishment of the Reichsbank in the Banking Act of 1875.

In many respects, however, the most interesting example of a national monetary union is that of the USA. Its monetary union formally began with the ratification of the Constitution in 1788 and has survived ever since, with a temporary break during the Civil War. Proponents of EMU want to emulate the power and influence of the American economy and the dollar, and the USA is often cited in evidence of the advantages that monetary union will bring to Euroland.

Clearly, the USA does now benefit from having a single currency, but in purely economic terms this was not always the case. America experienced a succession of economic crises that could have prised the continent apart had it not been held together within political framework that was settled, at least after the Civil War. The benefits of a single currency took time to emerge and did so because the role of central government expanded and because the USA developed some of the characteristics of an 'optimum currency area'. America has only been able to do that because it is a nation.

It was Robert Mundell who first used the term 'optimum currency area', in a famous paper published in 1961 in which he tried to define the optimum geographic area that should share a common currency. His starting point was to consider the implications of an 'asymmetric shock' and he used a hypothetical North America that was divided into two regions – the East, producing cars, and the West, producing lumber – to postulate a sudden rise in demand for western goods and away from eastern goods. A shift in demand from cars to lumber that would tend to create a boom in the West and a recession in the East.

If the two regions had separate exchange rates, a depreciation of the East's currency (an appreciation of the West's) would stabilise demand. Alternatively, if the factors of production – labour and capital – could move freely between regions, there would be no need for exchange rate adjustment. Resources would move from the depressed East to the booming West, factor (labour and capital) mobility would be a substitute for exchange rate changes. Mundell held that the East and the West should have different currencies if there was no factor mobility between regions, while they should have a common currency if factor mobility was high, since in that case there would be less need for exchange rate changes to stabilise regions experiencing an asymmetric shock.

Mundell's point was that the optimum currency area was a region or geographical area with boundaries unrelated to those of a nation state, so that, in the illustrative example, the East-West divide would not have been ameliorated by currencies based on a north-south (Canada-USA) axis. This optimum currency area, defined in terms of internal factor mobility and external factor immobility, had also to be relatively large for reasons beyond the scope of this book.

Mundell was not proposing anything as silly as changing the monetary areas in North America, but he did argue that the economic case for flexible exchange rates was only valid for single-region countries. Flexible national currencies cannot help solve British regional unemployment, or Italian problems in the Mezzogiorno, or US problems in the Appalachians or German problems east of the Elbe, so, Mundell suggested, if the argument for floating exchange rates is valid, it could be applied to every sub-region in any country, with a proliferation of new currencies.

This merely demonstrates that logic taken too far may not lead to sensible conclusions with relevance to the world in which we actually live. In this world, if a sufficiently large number of people within a national monetary union do have a stronger sense of identity with geographical areas smaller than the nation state of which they are part, there is indeed a strong case for separate currencies. This happened with the break-up of the USSR and Czechoslovakia, but that is a matter of politics not economics. But in viable currency areas people in regions still primarily identify with the nation state of which they are a part.

In a strict sense it may be true that flexible national currencies can do nothing to ameliorate regional disparities, but it is beside the point. It is precisely because people ultimately identify with their national economy and the political settlement underpinning it that any strains from any regional disparities can be absorbed and responded to, indeed political pressure will demand a response. People have a very different attitude and tolerance towards similar problems in other countries, and that applies in or out of a single monetary system.

Mundell recognised that, in the real world, currencies are mainly an expression of national sovereignty, so that actual currency reorganisation would be feasible only if it were accompanied by profound political changes. However, he believed such a process to be underway in Europe so that the case for EMU amounted to little more than an empirical question as to whether Euroland had sufficient degree of factor mobility to be delineated a single region. But to pose the question is to provide the answer and begs a further question. For Mundell, 'Europe's geography makes it a political entity.'[4] This might mean anything, but what sort of political entity? Euroland is clearly not a political entity like other successful monetary unions, which leaves in doubt whether its cohesion is sufficiently robust to withstand the political and economic tensions inherent in any monetary union, national or multinational.

The US experience is instructive.[5] Throughout its first 150 years, the country was wracked repeatedly by bitter regional disputes over monetary policies. Some of these, for example the so-called 'Bank War' that killed off the Second Bank of the United States in 1836, took place before the Civil War, but most came after. High-profile examples included major bank panics (in 1873, 1884, 1890, 1893, 1902 and 1907) as well as the Great Depression of the 1890s and the Depression of the 1930s.

Regional disputes over monetary policy arose because of real differences in regional interests: what was good monetary policy from the point of view of one region was sometimes bad from the point of view of another. In broad terms, the disputes pitted the north-east (and in general the Pacific) states against the farming interests of the Midwest and the South. The bitterest disputes arose when adverse monetary reactions occurred in a region already suffering from a real shock. A decline in the demand for agricultural products, for example, would depress incomes, leading in turn to a round of bank failures and bank runs, and declining regional money supplies, that reinforced the effect of the initial shock. From a strictly economic point of view, for a long period in its history America might have been better off had it been divided into regions with different currencies.

Certain regions of the USA clearly exhibited many of the features associated with candidature for separate currencies, at least until the 1930s. The regions of the USA were large economies by world standards and were subject to asymmetric shocks, the Midwest in agriculture and the South in cash crops, especially cotton. Capital markets became integrated by the turn of the century but labour mobility was limited. The South was pretty well cut off from the rest of America until the Second World War and although mobility between other regions was much higher, moving in response to regional shocks was still difficult in the 1930s.

In both the Great Depression and the Depression there were major errors in national policy and in the 1930s no region could have been immune from crisis, but, with separate currencies, the regions hit by severe asymmetric shocks would have been able to devalue, which would have reduced inter-regional loss of reserves and this might have ameliorated some elements of the crisis that were particular to the region.

Of course, within the USA there was no desire or prospect for separate regional currencies – though for a period after the Civil War there were two currencies, since the Pacific Coast had a separate currency, the 'yellowback' in contrast to the Yankee 'greenback', based on gold; and of course, during the Civil War, the Confederacy had its own currency (two, in fact, at one stage). This is not to suggest (any more than did Professor Mundell) that is it sensible to argue that currency reorganisation of America was either practical or desirable, but the US experience shows that regional differences can create serious economic and political tensions within a monetary union. Clearly the nature of these will be very different in twenty-first century Europe than in nineteenth and early twentieth-century America, but the basic problem remains and Euroland clearly lacks the political cohesion of America.

Since the end of the Second World War, the USA has continued to experience asymmetric real shocks. Examples include the oil-price fluctuations that periodically hit Texas, the changes in manufacturing affecting the 'rust belt' of the north-east in the 1980s or the fall-out in California from the high-tech bubble in 2001. But the institutional changes that took place in the Depression and the war weakened the old divisions.

The USA reaped the economic benefits of monetary union when capital and (finally) labour moved freely (the long-term isolation of the South's labour market didn't end until after the Second World War). Two other factors also played their part. A system of inter-regional fiscal transfers that helped to cushion regions suffering from asymmetric shocks was introduced, together with a system of deposit insurance that helped ensure that asymmetric real shocks are not aggravated by banking crises. This occurred because America was a country. There are no examples of enduring monetary unions that have not been accompanied by political unions, so much so that with the exception of the newly formed EMU all other economically and politically significant monetary unions are all nation states. Does that mean that monetary union can only work with a high degree of political centralisation and integration? Is this the inevitable outcome for Euroland?

Of course there are those that want this anyway for political reasons. The implications of this will be addressed later. However, there are others in Britain who favour participation in EMU on economic grounds but who believe that this can be combined with a decentralised political framework. It might be prudent to be sure of this before committing Britain to the single currency, but for a variety of reasons the history of previous monetary unions – whether multinational or national – is deemed to have little relevance to EMU.

First, it is suggested that EMU is attempting something different from anything tried in the past. EMU combines elements of both national (there is a single central bank) and multinational unions (there is no overriding political authority). There is no precedent for a group of monetary and politically independent countries surrendering their national currencies to form a common monetary union based on a new unit of account under the leadership of a common monetary authority, while still retaining political independence. However, this doesn't in itself tell us much about its future development and whether it will work without some of the features that have characterised successful monetary unions in the past. After all, designing a bicycle with oblong wheels would be different, but experience would tell us that it wouldn't run very well. EMU will have to withstand some serious economic and political strains and it is not enough to simply deny the relevance of previous monetary unions. It has to be explained how the framework of the single currency is to contain the tensions that would seem to be inherent in any monetary union, national or multinational. Although EMU may not be vulnerable to particular weaknesses of some earlier multinational monetary unions that tolerated multiple central banks, it may be vulnerable in other ways.

It is also suggested that there are limited lessons for EMU from the past because previous monetary unions, both national and multinational, were based on a metallic standard, particularly gold, that provided an anchor for individual currencies. Furthermore, the monetary unions of the nineteenth century were not concerned with the price level – as is EMU – or with sustaining economic growth or employment. They were mainly concerned with the complications resulting from the circulation of numerous coins of widely varying denomination and purity and with the absence of a single standard for denominating contracts. To that extent, the efforts to get rid of them by establishing multinational currency unions resembled more the single market than the single currency.

This is all very well – and the parallels with Latin and Scandinavian monetary union are limited – but if the comparison is with the single market, no one seriously suggests that this needs political union. It does not mean that genuine monetary unions (such as EMU and other national monetary unions are) do not need political underpinning that goes well beyond existing arrangements in Euroland.

The reasons why the Gold Standard provided a poor precedent for EMU were set out earlier, but this simply raises more questions about the political structure of Euroland. In the past, it was relatively easy to create national or multinational monetary currency unions because the members of the ensuing union, regardless as to whether they were different regions or different countries, already had their currencies tied to a metal such as silver or gold. The monetary system remained a metallic standard after unification and this provided an essentially politically neutral anchor for participants.

EMU is not like that at all. It is a multinational monetary union based on paper and in the absence of the metallic anchor it has established a nominal anchor (inflation targeting), which is based on political agreement. But the political landscape can change. This is very different to the Gold Standard when there was no dispute about the nature of the anchor. If EMU is to maintain its nominal anchor it requires that the initial political commitment remain undiminished; but differences about objectives may alter in the future. The process is far less automatic than using a metallic anchor. Politics is built into the very structure of EMU in a way that was not the case with gold. This may not make political union inevitable but it puts a premium on political cooperation and this is likely to lead to more political integration than presently exists.

It is further claimed that those who think that EMU will lead to centralisation ignore the unique nature of the coalition of nation states in Euroland. Earlier federations, it is argued, involving monetary unions coalesced at a time when the nation state and its powers were undeveloped. This left a vacuum for powers to develop at the federal, central level, and this is what happened in all cases, though to differing degrees. But the EU is a coalition of already developed states. Hence it is argued that this makes it less likely that Euroland will be centralised since that would mean nation states giving up major powers.

This is only partially true and misses the point. Even before the single currency the EU certainly led to considerable centralisation of powers, and examples of previous monetary unions suggest that pressures for this will increase. Even if we accept that established nation states will resist tendencies towards centralisation it begs the question as to whether this is a credible position with a single currency. It could be that it is the strength of national identity that prevents EMU working, since monetary union requires participants to see nations in same way as US citizens see their states. Indeed, it is precisely because nations are well developed that the EU requires supranational bodies in some areas and may require it in EMU.

The fourth reason put forward for discounting the relevance of previous multinational monetary unions is that their break-ups have come about as a result of political and economic shocks that were extraneous to monetary union, most notably the growing tensions in the lead-up to the First World War. It is argued that although it is possible to envisage circumstances in which the EU might split apart, the cost of doing so and the prospects of this happening are made more remote because the degree of interdependence between them is greater than in earlier monetary unions.

It may be true that EMU members are tied more closely together than in a number of previous multinational monetary unions, though much less closely than in national monetary unions. However, the perceived cost of exit merely makes it more likely that there are delays in dealing with an emerging political/economic crisis and that when it develops and the status quo is no longer an option the pressure will be for more integration.

Previous monetary unions may have buckled under political and economic events that originated outside the union, but this does not mean there are no implications for EMU. Such events will almost certainly reoccur in some form or another, although we can probably rule out war between the nations of Euroland. The issue that still has to be addressed is how they are handled within a multinational monetary union such as EMU.

What is clear from history is that although politics are crucial in founding monetary unions and this certainly includes EMU, they have also been important factors in sustaining or destroying them. If a monetary union is to survive it must retain political cohesion. In theory, this may not mean the creation of something close to a nation state, even if in practice it is the only model that has lasted any length of time. But, one way or another, Euroland has to create greater political cohesion since it has obviously less of this than in other surviving monetary unions where – as was previously envisaged in Europe – political union has preceded it.

In most monetary unions, governments have introduced a system of 'transfer payments'. This system acts as an extra safety valve and allows a significant proportion of GDP to be transferred from rich to poorer regions. The Delors Report expressed concern that, 'If sufficient consideration were not given to regional imbalances, the economic union would be faced with grave economic and political risks.' There are limits to the effectiveness of this and there is considerable literature on the significance of the role of the federal budget within large currency unions, both in reducing inequalities (the redistributive function) and in offsetting asymmetric regional shocks (the stabilisation function). Even in monetary unions with large fiscal transfers, severe regional problems can arise as they have from time to time in the USA, where federal taxes are used to iron out imbalances between regions. But the question naturally arises as to whether, when national monetary unions join together in EMU, it requires there to be a larger EU budget.

The Treasury's assessment in 2003 came to the conclusion that fiscal transfers within member states were already sufficiently large to reduce the need for a larger central budget. This may be true, but other reports (including one for the EU Commission as far back as 1977 under the chairmanship of the late Sir Donald MacDougall) come to different conclusions, and it is a fact that significant fiscal transfers are a feature of successful national monetary unions and are used to address imbalances that occur within their boundaries. When such things happen in a mature and cohesive monetary union – federal or unitary – the Government and the currency union will be taken for granted, or seen as a supportive institution. When oil prices fell or the technology bubble burst, Texans and Californians did not blame their plight on their fixed dollar. It is much less clear what the response will be in Europe if countries and regions are faced with serious economic difficulties. It is more likely that cases of recession or depression within EMU will be blamed, rightly or wrongly, on membership of the exchange rate regime. In such circumstances the EU will be unable to point to any overt provision of any financial support to a country, or a region, in particular difficulties. Almost inevitably, EMU will be perceived in due course as seriously damaging the economic interests of some large part of some member country.

Member states are very reluctant to increase the size of the EU budget and for understandable reasons. But if countries do not feel sufficient cohesion to agree a larger transfer of fiscal competence to the federal centre are they sufficiently cohesive to maintain a single currency when, as they surely will, economic and political tensions arise? Some proponents of the single currency suggest that over time a larger EU budget will be easier to accommodate. This is because with the single currency there are no balance of payments figures and it will become harder to estimate the net costs, or benefits, to any constituent nation of any fiscal measure. For example, it is argued, if each country in the UK had a separate currency and could assess and potentially veto every UK fiscal proposal that it did not like, nothing would ever get done at Westminster. However, the reason that the countries making up the United Kingdom do not have separate currencies is that they are in an established political union. Nonetheless, it is hoped that the very existence of a single currency could erode national selfishness in a manner that would facilitate the subsequent transfer of suitable fiscal competences to the federal centre. It has to be said that such a view is at odds with the pursuit of national interest that has generally characterised the EU, but in any case it does not resolve the political point that proponents of EMU fully recognise. EMU has first to get through the early years when the single currency is in place without either overwhelming political support or the perceived benefit of a sizeable federal budget.

For a long time, in purely economic terms, the USA was probably not an optimum currency area and it was decades before America reaped the economic benefits of a single currency. It did not do so until labour and capital markets were integrated and a system of inter-regional fiscal transfers had been introduced.

Before that, the USA experienced a series of economic crises that might have prised the monetary union apart if it had not also been a political union, albeit one that had to be finally settled on the battlefields of the Civil War.

Euroland, also in purely economic terms, is certainly less of an optimum currency area than the USA and clearly lacks the political cohesion of America. There is no example in history of enduring monetary union that is not accompanied by political union, but proponents of the single currency argue that it is because Euroland is set on a path that has not been attempted before, that history is no guide to its future. EMU is certainly breaking new ground: there is no previous example of politically independent countries voluntarily surrendering their sovereignty to a supranational monetary authority. Whether this argues for dismissing the lessons of the past is another matter.

It would be absurd to draw hard and fast conclusions from previous monetary unions for EMU. However, it would also be foolish to ignore some of the lessons from the past, not least that a viable currency union requires political cohesion to survive, whatever the economics underpinning it. Previous multinational currency unions were very different in origins and intent to EMU but for this very reason, in economic terms, were easier to establish in the first place. EMU involves a currency union spanning a set of sovereign states with relatively little federal centralisation of either political power or of fiscal competences. The issue is whether this is a sustainable position and, if it is not, what implications does this have for the political structure of Euroland and Britain's decision on the euro?

CHAPTER THIRTEEN

Democracy or Directorate

The Political Impact of EMU

In most of continental Europe, political union and EMU are two sides of the same coin. 'It would be senseless to unify the currency in Europe except with a view to political union... The Community's vocation is to become a political union and monetary union is an important part of the process.'[1] This is the view of Tommaso Padoa-Schioppa, Secretary to the Delors Committee, and shared by many others. But the form of political union will affect and be affected by the single currency and this chapter will examine the likely impact of the economics of the single currency on the nature of the emerging political union.

Peering into the likely political future of Europe, it is worth reflecting on some recurring themes from the past, and one of these has been the struggle for ascendancy between the 'federalists' and the 'intergovernmentalists', between proponents of a supranational Europe and a Europe of nation states. However, while it is tempting to see the political framework of the EU being determined by a battle between federalists and intergovernmentalists, the reality is more complicated, not least because of differences within the two camps.

There were at least two sorts of federalist. There were the so-called 'funda-mentalists' or 'constitutionalists'. At various times, they put forward blueprints for an overtly federal future, accompanied by proposals for a written constitution with executive, legislative and judicial functions spelt out. Then there were others who favoured political integration step by step as a result of advances in stages and by sectors, for example, coal and steel, the economy or defence. These have been termed the 'functionalists' and have generally advanced their cause through the cumulative impact of treaties rather than a specific constitutional settlement. This group has been the driving force of Europe for much of its history, with Jean Monnet a prime exponent (see Chapter 3).

However, the difference between the fundamentalists and the functionalists was about means not ends. The aim of both was some sort of federated Europe, but in the case of the functionalist it might creep up, if not by stealth, since many were open about the objective, at least in ways that blurred the ultimate destination. As more and more activities were progressively shared, the substance of national policies gradually and progressively came under shared sovereignty. The jargon of the EU describes this process as the 'community method', in which matters are slowly transferred from intergovernmental decisions to those of the 'Community'. Over time, this shared sovereignty has to acquire political powers and a political authority is established to cover the sectors already integrated, but the process itself blurs the lines of democratic accountability that feature, at least formally, in most of the federal schemes and blueprints from the fundamentalists.

The intergovernmentalists were not a solid phalanx either, with perspectives often reflecting different views about the role of the state. On occasion, France appears at one end of the spectrum and Britain at the other. Countries may use the same language and may appear to be sharing common objectives in supporting 'a union of sovereign states', but in practice British views have very different implications for the nature of such a union from much of the rest of the EU, particularly the French. A political tradition in which the role of the state is pervasive is one that, within the EU, puts a premium on harmonisation and a discount on diversity with the practical consequences of intergovernmentalism rather similar to the plans of functional federalists.

Furthermore, among some of the key players, support for intergovernmentalism has altered over time. For example, under de Gaulle, France saw further European integration as a threat to national sovereignty at a time when France was confident of its leadership in the Franco-German alliance. De Gaulle's exit and the consolidation of German economic dominance in Europe during the 1970s and 1980s (particularly during the ERM period when the deutschmark was the anchor of the system) changed French arguments for integration. 'More Europe' became useful for the French as a vehicle to dilute Germany's dominant position, and EMU the means to that end. Since then, there has been an apparent revival of intergovernmentalism in France and, after Chancellor Kohl, its emergence with talk of the 'German Way' from Chancellor Schroeder. However, at the Convention on the Future of Europe in 2003 it became clear that France also saw 'more Europe' as a means of corralling some of the new members from the former Soviet bloc and keeping the Franco-German partnership in control.

The various strands of thought that have gone into making the political framework for Europe are, not surprisingly, a mixture of the federal and the intergovernmental and this is likely to remain so for some time yet. However, in some respects at least, it has resulted in the worst of both: a political union that is centralised and largely undemocratic. How will the economics of EMU affect this?

The tussle between a federal and intergovernmental future for Europe had its parallels in the economics of monetary union, with two strands of thought identifiable in continental Europe. There were those often referred to as 'economists' and there were the so-called 'monetarists' who, despite the name, had nothing to do with monetarist economic theory. And each has generally been associated with particular notions about the appropriate political framework, with the economists favouring a federal system and the monetarists a political union based on the nation state.

The economists were the dominant tradition in Germany, including the Bundesbank, and they saw currency union as the final step to be taken after all the other aspects of economic integration had been completed in full. This view was based on the fact that economic integration between countries takes time, is difficult and will create economic and political tensions. But once integration was accomplished, currency union became a natural and relatively painless 'crowning' and for this reason the approach is sometimes referred to as the 'coronation' theory of monetary union. The monetarists, mainly from France and including Jacques Delors, took a different view, arguing that although a minimum degree of convergence between countries is required before embarking on monetary union, the single currency itself will subsequently stimulate and force through economic integration. For this group, EMU was an agent for change and if its introduction led to periodic crises these were seen as catalysts to force institutional changes that were thought to be desirable.

In economic terms, the monetarists won. Chancellor Kohl agreed to monetary union before economic integration had been completed. The institutional change that the monetarists have sought after most is an 'economic government' and any crisis that occurred as a result of insufficient integration to make EMU work smoothly would be used as an opportunity to push this objective forward. The rationale is economic but the purpose is political. It is argued that a single currency makes the coordination, and ultimately integration, of all other aspects of economic policy necessary too. The Werner Report (see Chapter 4) published in October 1970, was explicit about the objective: 'The development of monetary union will have to be combined with parallel progress towards the harmonisation and finally the unification of economic policies,' calling for a 'centre of decisions on economic policy which would exercise a decisive influence over Community economic policy and especially national budgetary policy'.

The French are particularly keen on establishing an economic government, argued for it during the Maastricht negotiations and continue to see it as a necessary political as well as economic counterweight to the ECB. The French tradition mistrusts markets and seeks to politicise as many economic decisions as possible. It was for this reason that Germany rejected the economic government proposal at Maastricht, maintaining the independence of the new central bank was vital if the German public were to accept the demise of the Bundesbank. Later, in May 1997, the new French Government of Lionel Jospin revived the idea of economic government which, in a watered-down form, was pressed on other governments by France and Germany the following November. This subsequently became the euro group and is seen by its proponents (especially the French) as the basis for a powerful and effective economic government. This aim was made clear in a Franco-German paper on economic governance to the Convention on the Future of Europe in 2003. This called for a reinforced euro group to be recognised in the protocol to the treaty and the election of a president of the euro group for a period of two years, and this was reflected in the wording of the EU constitution drafted by the Convention 'to develop ever-closer coordination of economic policies within the euro area'.

The economic justification for greater coordination reflects concerns about the implications for economic stability in EMU when fiscal policy remains in the hands of national governments. Before EMU started, this was a particular preoccupation of Germany and, after Maastricht, its finance minister, Theo Waigel, led the case for budget discipline in the face of French opposition. A settlement was reached at the Amsterdam European Council in June 1997 when the Stability and Growth Pact (SGP) was signed. This framework was designed to control the fiscal deficits of Euroland members by ensuring that they avoid 'excessive deficits' that might otherwise threaten the macroeconomic stability of Euroland. The SGP was intended to prevent 'free riding'. Without the SGP, it was argued, individual countries would be free to increase budget deficits, safe in the knowledge that in a single-currency area there would be no penalty either in terms of higher interest rates or an exchange rate crisis. Under the SGP, a country should have a 'medium-term orientation' for a deficit that was at, or close to, balance, and in March 2002 the date for this objective was set at 2004.

The details of how the SGP surveillance was supposed to work were arcane, but in essence there was an escalating process as a country's deficit moved or threatened to move, towards an upper limit of three per cent of GDP. The process could last several years and in theory fines could be imposed (up to 0.5 per cent of GDP) but in practice it became clear that this 'nuclear option' would not be used – indeed would be self-defeating by simply making a deteriorating budgetary position worse. Monitoring adherence to the SGP was to be the responsibility of the EU Commission and each year it was to make a report to Ecofin. The Commission has tried to use this process as a way to establish a central, indeed prime, role in running European economic policy and the process has led to several clashes between the EU Commission and member states as well as between member states.

The first of these was in March 2001, when the Commission rapped the knuckles of the Irish Government when it planned a tax-cutting budget. The Commission was supported by a majority of finance ministers (including those from France and Germany), but the Irish Government went ahead anyway. The difficulties intensified as the economic downturn developed through the year. At the beginning of 2002, the Commission recommended that Germany and Portugal be given an 'early warning' that they were in danger of breaching the three per cent limit, but on this occasion finance ministers did not support it. In July, the new Government in Portugal revealed that it had a budget deficit close to 4.5 per cent in 2001. Yet this was only a few weeks after the Commission, using similar economic assumptions, had calculated it at 2.6 per cent, conveniently within the SGP. As a result, Portugal became the first country to trigger the 'excessive deficit' procedure. Portugal promised to take action to cut the deficit to within the accepted guideline, but this implied a wholly improbable (indeed unbelievable) turnaround in a short space of time, and the deficit was only reduced by one-off revenue generating measures, such as the sale of the state telephone network.

In September, the Commission bowed to the inevitable and gave Germany, France, Italy and Portugal an extension of two years until 2006 to balance their budgets, to the fury of Spain, the Netherlands and most small countries that were close to balancing their budgets. France declined to join other countries with excessive deficits in a commitment to reduce them by 0.5 per cent a year starting in 2003 and as a result was isolated eleven to one in the euro group in October 2002. Finance Minister Francis Mer summed up the French position: 'We have decided there are other priorities in France,' a stance that was repeated at the beginning of 2003, when Germany again agreed to curb its deficit. In the event, slower growth made further deterioration of budgetary position inevitable and in October the French and the Germans admitted that they would break the deficit limit for the third successive year in 2004. By November 2003, the SGP was in tatters. The small countries, many of which had taken difficult and painful decisions to keep their budget deficits within the limits set by the SGP, were understandably angry at the way the big countries, especially France, were flouting the rules. The Dutch threatened to take the Commission to court unless it took steps to enforce the excessive deficit procedure. The Commission tried, but there was insufficient support for this among finance ministers and the SGP was effectively suspended with no more than a political promise of better behaviour from France and Germany, with only the Netherlands, Austria, Finland and Spain voting to uphold the letter of the SGP.

All this says quite a lot about the process for enforcing the SGP and the manoeuvring within the euro group. The process is intensely political. Some of the larger countries simply ignore the spirit as well as the letter of the SGP. It is wholly ineffective, entirely concerned with presentation and with no expectation that the disciplines of the system including the early warning or excessive deficit procedures will have any practical effect, at least on the large countries. There is no reason to expect that to change. The Commission will be sidelined, and the difficulties created by the SGP will be used by those who have always seen crisis as a means of pressing on with their agenda of institutional change, to use the euro group as a bridgehead for genuine economic government. And, by 2003, there were at least three forces at work helping them.

First, problems surrounding the SGP and its possible reforms were likely to encourage more coordination and intrusion into the fiscal policy of member states. Secondly, Germany's difficulties undermined its traditional resistance to the politicisation of economic decisions. Thirdly, EMU was creating particular problems for the smaller countries that could ultimately erode their economic independence.

It reached the stage where the President of the Commission, Romano Prodi, described the SGP as 'stupid' and the worsening public finances and rising budget deficits inevitably led in the course of 2003 to an examination of the working of the SGP. For the sake of clarity, attitudes towards the SGP could be categorised into three camps: 'purists', 'cynics' and 'reformers'.

The purists included Spain, Holland, the Nordics, Benelux and Austria and, for a long time, Germany, and this group appeared to take the view that governments with excessive deficits should take action to put things right by cutting spending or raising taxes. The problem for the purists was that tighter fiscal policy would only bring about sustained improvement in the budgetary and debt position of a country if it were associated with economic growth or at least the prospect of economic growth. Without this, raising taxes or cutting expenditure would result in a downward spiral in the economy and rising budgetary problems. This meant that fiscal consolidation in any country had to be accompanied by appropriate monetary policy, but in EMU this was not possible for individual countries. The ECB does give more weight to developments in the larger countries than in the small ones. However, even for the big countries, the degree of coordination between fiscal and monetary policy is a far cry from that of an independent central bank operating a domestically oriented monetary policy, so that they can get into serious difficulties. For example, after the election in 2002, Chancellor Schroeder's Government tightened fiscal policy in Germany, but when its economy continued to deteriorate, further attempts at this self-defeating policy were implicitly abandoned. For the smaller countries, the chance of an appropriate monetary policy is even less and the subsequent problems even greater.

The cynics were led by the French and included the Italians, which was no surprise since these two countries (and others) had to cheat to meet the Maastricht criteria and Italy was taken to task in 2002 for fiddling the figures for its public accounts, with the head statistician in the EU comparing Italian accounting methods, including the securitisation of lottery ticket sales, with Enron. This camp formally endorsed the SGP, but had little intention of taking it seriously, a position summed up by Jacques Chirac during a visit to the Prime Minister of Italy, Silvio Berlusconi, at the end of 2002. The President of France said, 'We both back the stability pact completely and without ambiguity,' before adding that, of course, 'the application of the stability pact requires an adaptation, without in any way changing its objectives, in a period of a growth downturn or weak growth.' On Bastille Day, 2003, President Chirac called for a 'temporary softening' of the SGP, saying that, although he respected the rules, they required a more political interpretation. He was criticised by the finance ministers of Austria, Belgium, Finland, Greece, Spain and the Netherlands, all of whom had taken measures to curb the deficits in their own countries. Gerrit Zalm (Netherlands) summed up their feelings when he said, 'France has already broken the three per cent in two consecutive years. That's enough flexibility.' This was all predictable and it might even be argued that, with the overall economic outlook at the time, a general relaxation of fiscal policy made sense for Euroland as a whole, even though it did nothing for the particular problems of some of the smaller countries. However, beyond the short-term fix, abandoning the SGP was hardly a long-term solution if it was to retain even minimal credibility with financial markets and this was one reason why the third camp became potentially important.

The third group were the reformers and Britain was to the fore in this camp, despite being out of EMU, with Gordon Brown apparently thinking that parts of Britain's fiscal framework might have wider application. Germany moved into this camp too, because of its own difficulties and because it still worried that without some sort of credible framework, certain profligate countries, including Italy, would return to type. The EU Commission also put forward proposals for reform, belatedly coming to see it was inevitable and desirable since attempting to stick to the original pact had lost all credibility: the Commission wanted more focus on debt sustainability and a more sophisticated assessment of the underlying fiscal position rather than the headline deficit. For this group, the design of the SGP was deemed too restrictive and the real problem was said to be that the SGP was a 'one size fits all' policy, which was a bit ironic given that the basis of EMU was a 'one size fits all' monetary policy.

It was argued that the SGP should be adapted to have a greater focus on the medium-term budgetary positions required for each country to achieve debt sustainability. The existing format of SGP made no distinction between the different levels of debt in the countries of Euroland, but the appropriate medium-term budgetary position to stabilise the debt ratio below sixty per cent as envisaged in the SGP will vary from country to country. Countries with high debt ratios required more ambitious targets for budget deficits than countries with lower debt ratios. Furthermore, it was argued that, subject to being compatible with debt sustainability, there needed to be greater willingness to allow budget deficits above three per cent of GDP when these were due to cyclical factors.

Superficially, this all looked sensible enough, but far less so within the confines of EMU. Stripping out the cyclical component of budget balances and focusing on the 'structural' position is not a simple matter. The structural deficit is difficult to estimate with any precision and there are significant margins of error. Such calculations open up a whole range of subjects for political haggling and bargaining, no doubt cloaked in the technical language of economics and given spurious precision by econometric models of one sort or another. This would all fit in very well with the political nature of the euro group: deals would be cut and compromises made, but the process is unlikely to be any more credible than the previous framework. Similar problems arise with the notion that different debt ratios should allow countries to have varied targets for budget deficits. There would be endless room for manoeuvre and bargains to determine whether this country or that should be allowed a more generous target than another.

Reforms along these lines would certainly require more 'coordination', either through the Commission or the euro group. But even if such a system were put in place, to have any more credibility than previously it would still have to be monitored and, more importantly, enforced. The more individual countries were to be differentiated, for example in the size of their permitted deficits, the more intrusion it would imply into domestic budgetary policy by the euro group as an institution, with the big countries inevitably calling the shots. In any case, even if the 'technicalities' could be agreed, the benefits in EMU would be limited. Separating the cyclical and structural components makes some sense for an individual country (like Britain) with its own domestically oriented monetary policy, but it would not function in the same way for Euroland.

There is a view that once a framework is in place that distinguishes the cyclical and structural components of the budget balance, it can be left on the equivalent of autopilot with the 'automatic stabilisers' taking any strain. This is not really tenable for a national economy with its own domestically oriented monetary policy, and it is certainly not the case in EMU. Monetary policy needs to vary with the economic cycle, but the economic cycles within Euroland do not move together. As noted several times during the course of this book, this means that for some countries monetary policy will periodically be inappropriate with the result that the budgetary position will be exaggerated in both the upswing and the downswing. This being the case, however well designed the fiscal framework, it is inevitable that it will break down for some countries in Euroland.

This conclusion leads into the other factor likely to bring about greater centralisation of economic policy within EMU. The structure of EMU is liable to produce a budgetary and financial crisis and the political response will almost certainly involve a further loss of economic independence. The smaller countries face the biggest risk, but they are not alone.

In 2003, the economic position of Germany within EMU looked dire and some comparisons with the problems confronting the Labour Government in Britain of 1929–1931 can help shed light on the nature, if not the scale, of Germany's predicament. At the time, Britain's unemployment was high, even during the 'roaring twenties', largely because the previous Conservative Government had in 1925 restored the Gold Standard at the pre-war parity. Germany entered EMU with an overvalued currency too, after the effects of unification (as noted in Chapter 8). In 1931, with the 1920s global boom collapsed and London badly hit by the financial crisis on the continent, unemployment in Britain soared and government finances were out of control. However, the Macmillan Committee on Finance and Industry, which had been set up in 1929, came to the conclusion in 1931 that it was impossible to come off Gold (with only the leader of the Transport and General Workers' Union and future Foreign Secretary, Ernie Bevin, arguing against). In the same year, the May Committee recommended cuts in spending to restore the budgetary position and to maintain foreign confidence in the parity, with some similarities to those in the EU Commission arguing in 2003 that Germany should cut its budget deficit to come into line with the SGP. Nine of the Labour Government's Cabinet refused to accept the May report and a new National Government took office, implementing the May cuts in an emergency budget. A few days later, the continuing run on sterling led the new Government to go off Gold. One of Labour's ministers, Lord Passfield, formerly Sidney Webb, said, 'Nobody told us we could do that!'

In 1931, the weakness of sterling provided both a thermometer and a safety valve: it showed the economic position was unsustainable and once the Gold Standard had been abandoned, opened the way to some degree of recovery, even though the May cuts were implemented. (There is an obvious analogy with the recovery of the British economy, during a period of severe fiscal retrenchment, after the country's release from the ERM, noted in Chapter 10.) If the Gold Standard had not been abandoned, unemployment would have risen further and the budget deficit would have worsened, despite the spending cuts. Deflation would have intensified; the real burden of government debt would have increased; fears of default would have emerged, driving gilt yields up despite deflation; and private-sector bankruptcies would have been widespread, leading to a banking sector crisis. In the 1930s, both Germany and France stayed on Gold and their recessions deepened and their political systems were undermined with the political class discredited. Today, Germany does not have the escape route available to Britain in 1931. It is stuck forever in EMU as it was stuck for a time at least on Gold.

Some people saw Germany's economic problems in 2003 as simply the result of 'labour market inflexibility'. Germany's relative disinflation was a relative price adjustment within monetary union, necessitated by relative decline in the demand for German goods as new sources of supply, notably from central and Eastern Europe, enter the market. This view implied that the phenomenon was in principle benign and bothersome only if there were real wage rigidities in Germany. This brought to mind elements of the 'Treasury view' in the inter-war years and was wrong.

It treated Germany's problem as being analogous to a relative price shift between two sectors of a single economy, but the comparison did not really stand up because Euroland is not a real economy, but twelve separate ones (with one monetary policy). An illustration may help make the point. Consider an economy made up of two industries of equal size. Call them agriculture and manufactures. The demand for manufactures increases relative to the demand for agricultural products (food). If there are no frictions, overall unemployment in the economy is unchanged and so are real wages. There is price stability in the economy as a whole, so economy-wide nominal wages, as well as real wages, are unchanged. But falling food prices and rising manufactures prices mean that real wages as viewed by food producers have risen and as viewed by manufactures have fallen. It becomes less profitable to employ labour in agriculture and more profitable to employ them in manufactures. Share prices in the agricultural sector will fall; they will rise in the manufacturing sector. Within the single labour market, labour flows from agriculture to manufactures. In this economy, it makes no sense to talk of either 'deflation' or 'inflation'. There is price stability.

Compare this idealised adjustment between sectors with the position of Germany within Euroland. First, the relevant sectors ('Germany' and 'rest of Euroland') were regionally concentrated and there is no single labour market. In the face of falling prices for German production, nominal wages in Germany had to fall in order to maintain employment. But a fall in nominal wages (relative to productivity growth) was difficult to achieve. In practice, it required rising unemployment. But rising unemployment reduced German demand, and German output was not independent of German demand (both because of the existence of non-tradables and because of the home bias in the consumption of tradables). So German output fell further, raising unemployment, further depressing demand and output and so on in the way that Keynes described.

But that is not all. The overall price level in Germany fell, at least relative to the Euroland price level, so real interest rates in Germany rose, since nominal interest rates were set for Euroland, not for Germany, producing asset deflation.

The banks began to suffer bad loan problems and borrowing constraints began to bite, further depressing demand. With home as well as foreign demand falling, German prices were subject to further downward pressure, so that real interest rates rise further. Moreover, the fiscal position deteriorated rapidly.

If Germany had still had its own currency and the ability to set its own interest rates, the circumstances that have in fact led to relative disinflation and to a real risk of deflation would have been easier to deal with. The adjustment of real wages would have been much more readily possible, without a need for nominal wage adjustment, if the deutschmark had still been there to depreciate and the demand effects of Germany's terms of trade loss could have been offset by reducing interest rates. By stabilising the overall German price level, this would have avoided asset deflation.

In abandoning the deutschmark, Germany has reduced its ability to resist the political objective of France for more political coordination and control of economic decisions within Euroland. But the trap for the smaller countries is even worse since, inside EMU, monetary policy is likely to be even less appropriate than it is for a big country. Even the EU Commission appears to have recognised their problem. The Annual Economic Report (2001) of the EU pointed out that, 'Financial crises are generally associated with boom and bust cycles and the limited – or absent – monetary or exchange rate adjustment in response to cyclical pressures.' The report suggested that:

> Financial and banking systems often seem extremely healthy in periods of buoyant economic growth and rising assets prices, as the measures of solvency and liquidity tend to be highly pro-cyclical. This pro-cyclicality of capital requirements is challenging for all economies but more so for small member states in a monetary union that risks overheating, due to the lack of interest rate and exchange rate equilibration.

Previous chapters have explained the particular vulnerability of small countries to inappropriate monetary policy set by the ECB: real interest rates too low in the economic upswing and too high in the downturn. In these circumstances, it can become impossible for a small country to achieve budgetary adjustment once its economy goes into a downturn relative to the rest of Euroland. In such conditions, the public finances deteriorate very rapidly. Cutting expenditure only deepens the economic downturn, while any attempt to get out of the downward spiral by a 'Keynesian' fiscal expansion only brings about a further deterioration in public finances.

It may take several more years for the full effect of inappropriate monetary policy to work its way through, but a number of smaller countries, including the Netherlands, Spain, Finland and Greece, as well as Portugal, already look vulnerable. However, credit markets have been slow to recognise the pending danger. For example, despite the deteriorating position of Portugal through 2002 and 2003, the differential between yields on Portuguese and German government bonds ('credit spreads') had not widened significantly. In these circumstances any small country that gets into difficulties will be left to its own devices: worsening budgetary position, slow growth and rising unemployment and (eventually) a political crisis.

If markets did react and credit spreads widened, it would happen quickly, pushing up the cost of debt. This would lead to a downward economic and financial spiral and ultimately the threat of default. The process would be different from more usual defaults that are often triggered when sharp movements in currency put up the cost of servicing foreign denominated debt, but when it happens it is still default and real enough. A government can't borrow by issuing bonds or only at punitive and self-defeating rates of interest. The cost of servicing existing debt will take a larger and larger share of national income and the last resort of printing money in order to 'monetise' the debt is not an option available to a national central bank in Euroland. A finance ministry might lend to the banking system, but that would only make the debt position worse. Long before then, individuals and companies within the suffering country would have transferred their euro-denominated assets to banks in another country while the euro-denominated liabilities of domestic and foreign residents would have been parked in the banking system of the country caught in the trap.

The ECB is a potential safety valve – a cut in short-term interest rates could bring relief both by stimulating demand and by reducing government debt interest. The ECB has the task of setting interest rates that will keep inflation low for Euroland as a whole, and it is unlikely to deviate from this objective because of conditions in a small country. However, if a government in one of the large countries were in budgetary crisis, or if several smaller countries were in similar predicaments, pressure to cut interest rates would increase even if this meant higher inflation in Euroland as a whole.

In addition to controlling inflation, the ECB is mandated to 'contribute to ensuring the smooth functioning of the payments system'.[2] If depression in a small country created a crisis for the banking system, and its government could not do anything about it, the ECB would have to act by holding down interest rates. (In the extreme, the ECB could be forced into buying the debt both of the banks and the government.) In the end, the ECB would simply have to act as though it were a national central bank. However, there could be very limited scope for the ECB to ease any financial crisis by means of inflationary finance (and if the dollar were to weaken to the extent that a sustained US recovery required it to weaken, the ECB could be forced to cut short rates close to zero, as in Japan and the USA); but if inflation were take hold at some stage, possibly as a result of some governments disregarding the SGP and resorting to deficit spending, it would only provide temporary relief at the expense of greater pain later. At some point, the ECB would be forced to react by raising rates higher than they would have been without the inflation, bringing back the very conditions that motivated the softer interest rates policy in the first place.

Long before that, there would be calls for financial assistance to prevent actual default. The EU treaties allow for financial assistance to be granted to a member state in certain circumstances, but the funds that could be found within the existing budget are very small. So the richer EU countries, not excluding Britain, would come under pressure to provide handouts or cheap loans, to act as guarantors to the government of the particular country in trouble to see it over its 'temporary' downturn.

Without financial assistance, the crisis would get worse. There are plenty of examples – including Argentina in 2001 – that illustrate the political limits to coercion. It becomes impossible for governments to enforce tax increases to deal with a budget crisis while reneging on commitments to paying their own employees. In the end this can't be sustained and this becomes apparent long before fiscal adjustment is anything like sufficient to avoid a crisis. Political will is not enough if the economy is out of control.

If a country in Euroland got into that sort of mess, one option that would have to be considered would be leaving EMU. Countries have re-established their own currencies in the past, most recently the Eastern European members of the former Soviet Union. But this has usually happened in conditions of considerable political turmoil and regime change. In such circumstances, Euroland countries would be subject to a complicated and often ambiguous relationship between national law, international law and Community law, which would make leaving the single currency much more problematic. Another factor would be that while the financial systems of the former Soviet countries were primitive, debt markets in Euroland are well established and ownership more dispersed.

One example of the sort of intractable financial, legal, social and political problems that can arise when a country abandons a fixed-rate regime is that of Argentina in December 2001. Having no control over its own monetary conditions, Argentina was subject to a one-size-fits-all interest rate and exchange rate that inevitably produced boom-bust. In the bust, deflation set in, causing very high real interest rates and threatening government and private sector solvency. Repeated IMF austerity packages merely postponed the unavoidable break with the fixed peso-dollar peg. When that finally occurred, it brought major problems of its own, because most private-sector debts and nearly all private debts to foreigners were denominated in dollars. Released from its dollar peg, the peso and the burden of these debts, measured in pesos, rose in proportion.

In EMU countries, nearly all government and private debts are obligations to pay euro. This would make departure from EMU a costly and uncertain undertaking. If a country were to leave EMU, its government might be just able to get away with rewriting its debts into the new national currency,[3] but firms with earnings in 'soft' national currency and debts in 'hard' euro would be in an impossible position. Moreover, if corporate debtors tried to convert their obligations back into the national currency, foreign holders would undoubtedly seek redress. It is difficult to see the outcome of the legal arguments that would ensue. However, since there are no provisions for withdrawal from EMU, there would undoubtedly be conflict between the national government (and perhaps national courts) and the European Court of Justice, and indeed between Community law and international law. The financial crisis would provoke a constitutional crisis.

The implications make departure from EMU unattractive for any individual country and for the remainder of the EU. With a probability that financial disruption in the particular country in crisis would spread beyond its borders, other EU countries might well be persuaded to find some cash to bail out a country in an attempt to arrest its debt default. This would inevitably be accompanied by increased monitoring and more overt interference by the Commission and the euro group in the budget and fiscal decisions of the country in trouble, which in turn might well be inclined to accept, given the alternative. Any bail-out of a country would make it more difficult to maintain the pretence that, within the SGP, overspending carries penalties. It would just perpetuate 'moral hazard' (the problem whereby insurance encourages greater risk-taking).

Moreover, there are limits to the extent to which the EU members would be able and willing to provide finance to an ailing partner. As long as it was just (say) Portugal or Greece (and maybe Ireland or Finland) that had to be supported, the politicians might just get away with forcing the populations of the rest of the EU to stump up the money. But it is a stretch to see how it could be extended to Spain, which might happen albeit with a lag to some of the more obvious candidates; and even harder to see how populations of existing members of the EU could be made to accept that they would have to provide large, ongoing transfers to the new accession states.

There would have to be a Treaty change. At present, the so-called 'no-bailout' provisions say that no government or Community institution shall accept responsibility for the debts of any other Euroland government. Jacques Delors always saw this as an untenable position and, as long ago as 1995, said that, 'Monetary union means that the Union acknowledges the debts of the member states of the monetary union.' He was right.

One option would be to establish a clearly federal structure for the EU that would allow funds to be transferred from a EU central budget to a particular country. However, this would potentially increase the scale of moral hazard by reducing the responsibility of national governments and also require the readiness of national governments to dilute their control of fiscal policy to a supranational institution. It is improbable that many – certainly not the bigger ones – would agree.

In this area at least, the intergovernmental model would be likely to triumph. All countries would accept some dilution of fiscal sovereignty, but not to a supranational body, and it would not be shared equally. A new treaty would have to abolish the no-bailout provision and, in return, smaller countries in trouble would be forced to accept the conditions, including the issuance of debt, determined by the bigger countries within an institutionalised euro group. The decisions would be behind closed doors, with little or no accountability to the various electorates. The idea had already been discussed in Brussels: in 1999, Yves-Thibault de Silguy, the EU Commissioner for Monetary Affairs, called for the creation of a Euroland debt management office with the power to issue bonds.[4]

This is an outcome that would fit all too well with the emerging political framework of the EU and would also be a logical conclusion given the economics of EMU. The single currency is incompatible with dynamic economies, since they require the nominal exchange rate to be free to appreciate and depreciate. EMU is unsuitable for a world in which capital flows to the highest anticipated rates of return. In economic terms at least, EMU could have been more successful in the 1950s and 1960s when private-sector capital flows were small and rates of return played little or no part in economic decisions. EMU would have been better suited to the corporatist economic system that then prevailed. A system in which large companies, unions and governments settled matters as best they could between themselves, a world that supported the so-called European social model. Much of that world has been dismantled, but its culture still remains instinctive in much of continental Europe's political class and EMU gives them a vehicle to pursue their ends. In this they will gain encouragement from the emerging strains identified earlier in this chapter. EMU would be shaken apart by economic dynamism so this has to be curbed or suppressed and the method is a bureaucratic – like an economic government – rather than market-oriented response to economic issues. Unsurprisingly, political union is developing the same way, with a predominantly bureaucratic rather than democratic framework.

CHAPTER FOURTEEN

Deceivers
and Dreamers
The Grand Vision of Europe

Britain joined Europe late and many of the British remain 'reluctant Europeans'. Some people put the latter down to the distorting influence of the press in Britain, particularly the tabloids, that 'prevent an informed debate' about Europe. This is contrasted with the more sober coverage of such issues on the continent, and this is seen as proof of their greater maturity and sophistication. Is it? Britain does have a lively, not to say strident, press that periodically offends sensibilities and good taste about Europe and many other matters too. But this has always been the case, reflecting a robust political culture; and indeed many attacks on contemporary figures are mild in comparison to the vilification that politicians and monarchs experienced in the past. In Britain, supporters and opponents of EMU and the EU constitution have their views reflected in both the broadsheets and the tabloids. In much of continental Europe, the press is more compliant and is almost universally in favour of the single currency and supportive of more economic and political integration.

There are many reasons for this contrast, but the British media as much reflects as it forms the views of the British people, who do have very different perspectives on Europe from those of most other peoples in the EU. And it is noticeable that in other countries too, when the electorate is actually asked for its view, enthusiasm for further political and economic integration is less entrenched than that of their political elite. Denmark rejected the euro in a referendum in September 2000 and Sweden did the same three years later.

In September 1992, the majority in favour of the Maastricht Treaty in France was only two per cent. Denmark had already voted against it three months earlier and Ireland rejected the Nice Treaty in June 2001. When this happens, the response of the political establishment in Europe is to tell voters to have another go until they get the 'right' result: the Danes voted 'yes' to Maastricht in May 1993 and Ireland did the same over Nice in October 2001. Within the EU, when the politicians' plans are exposed to the electorate and rebuffed, for example, Sweden's rejection of EMU in 2003, it is put down to the electorate's lack of understanding or misinformation.

It is all rather reminiscent of Bertholt Brecht's comment on the reaction in so-called Peoples' Democracies, when the voters misunderstand the purpose of elections or plebiscites in such regimes, 'Would it not be better in that case for the Government to dissolve the people and elect another.' On the whole, electorates are not stupid. In Britain the press may be unhelpful and inconvenient for those in Westminster, Whitehall and Brussels. But at every stage in the European journey too many British politicians, including prime ministers, have simply not told the truth about the extent to which Europe has reduced Britain's ability to remain in control of its own affairs. Individuals will differ as to whether the effect has been desirable or otherwise, but all democrats surely must accept that the extent of such transfers of power should not be hidden from the people. The electorate's trust has been wilfully misused in the past so that it is not surprising that it was suspicious when it was told in 2003 that Europe's proposed constitution was merely a matter of 'tidying things up' with no particular significance for the way Britain is governed, and this suspicion can only have been increased by what others, including the leaders of both France and Germany, said about the same issue. As a former prime minister of Italy, Lamberto Dini, remarked, 'Anyone in Britain who claims the constitution will not change things is trying to sweeten the pill for those who do not want to see a bigger role for Europe.'[1]

Harold Macmillan was the first prime minister to try to take Britain into the European Economic Community (see Chapter 5) and the first approach in 1961 set the pattern for the way in which Europe was presented to the British people on many subsequent occasions by their leaders. The political implications were deliberately played down or glossed over. Macmillan and Heath certainly knew what they were doing when they sought entry to the EEC and, presumably, Tony Blair also understood what was at stake in signing up to the broad terms of the draft constitution in 2003 and when he urged a speedy agreement when discussions resumed in 2004.

In December 1960, the Prime Minister, Harold Macmillan, and Edward Heath (as Lord Privy Seal) wrote to the Lord Chancellor, Lord Kilmuir, formerly David Maxwell Fyfe MP, seeking an authoritative assessment of the impact on sovereignty of accepting the Treaty of Rome.[2] Kilmuir examined the question under three headings: the position of Parliament, treaty-making powers and the independence of the courts. In his conclusions, the Lord Chancellor said that the first two were the most important. He went on to say:

> I must emphasise that in my view the surrenders of sovereignty involved
> are serious ones and I think that, as a matter of practical politics, it will
> not be easy to persuade Parliament or the public to accept them. I am
> sure that it would be a great mistake to underestimate the force of the
> objections to them. But these objections ought to be brought out into
> the open now because, if we attempt to gloss over them at this stage,
> those who are opposed to the whole idea of joining the Community will
> certainly seize on them later on.

He conceded that some loss of sovereignty might be balanced by other factors, but the trade-off should be brought out into the open:

> In the long run, we shall have to decide whether economic factors require
> us to make some sacrifices of sovereignty: my concern is to ensure that
> we should see exactly what it is that we are being called upon to sacrifice,
> and how serious our loss would be.

Between April and June 1961 there was a series of Cabinet and ministerial meetings to discuss the implications of joining the EEC. In the official minute of the Cabinet discussion in April, running to around 6,000 words, only five sentences are devoted to the question of national sovereignty. The last one stated that, 'A major effort of presentation would be needed to persuade the British public to accept these encroachments on national sovereignty.' The substantive issue was ignored; all that mattered was persuading the public.

In further meetings, on 9 and 17 May, ministers had before them official papers that had been prepared in Whitehall by the Treaty of Rome Working Group. The topics covered included, Sovereignty, Commercial Policy, Economic Policy and Balance of Payments, Associated Overseas Territories and the future of EFTA. However, nothing is recorded as having been said about sovereignty at these meetings, which is surprising given its importance later and the attention it received in the official papers. The sovereignty paper covered much the same ground as the Lord Chancellor had done the previous year:

> In the past, the loss of national sovereignty has been the most potent
> argument against United Kingdom participation in supranational
> institutions. It was to a large extent responsible for our decision, in
> 1950, not to join the European Coal and Steel Community and, in 1955,
> to withdraw from the discussions that led eventually to the drafting of

the Treaty of Rome. Although the Treaty of Rome does not express this explicitly it has underlying political objectives that are to be brought about by a gradual surrender of sovereignty. Continental opinion would not think we were in earnest in establishing a new relationship with the Six unless we were prepared to abandon a significant degree of sovereignty.

The paper went on to say that:

the United Kingdom would, in accordance to the Treaty of Rome, be committing itself to a range of indefinite obligations over a wide field of action within the economic and social sphere which might subsequently be translated into specific obligations by means of a decision, directive or regulation with which we would not necessarily agree. This is a commitment of a kind different from obligations under other treaties [such as the GATT and NATO].

However, these sorts of assessments played no part in the Government's case in public, at the time or later.

In July 1962, the Cabinet decided to open negotiations with the Six and the public statement announcing this was drafted to head off a motion tabled in the Commons opposing any material derogation of British sovereignty or any endangerment of the future expansion of trade with the Commonwealth and EFTA. A specific undertaking was included in the statement from the Government to consult Parliament before entering into an agreement. However, once the House had approved the Government's motion it would have been very difficult for it to oppose entry unless the terms were clearly unsatisfactory, and the Government got approval on the narrow technical grounds that it was only seeking approval to seek out the terms of entry.

In the event, de Gaulle vetoed Britain's application in 1961 and again in 1967 (the background was set out in Chapter 3) but, twelve days after taking office in 1970, Edward Heath began negotiations with the Six, as Wilson was preparing to do if Labour had been returned to power. In July 1971, the Heath Government's case was set out in the White Paper 'The United Kingdom and the European Communities'. The economic case was little more than a series of assertions that put a lot of emphasis on the benefits of a large single market. This is something that few people would have disagreed with then or now, but to reap these potential benefits it was not, and is not, necessary to construct the political framework of the EEC or the EU or to embrace the other policies and institutions associated with either. But then, as now, an economic case for Europe had to be made and it fell to the Treasury to make it. The economic staff examining the costs and benefits of entry concluded that the overall economic impact of entry was at best broadly neutral. They were informed that this was not what the Prime Minister wanted to hear and so a 'dynamic effect' was introduced over their heads. Subsequently, the Government's chief economic adviser, the late Sir Donald MacDougall, asked his team of economists involved in the assessment, including Hans Liesner and John Shepherd, who was still at the Treasury when I worked there with Denis Healey, whether the economic case for entry to the EEC had been made and not one of them thought it had. Economics aside, concerns about the loss of political sovereignty were dismissed in the White Paper:

> Like any other treaty, the Treaty of Rome commits its signatories to support agreed aims; but the commitment represents the voluntary undertaking of a sovereign state to observe policies which it has helped to form. There is no question of any erosion of essential national sovereignty.

Heath must have known this to be untrue. As noted earlier, the Lord Chancellor's paper, commissioned by Macmillan when Heath was his negotiator prior to the first application for Community membership, had specifically dismissed the notion that the Treaty of Rome was just another treaty, as had the official papers considered by the Cabinet. But in 1971, Heath and the Foreign Office were determined to press on.

A Foreign Office paper of 1971 entitled 'Sovereignty and the European Communities'[3] is worth quoting at some length. It:

> set out to clarify the various ways in which the term [sovereignty] is used in present circumstances; to identify the relevant changes which will be involved in joining the European Communities; and to suggest a number of conclusions and implications for policy.

The paper distinguished between external and internal sovereignty and acknowledged, yet again, that 'it is not correct to regard the European Community Treaties as involving solely matters of a legal significance equivalent to that of other existing treaties.' However, the paper argued that at the time of writing the practical diminution of external sovereignty was limited. But the paper went on: 'The loss of external sovereignty will however increase as the Community develops, according to the intention of the preamble to the Treaty of Rome.' Furthermore, the paper argued:

> The implications of membership for parliamentary sovereignty and for the legal system which is closely related to it, are more immediate. By accepting the Community Treaties we shall have to accept the whole range of subsidiary law that has been made by the Communities.

Not only this but we shall be making provision in advance for the unquestioned direct application of community laws not yet made.

But the intentions of the Foreign Office were clear:

It will be in the British interest after accession to encourage the development of the Community toward an effectively harmonised economic, fiscal and monetary system and a fairly closely coordinated and consistent foreign and defence policy. This sort of grouping would have major politico/economic advantages but it would take many years to develop and to win political acceptance. If it came to do so then essential aspects of sovereignty both internal and external would indeed increasingly be transferred to the Community itself.

By the end of the century [i.e. 2000], with effective defence and political harmonisation the erosion of the international role of the members states could be almost complete. This is a far distant prospect; but as a member of the Community our major interests may lie in its progressive development since it is only when Western Europe of which we shall be a part can realise its full potential as a political as well as economic unit that we shall derive full benefits from membership.

The Community, if we are to benefit to the full, will develop wider powers and coordinate and manage policy over wider areas of public business. To control and supervise this process it will be necessary to strengthen the democratic organisation of the Community with consequent decline in the primacy and prestige of the national parliaments. The task will not be to arrest this process, since to do so would be to put considerations of formal sovereignty before effective influence and power, but to adapt institutions and policies both in the UK and in Brussels to meet and reduce the real and substantial public anxieties over national identity and alienation from government, fear of change and loss of control over their fate which are aroused by talk of the 'loss of sovereignty'.

This was all very percipient of what was to happen during the following forty years but was very different to what the country was being told by the Government at the time. There was no suggestion from it that signing up to the Treaty of Rome was not 'just like any other treaty'. Still less that 'successful' membership would entail further erosion of Britain's sovereignty on a broad front and in its ability to control its own affairs. Thirty years later, Sir Crispin Tickell, Edward Heath's private secretary, admitted that although the issues involving Britain's loss of sovereignty 'were very much present in the mind of negotiators', the line was that, 'the less they came out in the open the better'.[4]

In the referendum campaign of 1975, the political aspects of membership of Europe were discussed, although much of the campaign focused on economics, particularly prices. The 'Yes' campaign was not silent on sovereignty but it was disingenuous in its arguments as pro-European and pro-EMU commentators have admitted. One of these observed that there was:

> no major document or speech that said in plain terms that national sovereignty would be lost, still less one that categorically promoted the European Community for its single most striking characteristic: that it was an institution positively designed to curb the full independence of the nation state.[5]

Indeed, the same commentator said that the 'entire "yes" campaign' conformed to:

> [the] golden thread of deceptive reassurance that runs through the history of Britain's relationship with the European Union up to the present day: our entry was essential, our membership is vital, our assistance in the consolidation imperative – but nothing you really care about will change.

The official document of the 'Yes' campaign argued that, 'so much of the argument about sovereignty is a false one.' It was not a matter of dry legal theory but had to be tested against British interests in the real world. 'The best way is to work with our friends and neighbours.' Well, yes, but would anyone deny the desirability of working with our friends and neighbours? Jean Monnet recognised that Europe required not just cooperation between nations, but 'a fusion of the interests of the European peoples' (see Chapter 3). However, 'the extent to which the project was political at all became masked',[6] even though Roy Jenkins later claimed that the campaign had been all about politics. Recalling sitting on a sofa at a celebratory dinner after the referendum reminiscing with Edward Heath, Roy Jenkins said:

> We both agreed that we had had some great meetings, very well attended, two thousand, three thousand people. In all of them it was when one talked about the political issues that one got those moments when there was that sort of silence, a positive silence that meant one was gripping the attention of the audience.

And thus it came to pass, in 'a positive silence' interpreted by the leaders of the time.

Subsequently, the electorate's concerns about the implications of being in Europe were only increased by the way in which prior assurances were set aside later by the politicians or were transformed by the rulings of the European Court of Justice (ECJ). Lord Kilmuir's wish to bring the issue of sovereignty into the open has consistently been ignored by the British political establishment and his analysis of the loss of sovereignty was made as it stood in 1960, before the treaties of Maastricht, the Single European Act, Amsterdam and Nice, let alone a European constitution, and it was made before a series of judgements by the ECJ further impinged on British sovereignty. If the erosion of sovereignty was serious in 1960 it is much more significant now and even those who voted 'yes' in 1975 may have changed their minds or seek another opportunity to let their voices be heard. People supported entry to the European Community in 1973 or voted 'yes' in the referendum in 1975 for a variety of reasons, as did those on the other side and both sides may feel their hopes and fears vindicated or otherwise. But, despite all the reassurances to the contrary and whatever a person's own preferences, everyone has seen the process at work by which the authority of 'Brussels' is extended, never retracted.

Many years after Britain had entered the Community, one long-standing pro-European made some pointed observations about the nature and implications of the methods employed in the early 1970s by his allies. Roy Hattersley said:

> Not only was it wrong for us to deal superficially with what Europe involved but we've paid the price ever since, because every time there's a crisis in Europe, people say with some justification, 'Well, we wouldn't have been part of this if we'd really known the implications.' Joining the European Community did involve significant loss of sovereignty but by telling the British people that was not involved I think the rest of the argument was prejudiced for the next thirty years.[7]

Hattersley was right, over twenty-five years after the event. At the time, the truth could not be told because the British people would have rejected it. And the same pattern can be seen today in the dissembling of politicians about both the single currency and the implications of any new constitutional settlement for Europe.

For Tony Blair, membership of the EU represented 'the pooling of sovereignty in order to extend the reach of democratic action'.[8] He saw sovereignty 'not merely as the ability of a single country to say no, but as the power to maximise our national strength and capacity'.[9] Others, including the Foreign Secretary, Jack Straw, insisted that sovereignty was just a relative concept, suggesting that if Britain gains more influence on the outside world, its sovereignty is increased. Along similar lines, Edward Heath has said that sovereignty isn't something you hoard in your cellar like a miser, and go down there once a year with a candle to check it's still there. It's something you spend and use. On this argument, the way a country gains more influence is by pooling sovereignty with other countries: therefore Britain will somehow become more sovereign if it shares its sovereignty with the rest of Europe.

This is confusing power and sovereignty. Power is indeed a relative thing, which can grow and diminish in relation to external factors, but sovereignty is a matter of authority. While some states are more powerful than others, every sovereign state in the world is equally sovereign. In the same way, a rich person may have more financial power than a neighbour with a modest income, but each has the same final authority to decide how to spend his or her own money. If someone of modest means pooled their bank account with a group of neighbours, the whole group would have more power, but that individual would only have one vote among many. Each time the vote went against him, he would find not that he had gained financial power, but that he had lost financial sovereignty. Sovereignty is a matter of authority – the final legal and political authority to make decisions. In the EU, once competence is handed over, sovereignty has gone. People may have different views as to whether this is a good or bad thing, but it is misleading to pretend it hasn't happened.

The official document of the 'Yes' campaign in 1975 stated that if Britain said 'No' then, 'the Community would go on taking decisions which affect us vitally – but we should have no say in them. *We would be clinging to the shadow of British sovereignty while its substance flies out of the window.'* [italics in original] But the argument then was about the substance, not the shadow of sovereignty, and this is even truer about any decision to enter EMU or the adoption of a new constitutional settlement for the EU.

Proponents of EMU dismiss such concerns. Other countries have joined the single currency, so what's the problem for Britain? Are the French less French in Europe? Do the French feel less French inside EMU? Will Italy find itself removed from the map under the new constitution for the EU? The answer is 'probably not', but irrelevant.

First, because even for those countries that have joined EMU, the story is not yet played out. It is true that, unlike Britain, other countries entered EMU for political not economic reasons, but there was little or no real debate about its political and economic implications. The political elite led; and the people, by and large, followed, although sometimes it was a close-run thing (in France, as noted earlier in the chapter, the Maastricht Treaty was endorsed only narrowly, by just fifty-one per cent to forty-nine per cent). But that does not make the actual loss of sovereignty less real, and support in 2003 for a new constitution was very weak among the electorates of many countries in the EU, including the 'core'. And as voters in other countries come to realise the economic implications of EMU, it will have political consequences whatever the apparent initial lack of concern for the loss of national sovereignty in joining the single currency.

Secondly, while all countries are different, Britain is set apart from other nations in Europe. This view is not some anachronistic post-imperial nostalgia, nor is it some idealised 'thousand-year story of an island race'; it is merely to recognise an historical fact. For much of the past four hundred years, Britain has striven in one way or another to prevent the continent of Europe falling under the control of absolutism in its various forms. If Britain had succumbed and the Habsburgs, Bourbons, Bonaparte or their twentieth-century heirs prevailed, Britain would have been profoundly different today. And this does matter, since it is the attitude of minds, the political and legal institutions that evolved in the course of these earlier struggles that, in part at least, gave Britain the distinctive characteristics that do set it apart in important ways from countries that have in the past succumbed to European territorial empires.

Geography matters too. It affects how Germany and France view their place in Europe: for them Europe is so intimately 'us' it could never be 'them'. For Britain, it is always both 'us' and 'them.' Britain has cultural, political and linguistic as well as economic links across the globe that are at least as deep as those with a continent that in turn has been a threat as well as a benefit. Britain may seem to want it both ways, but that is because Britain does face both ways, neither wholly part of one nor of the other of its two worlds.

The British Isles have always been and will always be entwined with the continent, but that is not the point. Because of its geography and history, Britain is a country with institutions and a prevailing political and economic culture that, while far from uniform, is recognisably distinct from most of the continent, as is its legal framework and tradition. The system of English common law is aberrant to many on the continent, reflecting a very different notion about the role of 'the State'. It embodies the principle that law is something to which the state is subject instead of being the enforcer of the General Will. In common-law systems, the state must uphold the law; in continental systems, law is the upholder of the state.

Given all this, it is bound to be more difficult for Britain than for other countries to accommodate and feel at ease in an arrangement that inevitably bears the footprint of the predominant political, economic and legal culture of the continent and which represents a discontinuity with our history and political sense of identity, to a far greater extent than for France or most other countries in the EU. This is one of the reasons why Britain was so reluctant to join the Six and explains why many British politicians favouring further integration feel the need to deny the full political implications of membership. But as the project has been taken forward it has become more and more difficult for British politicians to dissemble in the face of observable facts. Politicians in other countries of the EU have generally been more straightforward about the objective of political union. And all recognised that the decision to join the single currency is more significant for national sovereignty than any other single step in the institutional development of Europe. As Joschka Fischer, Germany's Foreign Minister, said in 2000: 'The euro is not just an economic matter; it is a profoundly political act, for the euro symbolises the power of the sovereign who guarantees it.'[10] And the same man was in no doubt about the significance of the proposed new constitution in 2003: 'The constitution is the most important treaty since the foundation of the European Community.'[11] For Romano Prodi, the legal personality outlined in the draft constitution for the EU had implications beyond the continent: 'Europe can now play its role on the world stage.'[12] On the continent of Europe, the single currency and proposals for a constitution are part of a grander vision: to project the economic and political power and influence of Europe and its particular 'values' across the world or, in the words of the Amsterdam Treaty, 'Europe must assert its identity on the international scene.' But what is to be the basis of this objective and what are these 'values' that Europe seeks to spread?

According to the official record, at the beginning of the second day of the meeting at Chequers in November 1961, Macmillan told de Gaulle that:

> European civilisation was what we must at all costs preserve. It had
> survived 3000 years, but it was menaced on all quarters, by Africans,
> Asians and Communists and, in a quite different way, even by our
> Atlantic friends such as the North Americans and New Zealanders and
> Australians. More than ever there was need for political unity in Europe.

Had Macmillan's assessment been made public at the time it would have come as a surprise. Not least to the relatives and loved ones of the thousands of men from these same countries who had been killed or wounded only a few years earlier in saving this so-called European civilisation from the murderous tyranny imposed by one of its own.

Faced with that fact, the establishment of the Common Market half a century ago was accompanied by the emergence of a new European ideology that sought to identify Europe with the defence of freedom, a convenient way of underscoring its alignment with the Free World and distancing itself from Europe's recent Nazi and fascist past. Its intellectuals stressed the origins of what they regarded as distinctly European values in a symbiosis of Christendom and Roman law. This overlooked the fact that Christendom had started as much an Asian and African as a European religion or that Byzantium had been as much a Christian descendant of the Roman Empire as Western Europe. The point was that Christian Democrats – the great winners of post-war European politics – needed this kind of history particularly badly because Catholic political sentiment before the Second World War had certainly not been overly concerned with freedom and had often taken an authoritarian and anti-democratic line. The rapprochement of Catholic thought and parliamentary democracy that took place after Hitler's defeat thus required a new reading of Europe's past. Perhaps it did not matter much during the Cold War that this history consigned the eastern half of the continent to oblivion, or that it wrote Muslims, Jews and even Orthodox Christians out of the script. But it does now. With its new entrants, Greece will not be the only predominantly Christian Orthodox member of the EU, Europe's Muslim population is growing rapidly and politicians are a bit selective in the choice of values with which they wish Europe to be associated. Values à la carte, keeping Europe's darker side off the menu.

For Tony Blair, democracy, freedom and the rule of law 'are the values that unite the European Union'.[13] On another occasion, when he accepted the Charlemagne Prize, the basis for building Europe's 'strength, power and responsibility vis-à-vis the outside world' were the values of 'freedom, solidarity, democracy and enterprise'.[14] The notion that these values are the ones that had characterised the EU in the past fifty years or Europe in the past hundred or more might be questioned, and in any case these are hardly distinctive European values. If an Australian is asked whether he believes in 'freedom, democracy and enterprise' he does not reply, 'Ah no mate those are European values.' They are values shared by all other liberal democracies of the English-speaking world and a number of other nations besides. At times, Tony Blair seems to recognise this but, as such, they cannot be the basis of a distinctive identity for Europe. This has to be on the basis of something else. So what is the basis of this identity?

In a speech in Warsaw in October 2000, Tony Blair said that, 'Europe can, in its economic and political strength, be a superpower; a superpower, but not a super-state.' Just how Europe could be a superpower without being a super-state was not explained, indeed can't be explained since it is meaningless. Superpowers only get to be political superpowers if they are held together by a strong sense of national identity or perhaps, for a period, by force. Europe cannot become a political superpower precisely because it cannot become a super-state in the way that the USA is or others may become. Not that this will stop some people from trying. 'Superpower not super-state' was a classic piece of 'Third Way' triteness that attempts to reconcile two irreconcilable themes while seeking to soothe fears among the British electorate about the development of a European federal state. But at the moment the political threat is not the creation of a recognisably democratic federal state in Europe, which might in theory enable it over time to become a superpower, because there is too much opposition to such a notion. The most likely outcome is the creation of an undemocratic and unaccountable political structure: the antithesis not only of federalism but also of effective democracy within member states.

Europe cannot become a superpower in economic or military terms either. The economic arguments were covered in detail in the core economic chapters of this book. Although the US economy reaps gains from having a single currency, it only does so because it is also a country. In Euroland, on the other hand, the single currency actually penalises economic dynamism and makes it more difficult for the participating countries, individually or collectively, to embark upon economic reforms. Yet these are not only necessary in themselves but a precondition for any attempt to match the economic strength of the USA. And in military terms there is not the slightest evidence that the generality of countries in the EU are prepared to devote the scale of resources to maintain their own security or carry out minor military actions on their own continent, let alone a world role to match the USA. But even if it were possible, it is undesirable that Europe seek to become a superpower, for two very good reasons, one internal to the EU the other affecting its external relations.

There is a tendency, for obvious reasons, to treat nationalism as a dangerous instinct, but there were tribal, dynastic, feudal and religious wars that tore Europe apart long before there were wars motivated by nationalism. Today, war and strife is as likely to be caused by the suppression of nationalism as by its worship. It is no answer to say that nations in Europe are in no danger of losing their identity. Indeed, if they could lose it there would be no problem. Member states remain nations. The bigger threat to stability and tolerance comes when a nation finds itself without real voice in a political structure that is largely unaccountable to anyone. More and more, Europe erodes the institutions that define and give expression to the political sense of national identity. Europe undermines national identity without replacing it. In these circumstances, the danger is that people will define themselves in other ways – colour, language, religion or ethnic origin. This has already happened in Belgium, where a Belgian political identity has always been weak. The country was an artificial one, put together by the great powers. Now, Europe is seen as an excuse for overthrowing that identity and, in consequence, people are defining themselves in tribal terms. The linguistic conflict in Belgium is nothing new, but it has gained intensity. Worse, neo-Nazi notions of ethnic purity have gained ground with the ethnic Vlaams Blok, the biggest party in the Flemish-speaking region. There are several other recent examples, including the sudden rise of Pim Fortuyn in the Netherlands and the success of Jean Marie Le Pen pushing Lionel Jospin out of the final ballot for the presidency of France. These are warnings that need to be heeded if voters think that traditional politicians have lost touch. In Britain, support of the BNP and UKIP, though in other ways very different, in part reflect similar forces at work. Of course, the British sense of nationality is much stronger than in Belgium, but if the political notion of Britishness and the institutions that define it are undermined or destroyed by Europe, no one should be surprised at the consequence. If people see that the politicians they elect have less and less real power over the things that matter to them and their families, our multiethnic and largely tolerant society could also be at risk. The great genius of the British and French polities – something they have in common with the USA – was that a nation was successfully created out of allegiance to political institutions. This has allowed those nations to become, to a greater extent than in any of the other European countries, genuinely multicultural and relatively tolerant. Let Europe take away that allegiance by destroying the relevance of domestic institutions, the ineradicable desire of human beings for a sense of belonging would then be expressed in tribal ways: through race, language, religion and through hostility to anyone with different tribal characteristics.

But beyond these problems within the EU, any attempt to create a superpower would have wider implications too. What would this superpower do? Challenge the other superpower, or just create conflict and tension with the USA? Of course, nothing could be further from the mind of Tony Blair; his commitment to maintaining Britain's friendly alliance with America is proven, but on occasion he too gets carried away, expressing the view that for him Europe 'is about projecting collective power'.[15] And others who want to 'project Europe's power' do so from a position that is fundamentally antipathetic to America. Now, there are many things wrong with America, as there are in every country, but for too many on the continent of Europe and not a few euro-enthusiasts in Britain, not being American or even being anti-American is the basis for the new identity of Europe and for some the euro is part of this agenda. This is often unconscious and unsaid or simply regarded as the inevitable by-product of the steady integration of Europe, but on occasions it is clear and explicit. In 1996, the Belgian Finance Minister, Philippe Maystadt, declared, 'The purpose of the single currency is to prevent the encroachment of Anglo-Saxon values in Europe.' That means us.

De Gaulle was in no doubt about the purpose of Europe and it is a recurring theme. During the Cold War, de Gaulle withdrew France from NATO's military structure, offering instead 'a third force', as an alternative to America and Soviet Russia. That posturing got nowhere because France, like everyone else, ultimately depended on American power for defence against Russia. With the end of the Soviet threat, France has renewed its efforts, arguing that the unipolar world is unsafe and that the world needs an alternative pole that just happens to run right through the Elysée Palace. France is not alone in this. In March 2003, Sweden's Prime Minister, Goran Persson, urged his fellow citizens to join EMU to help counter the supremacy of the USA. Sweden's voters rejected his appeal and a European identity established on such a basis can only force America and Europe further apart, which is contrary to British interests and instincts. In Warsaw in October 2000, Tony Blair repeated a theme of previous prime ministers. He said, 'Britain can be a bridge between the EU and the US', and 'there is absolutely no doubt in my mind, that our strength with the US is enhanced by our strength with the rest of Europe and vice versa.' This is obviously true: the more power and influence Britain has in Europe, the more powerful will be its voice with the USA. The issue is how best this is addressed, how best to increase Britain's power and influence in Europe, and how this is affected by any decision on the single currency and an endorsement of a new constitutional settlement.

CHAPTER FIFTEEN

The Art of Persuasion

Tony Blair and Europe

In Britain, views about EMU can be divided into three camps. First, those for whom the economics of the single currency are irrelevant. This is a particular characteristic of the older generation of pro-Europeans such as Edward Heath or Roy Jenkins, but not confined to them. Such people would have already taken Britain into EMU. They assume that any economic problems would be fleeting and easily manageable, with the political benefits large.

Next, there are those who think that both economic and political arguments point in the same direction: EMU is economically flawed and politically a step too far. Joining EMU is not sensible for the foreseeable future. Some of these people would take Britain out of the EU, but most remain supportive of the EU in one form or another. This view is reflected in this book. It should be noted that this group is quite distinct from those other people that Tony Blair and Gordon Brown have claimed to identify: those who oppose entry into EMU, even if they believe it to be in Britain's economic interest. Although such people might exist in theory it is difficult to identify any in practice. There are many who oppose joining the single currency for economic and political reasons, but that is a very different matter. I have never met anyone who actually thinks EMU would benefit Britain economically, but is opposed to it because of its political implications. To that extent, the 'principled' position of Tony Blair and Gordon Brown is based on a straw man, a phantom that doesn't exist in flesh and blood.

A third group wants to join EMU because they believe that there are distinct political advantages in Britain being a member, usually expressed in terms of 'influence'. This camp assumes some longer-term economic benefits, but unlike the first group it thinks that the economics have to be 'right' before it is sensible to join, though it is not always clear what 'right' means.

Tony Blair is in the third group. He is convinced of a political case, although only expressed in the most general terms, but he worries about the economics. However, after working as Tony's economic adviser in and out of government for the better part of ten years, I do not think that his concerns reflect a genuine grasp of the economic issues involved, but rather are based on a political calculation that, unless the semblance of an economic case can be sold, it will be impossible to persuade the electorate of the purported political advantages upon which he puts great store. The distinction is very important, since if he truly grasped the economic implications it would lead him reluctantly to keep postponing the attempt to take Britain into EMU for the reasons set out in this book while, if it is actually a matter of tactics, as Prime Minister, Tony Blair would always be tempted to use a window of temporarily benign economic congruence with Europe to gain his place in history and use the euro referendum as the defining moment of his period as Prime Minister before handing over to his successor.

When Tony Blair first stood for parliament, at the Beaconsfield by-election in 1982, it was on a manifesto to pull out of Europe. Of course, it is very difficult for a new, young candidate, let alone one in a by-election, to have much influence on the contents of his election address, but there is no evidence that he was ill at ease with the stance taken by the Labour Party led by Michael Foot. He endorsed Labour's General Election manifesto in 1983 with no qualifications, but as the Labour Party shifted, so did Tony Blair. When he was leader of the Labour Party, Neil Kinnock decided that dumping Labour's virulent hostility to Europe was essential if Labour were ever to win an election. Together with the shadow chancellor, John Smith, and Gordon Brown, Kinnock swung Labour to support membership of the ERM as a means of remedying the party's previous lack of 'credibility'. John Smith became leader just before the ERM fell apart, but there was little or no attempt to review the wisdom of entry or the merits of the case, let alone the implications for EMU, other than the assertion that Britain 'joined at the wrong time at the wrong rate'. Tony Blair and Gordon Brown have both taken this line, although the arguments don't stand up to scrutiny (see Chapter 10).

When Tony Blair stood for the leadership of the Labour Party, his commitments on Europe were inevitably set out in general terms, with the obligatory references to providing 'leadership'. A single currency was said to 'have clear financial and industrial benefits', but it could not be 'forced in defiance of the economic facts'. As Leader of the Opposition, repositioning on

Europe provided a hook for re-establishing Labour's credibility; it helped to distinguish 'New' from 'Old' Labour and served as a stick to beat the Government. Tony Blair was able to play on the problems of John Major in a merciless way and the disarray of the Conservatives enabled him to vent his pro-European inclinations without being too specific about the details. Europe and EMU were part of New Labour's political positioning ahead of the 1997 election.

Tony Blair is most unusual among successful politicians in that his early adulthood was not dominated by politics. He spent time in France as a young man, enjoys holidays there and in other parts of continental Europe. He feels comfortable on the continent and speaks French reasonably well, making a good impression when he addressed the French National Assembly in 1998. He is like many others of his age and background, and that is what made him an attractive political personality. But his engagement with Europe never seemed to have gone beyond that of thousands of his fellow countrymen and women. There was nothing in Tony's early travels to match, for example, the intellectual or political engagement that accompanied Denis Healey on his cycle ride to Salzburg or Edward Heath on his sojourn to Germany, in the 1930s. That may just be a matter of being of a different generation, but when Tony Blair arrived at No. 10, as he admitted himself, he had been too busy reforming the Labour Party to engage in serious thought on Europe. He had read little British or European history and had shown little interest in the forces and motives that forged post-war Europe or Britain's position in it.

Prior to the 1997 election, the most comprehensive statement of Tony Blair's attitude to Europe was the speech he made at Chatham House on 5 April 1995. This was titled 'Britain in Europe' and, like the pre-election address on economics in the Mais Lecture at the City University a month later (noted in Chapter 1), it was a carefully drafted exposition by the Labour Party's new leader on an important topic. There was nothing of any substance about economics, let alone EMU, in the Chatham House address and I was preoccupied with the forthcoming economic speech, so I was not involved in its drafting. But it is worth quoting at length because it sets out Tony's political case for Europe and it is as good an example of how he will seek to persuade the electorate about EMU, and Europe more generally, including the new constitution, as you can get. And from the inside I watched closely as its tone and substance were reflected not only in many subsequent speeches on Europe but also in many of the decisions in No. 10 Downing Street.

At Chatham House, Tony summarised his argument with three points. First, 'to be a significant influence in the world Britain must be a significant influence in Europe.' Secondly, 'such a role at the centre of Europe is fully consistent with Britain's history, not a rejection of it, and is indeed the only way today to fulfil our historic position in the world.' Thirdly, 'at the centre of Europe, Britain can then play a leading role in reforming Europe, making it more accountable, efficient and more open; shaping the future path of integration and setting limits to it.'

Few people will have any problems with the first point. Unless Britain has influence in Europe it is indeed very difficult to see how it could have much impact on the rest of the world. But it begs the question as to how best to ensure Britain's influence in Europe. Influence is a matter of geography and economic strength. The former is fixed, the latter is not and, for reasons set out earlier in this book, is more likely to be secured outside EMU. Others may disagree, but the point is that there is no dispute that Britain should be influential in Europe. The issue is how that is best achieved. However, by sleight, Tony suggested that 'influence in Europe' is the same as 'a role at the centre of Europe', but these are not the same things at all, or at least they do not need to be. He cannot have meant geographically at the centre, so that his argument must either have been another way of saying again that it was desirable that Britain should have influence in Europe, which is uncontroversial but raises the question: how? Or he was saying that Britain should be a full participant with France and Germany in the process of integration.

Having been taken to the centre of Europe by Tony Blair, Britain then became the 'leader'. In this position the British could reform Europe, on the basis that, if left to themselves, other countries would be incapable or unwilling. But it turns out to be an odd form of leadership. Later in the same lecture, Tony made it clear that, 'we are not setting out to break up the Franco-German partnership or engage in a new round of "balance of power" politics. Rather our aim is to join others in the leadership of Europe in the pursuit of our aims.' How others are to join us in pursuit of our aims was not explained, nor how others cooperating in pursuit of their aims might be resisted should they conflict with British interests. In other respects too, it is not really clear where we are being taken. The lecture slid from 'influence in Europe' to 'influence through Europe'. We were told that, 'all routes to influence travel at some point through Europe. There is no serious alternative. Unless we build our global influence through Europe we run the risk of being marginalised.' This rather suggested that Britain could have no influence beyond Europe unless it was speaking as a representative of Europe or at least on the basis of collective agreement.

At Chatham House, Tony argued that while relations with America were essential, 'our transatlantic relationship is multiplied in strength if we are also at the centre of Europe.' As Prime Minister, he was never in any doubt about the 'essential' nature of relations with America. But any influence with the USA on Iraq, for example, was not because it came 'through' Europe. Quite the contrary, Britain's attitude was distinct from several other members of the EU, particularly Germany and France. Whether Britain's influence within the EU reflected a position at the 'centre of Europe' is a moot point, but this influence and position was clearly not dependent on being in EMU. However, the relative performance of the British economy certainly did help Blair pursue a policy of 'constructive engagement' with others in the EU.

Tony Blair then presented us with what were described as 'two basic questions that had to be addressed'. The first of these was, 'Do we accept that it is through Europe, that we will, in the future, exercise greatest power and influence as a nation?' Again the phrase 'through Europe' might mean the loss of an independent voice or at least a submerged one, for Britain. But Tony apparently did not want to imply that since, for him, working through Europe was seen as the means to exert Britain's 'influence as a nation'. Again, this merely raised the question as to how this influence was best secured.

The second question that Tony posed was this. 'Are we as a country in basic agreement with the notion of closer cooperation between member states in the European Union over time?' The use of 'cooperation' was an interesting and disingenuous choice. Not many people would disagree with the proposition that more cooperation between countries is desirable. Certainly those who want to remain in the EU but stay out of EMU would be in favour of more 'cooperation'. And even those who might want to pull out of the EU altogether would still favour cooperation since even the most fanatical sceptics do not question the incontrovertible assertion made in this same speech that 'we have always been a European power.' But Tony Blair converted these two 'basic questions' to a personal referendum for us all: 'The real issue was and always has been: in or out.'

Blair briefly reviewed Britain's position as a European as well as world power. 'We are Europeans.' Nobody is going to challenge that and putting it forward made no distinctive contribution to Britain's relations with the EU, still less EMU. Nobody opposed to the single currency has to deny, or be implied to deny, that Britain's history is entwined with and part of European history.

He went on to say, 'Disraeli with his role in the Congress of Berlin and Gladstone, with his preoccupations with the Concert of Europe, were acting first and foremost as European statesman.' This was either a tautology or a distortion. At Versailles, in the aftermath of the First World War, Lloyd George might also have been described as acting as a European statesman. However, this tells us little more than British leaders have often found themselves pre-occupied with European affairs and always will be. The question for Britain as for other countries is how best to secure its influence within Europe and it can't simply be asserted that this will be increased with more integration and EMU.

Tony Blair recognised that in the past British interests were secured by the balance of power in Europe. 'When the balance of power was not maintained at the end of the nineteenth century, disaster descended on Europe... having tried to turn our back on the continent, we were dragged back in and had to pay a heavy price in the First World War.' Similarly, before the Second World War, 'we failed to intervene early enough... and millions had to pay with their lives.'

His reference to the deleterious effects of the breakdown in 'the balance of power' was in contrast to his earlier comments about Britain's potential leadership in Europe and the Franco-German relationship. There, the concept of the 'balance of power' was rejected – Britain was not about to 'engage in a new round of "balance of power" politics.' But the concept of the balance of power goes way beyond concerns about trying to muscle in on the Franco-German axis within the EU, which is presumably what was meant by the disparaging reference to engaging in 'balance of power politics'.

It has always been against Britain's interest for continental Europe to come under the control or influence of a single power or coalition of powers. For reasons set out in Chapter 13, the economics of the single currency will reinforce the tendency of the EU to become centralised, undemocratic and in sway to France and Germany, if not always dominated by them. The serious political and economic questions about EMU and any future EU constitution are similar to previous eras in which the 'balance of power' preoccupied policy-makers. How best to influence the outcome in ways that are more conducive to Britain's interests? Sometimes, in the past, Britain joined a European coalition to head off the threat of dominance by one or more countries. In contemporary times, entry to the Economic Community was partially motivated by such a concern and today Britain correctly tries to work with shifting coalitions of countries with similar interests on particular issues. But at all times in history it has been Britain's economic and financial power that has in the end underpinned its efforts to maintain its influence in Europe and either defeat or prevent the emergence of hostile coalitions. And so it is today. Economic strength is a key determinant of political influence – and for the reasons set out earlier in the book, this is best achieved outside the single currency.

In his Chatham House address, Tony Blair repeated the familiar argument that in the 1950s Britain 'lost our opportunity to influence the creation of the European Community'. This is a theme he has repeated on a number of occasions and the earlier 'lost opportunities' were seen as setting a pattern for 'missing buses'. However, the notion that more imaginative British 'leadership' would have allowed Britain to have held the ring or otherwise assisted the reconciliation of France and Germany is pure fantasy and the plan for the European Coal and Steel Community (ECSC) was prepared without informing or consulting the British. When the Messina Conference met in 1955 (see Chapter 3), the British did underestimate its potential, but it is facile to suggest that Britain could have altered the basic structure of the European Economic Community (EEC) had it signed the Treaty of Rome. Some aspects would have been different, but some conditions were changed after Britain entered, as Tony Blair acknowledges, for example the budget rebate. However, even if Britain had entered in 1958 or even 1962, it would not have been possible to head off the political aims of the new enterprise that the British well understood and which were the main reasons for not joining in the first place. If Britain had signed the Treaty of Rome with the other six, it would not have changed the basic structure and organisation of the EEC. Just being a member of a club does not enable you to influence the rules if all the other members – and in this case France and Germany in particular – want different things. It is wrong to suggest that if the British had entered the Community at the beginning and thus participated in the negotiations, the Common Agricultural Policy would not have taken the form it did. The French saw agricultural protection as a sine qua non, without which the project would never have started. Even the 'helpful' President Pompidou made certain that this was signed and sealed before Britain entered the EEC.

On the single currency itself, Tony Blair's address at Chatham House was short. For him:

> There is only one immediate question on EMU: is it inconsistent with the nation state? If it is, then we must reject it, even if it would be economically prudent to join. If it is not, as we believe, then we are free to participate fully in the formation of its institutions and structures, whilst deciding finally on whether to join on the basis of our national economic interest.

'Inconsistent' is a peculiar word to use. When the single currency came into operation, the participant nation states were not wiped off the map, men and women still thought of themselves as French, German and Dutch. But EMU does reduce national sovereignty in a more significant way than any other single step in the long history of Europe. The right to issue a currency is par excellence the mark of an independent state. As Keynes noted, 'Who controls the currency controls the country.' And as made clear earlier in the book, the ability of a country to set interest rates to meet the needs of its own economy is an absolutely essential component of national economic sovereignty in the modern world.

The Chatham House lecture, given before the 1997 election, has been quoted at some length because, in many respects, it sets out Tony's political manifesto for Europe and its themes were repeated in one form or another on many occasions in government. However, what was striking about the Chatham House lecture and subsequent speeches was the lack of content in the political case Tony Blair tried to make. There was no serious attempt to address the genuine fears that many British people have about where the EU is heading. 'Subsidiarity should be given real effect,' but nowhere, at Chatham House or on any subsequent occasion since, did Tony address the need to roll back the powers of Brussels if this is to mean anything in practice. There was no attempt to argue why membership of the single currency was necessary in political terms let alone economic ones, just a series of assertions and red herrings. The

British people should be wary of how Tony Blair caricatures the arguments of those thinking differently to him on Europe. It is all too easy to be taken along by him in a series of superficially logical steps. Apparent reasonableness leads to conclusions little more than assertions. The uncontroversial desire to be 'influential in Europe' slips effortlessly into being at the 'centre' and then 'leading' Europe. But this 'leadership' is ultimately precluded unless Britain joins the single currency since, without that, Britain cannot be a 'full member of the club'. All this is presented as a self-evident truth. Those opposed to such a notion are portrayed as being out of date, stupid or both, denying the 'European dimension' to British history, buttressed by a variety of straw men: '"Splendid isolation" was never an option!' Who ever supposed it was or is? Those with doubts about the wisdom of joining the single currency should ignore these verbal smokescreens and concentrate on the economic and political issues at stake. Europe illustrates the strengths and weaknesses of Tony Blair and New Labour. One of his strengths, in addition to natural charm and un-stuffiness, was his lack of inherited intellectual or political 'baggage'. This meant that he approached issues in a more open-minded way than many other politicians, but his lack of historical perspective was reinforced by New Labour's political strategy, including naive attempts to emancipate itself from the past: Britannia was 'cool' and Britain was 'a young country'. But there are many problems that can't be understood or addressed without a grasp of their historical roots, and Europe was one of these. In a political leader, open-mindedness not tempered by earlier exposure, discipline, experience or knowledge can lead him or her down paths that are naive and dangerous for the country.

Tony did not have the background knowledge that could be taken for granted in the other politicians with whom I had worked closely, Denis Healey, Jim Callaghan and David Owen, and, from my own reading of history. I simply didn't recognise his descriptions of Europe or Britain's contemporary position in it. My first discussions with Tony about this were in opposition and inevitably these centred on the economic issues, but my economic views on the single currency, outlined in this book, struck at the heart of his political case too. I found Tony's basic political argument that adopting the euro would increase Britain's political influence in Europe wholly unconvincing, since membership would sap not enhance Britain's economic strength and this in turn is a key determinant of political influence in the EU. These views were first sketched out for Tony in a brief paper I prepared for a meeting on EMU in his office in the House of Commons in July 1996. In addition to Tony, Jonathan Powell, David Miliband and myself, this gathering included Gordon Brown and Ed Balls, as well as Gavyn Davies and David (now Lord) Currie. This was still at a time when there were doubts about whether monetary union would actually go ahead and if it did how many countries would qualify under the Maastricht criteria. There was a pretty rambling, inconclusive discussion in Tony's office on the prospects for monetary union and its implications for Britain if it went ahead. My paper trailed some of the economic arguments covered earlier in this book. It concluded with the observation that 'a judgement has to be made of the wider political repercussions and the potential loss of influence should Britain stand aside, though ultimately this will be most affected and sustained by its economic strength.' There was nothing very controversial in the paper back in 1996, but afterwards Tony was very careful to make sure that no copies were left lying around where others might pick them up since anyone reading it 'will think we're never going to join the thing'.

After the election landslide in 1997, one or two euro-enthusiasts close to Tony Blair, including Roy Jenkins and Peter Mandelson, wanted an early 'enabling' referendum on the euro. This would have cleared the decks for the Government to take Britain into the single currency without the further need to consult the electorate. This idea was never a runner with either the Prime Minister or the Chancellor, since both thought that taking advantage of an election landslide in such a transparent manner would not establish adequate legitimacy for a subsequent decision to enter EMU. As Gordon Brown put it later in the House of Commons: 'Any serious gap between the referendum and the actual entry date would undermine the conclusions of the referendum.'[1] This notion was reinforced later, in the run-up to the 2001 election, when some commentators had suggested that Tony Blair might use victory to 'bounce' the electorate into a euro referendum. The Prime Minister's official spokesman said, 'It would not be right to have a general election and then immediately on the back of it have a referendum.'[2]

In fact, in 1997 neither Tony nor Gordon expected early entry, but the Prime Minister was careful to leave open the position in any discussions with other significant political actors Europe. After about a month in Downing Street, Tony told the President of the EU Commission that, although Britain would be unable to join in 1999, he hoped any delay would be short. Some of the peripheral players were keen to keep open the option of entry during the first parliament but most, including Peter Mandelson, had no grasp or interest in the economics involved in a decision to enter EMU. The Prime Minister and the Chancellor knew that a decision not to join the single currency at the start probably meant staying out for the whole parliament, but neither wanted to declare their hand at the beginning of the new administration.

Nonetheless, when Blair arrived in government he was certainly ready to engage more actively with members of the EU in other areas and he was kicking at an open door. The previous administration's relations with fellow EU politicians had become so dire that even when the Prime Minister (John Major) or the Chancellor (Ken Clarke) said sensible things they were ignored. Tony Blair's desire to engage was helped by the EU's own calendar: the new Government had to prepare to take over the presidency of the European Council in January

1998 and this inevitably meant that its tone was upbeat. It also put a premium on being seen to be treating the pending start of EMU in a fair-minded manner at a time when its start date and participants were still unclear.

Within a few weeks of the election in 1997, the Prime Minister sent a note to the Chancellor commissioning a paper on handling EMU over the summer. This was to include an assessment of the likely economic performance of EU economies in the next five years, the extent to which they would or would not meet the convergence criteria, the likelihood of EMU starting on time and the implications of any delay for Britain during its forthcoming presidency and beyond. Tony asked for a response from Gordon in three weeks. However, this had still not been received when the Chancellor made his own speech on Europe a month later.

Gordon Brown set out his views at Chatham House on 17 July 1997. Many of the themes echoed those of Blair two years earlier from the same platform and this was reflected in the title of the Chancellor's speech: 'Britain leading in Europe'. There was similar potted history from medieval times, through the Tudor era, Empire and into the twentieth century, the dangers when Britain diverts its eyes from the continent; and similar assertions of the obvious: 'Britain has been and will remain a European power.' In this speech, Gordon spent less time than had Tony on the so-called missed opportunities of the 1950s and 1960s, but in his search for Britain's role today, he followed Blair's example. More straw men were created to knock down. 'Britain's future cannot lie in low-wage competition.' He attacked the notion that Britain could become the Hong Kong of Europe, 'as a trading post or as a tax haven servicing major trading blocs'. He went on, 'The idea of the UK as a greater Guernsey, only needs a minute's consideration to be rejected.' Which is presumably why no serious person had put the notion forward; Brown was merely caricaturing the views of Conrad Black, sometime owner of the *Telegraph*.

Gordon Brown proclaimed his belief in 'a close constructive relationship with our European partners' and set out his agenda for economic reform, before returning to the theme of leadership. 'In order to shape an agenda that is right for Britain and Europe we need to be in and leading in Europe.' He announced the intention of publishing a guide to the practical implications of the single currency and creating an advisory group to allow an exchange of information between government and business. Exaggerating somewhat, Gordon declared that 'today the Government is throwing open the EMU debate,' and to help the process along the Treasury published a summary of a report, by the academic David (now Lord) Currie – first produced earlier in the year – setting out the pros and cons of EMU.

Although the contents of Gordon's speech were ones that Tony might have uttered himself, it caused its own tensions between No. 10 and No. 11, which also have to be seen against the other problems at this time that were referred to in Chapter 1. It had been very difficult for No. 10 to find out what Gordon had been planning in his first budget (a couple of weeks earlier) and he was being even less open about his future intentions. Gordon's Chatham House speech was discussed between No. 10 and No. 11, but as late as the Wednesday of the week before the speech we were told that it was not about EMU, but that it would be about 'stability, economic growth and employability'. In the event, the Prime Minister was relaxed about the content but he did not want it to be a big story and both he and Alastair Campbell felt that, without careful handling, the speech would inevitably be interpreted as a very positive signal about the Government's intention to enter EMU. That is exactly what happened because Gordon's team spun it that way with the journalists, despite an agreed line between Alastair Campbell and Charlie Whelan, Gordon's press secretary.

The Prime Minister was further irritated by the fact that Gordon chose the very morning of the speech to send over the delayed response to his earlier request for a note on handling EMU over the summer. Gordon's reply was accompanied by the suggestion that it might be useful to have a strategic discussion on the prospects for EMU before the end of the month. The day of Brown's own speech on Europe was perhaps a bit late for strategy, though Gordon commented, apparently without irony, 'It's not like the old days when Ken Clarke didn't tell John Major what he was up to.' Those who have worked closely with some of the principal players in the previous administration say that, whatever its failings, no one would have dared treat John Major in such a cavalier fashion.

Nonetheless, by the summer recess things had calmed down. There was a formal discussion on EMU between the Prime Minister and the Chancellor, accompanied by Ed Balls and including Jonathan Powell and myself. The focus of the meeting was the Prime Minister's questions a month before. Prior to the meeting, in a brief note, I had reminded Tony of the inevitable problems that would arise in monetary union with just one interest rate for several countries (at the time German short rates were three per cent and Italy's seven per cent) and I drew attention to what I saw as the failure of potential participants to grasp the significance of 'structural reform'. The note recalled that restructuring in the US had taken the best part of ten years and even longer in the UK. And in both instances there had been governments which were determined to press ahead with deregulation and to open up their economies in a way that was absent in most of continental Europe.

However, although the economic prospects of the EU were discussed at the subsequent meeting, more time was spent on the likelihood and implications of any delay in the start of EMU. I felt that in purely economic terms delay was most unlikely since if the markets once got a hint that this was a serious possibility the reaction in the bond markets of some of the peripheral economies would put the whole enterprise in jeopardy. And of course on top of this there was the determination to press on with what was seen as a political project in most countries of the EU.

Some commentators have said that the notion that the UK could play an active role in postponement showed the naïveté of the new government. But this was never really its position. The Prime Minister did toy with the idea of combining a controlled postponement with more explicit commitment to EMU from Britain, but he remained doubtful whether Britain could in practice play any role. However, the possibility of postponement was under serious consideration in a number of capitals. The Bundesbank had always been hostile to EMU and it was particularly worried about the participation of Italy. There were also concerns about the state of the French budget. In Germany, a number of serious players sought out British views on controlled postponement. The one, and vital, exception to all this in Germany was Chancellor Kohl, who would have seen any intervention by Britain as wrecking tactics. After some discussion with ambassadors and foreign-policy experts, it was decided that there was no role for the British and it was recognised that the decision to go ahead with EMU was a matter for Germany and France.

The Prime Minister wanted to follow up the July meeting with Gordon with another one in the autumn. In the event, this did not take place, because it became impossible to tie the Chancellor down to a date at a time when relations had again become strained between No. 10 and No. 11.

On the Friday before the Labour Party Conference, an article appeared in the *Financial Times*. In it, Robert Peston reported that the Government 'is on the point of adopting a much more positive approach to the European economic and monetary union, with a statement shortly that sterling is likely to join at an early opportunity after the 1999 launch'.[3] The pound fell on the news and Ed Balls telephoned me in my office expressing apparent surprise at the turn of events, volunteering the information, an unusual occurrence in itself, that the market reaction had nothing to do with him!

A couple of weeks later, the *Daily Mail* suggested that Blair would tell other leaders at Luxembourg on 21 October that the UK would join as soon as possible after the start date of the euro.[4] Both these articles implied that Brown was setting the pace on EMU. An article in *The Independent*, whose correspondent was known to be particularly close to Alastair Campbell, gave the story an anti-Brown twist, reporting attempts 'to bounce Blair into a decision which could lead to the early death of the pound'.[5] None of this had much to do with the actual views of the two men, but it set the background to an article in *The Times* by Philip Webster a few days later.[6] This had been carefully scripted between No. 10 and the Treasury with both Gordon and Tony recognising the need to dampen down the notion of early entry. Beyond that, there was no real disagreement between the two of them though, as Chancellor Gordon had been taken aback by the speed of the market reaction to the article by Robert Peston, and this reinforced his inclination to try and close down the option of joining for the parliament, while Tony wanted to allow a bit more ambiguity in public – although in private he recognised that entry in his first term was improbable. In the text of the interview with Webster, Gordon's remarks were careful. On the option of joining EMU in 1999, he said, 'We said in our manifesto and it remains true today that it is highly unlikely that Britain could join in the first wave.' The headline – 'Brown rules out single currency for lifetime of this Parliament' – was probably a bit stronger than Brown (and certainly No. 10) wanted, but it was the subsequent briefing by Charlie Whelan that fed not only the impression that Brown was deciding government policy, but that the policy itself had come down firmly against entry in the first term. The headline in *The Sun* summed it up: 'Brown Says No To Euro'. Whelan was seen popping in and out of the Red Lion pub in Whitehall, briefing other journalists along similar lines. According to one commentator, the Prime Minister, temporarily cut off from both Brown and his own press secretary, had to contact Whelan at his unusual, if familiar, venue to tell him to row back the story only to be told 'Sorry, Tony, it's too late'.[7]

After this, the Government had to restore some semblance of coherence to its policy towards EMU entry. This concern lay behind the 'five economic tests' and the Chancellor's statement to the House of Commons on 27 October 1997, when entry to EMU was effectively ruled out for the parliament. Gordon Brown emphasised that the Government wanted to join, 'provided the single currency is successful and the economic case is clear and unambiguous', which put the onus of any decision even more with the Treasury, though it was Tony Blair and not Gordon Brown who insisted on the phrase 'clear and unambiguous'. However, the current assessment was that 'British membership of the single currency in 1999 could not meet the tests' and 'there is no realistic prospect of our having demonstrated before the end of this parliament that we have achieved convergence that is sustainable and settled rather than transitory.' A decision to join in the first parliament of the new government was not realistic, 'barring some fundamental or unforeseen change in economic circumstances'. The last caveat potentially still left the door open for entry during the first parliament but, to all intents and purposes, any possibility of entry had been kicked into a second term.

This didn't stop periodic flurries of speculation as to the possible timing of any decision in the second term and, just over six months after his October speech, Gordon Brown suggested for the first time that the Government would be in a position to judge the case for entry 'early in the next parliament'.[8] This provided some clarification and was made without any consultation with the Prime Minister, who nonetheless seemed reasonably relaxed when I raised it: the laconic response was simply 'Don't worry, I'm watching it.' However, it still left open what 'early in the next parliament' meant, and this was not settled until near the end of the first term when the Leader of the Opposition, William Hague, asked Blair during Prime Minister's Questions in early February 2001, 'Does "early" mean the first two years of that parliament?' Tony's reply was, '"Early in the next parliament" means exactly what it says. It would of course be within two years.' Gordon now had a deadline for the five tests. He was furious at not being consulted, but the reality was that Hague had taken Tony by surprise.

After the 2001 election, there was no indication that the Prime Minister was in a rush to join EMU. The priority was delivering reforms of public services. When sterling started to depreciate against all major currencies some weeks after Tony was back in Downing Street, some commentators started to suggest that Britain was converging with the euro. The relief on the Prime Minister's face was palpable when I dismissed this notion during a brief meeting with him in his den in the second half of June. Despite all the press speculation and his desire to join the single currency, the last thing Tony Blair wanted to be told at that particular moment was that, on top of everything else, this was the time. He could only fight on so many fronts and his priority on re-election was reform of the public services.

My own concerns and warnings about the economic implications of EMU expressed in opposition only hardened during my six years in Downing Street. There were extensive if intermittent exchanges on the subject with Tony, either face to face or through short notes that he generally read at weekends, very often responding with comments or further questions, though there would always come a stage when these exchanges, verbal or on paper, would trail off. Of course, the Prime Minister was very busy, but exposure to the economic arguments, it seemed to me, left him uncomfortable. Communication and discussion could end rather abruptly. For example, towards the end of 2001, in a series of brief notes over several weekends, I outlined the pending problems within Euroland. Tony said that there were clearly problems with a single currency but that he had the answers and would return to it later in a note.

Of course I didn't expect a note from the busy Prime Minister, but neither did I think he had the answers and this could show itself in quite small comments as well as in more detailed discussion. Sitting in the back of his car in July 1999 on the way to a speech in the City, the Prime Minister told me that if Britain were in EMU, he thought it would clean up on investment. I doubted this and pointed out, as I had previously on many occasions, that even if we did clean up and there was a surge in investment coming into Britain, the loss of the freedom for the pound to appreciate and depreciate would mean particularly serious consequences, for reasons spelt out in this book.

The problem was that my arguments bypassed many of the traditional and irrelevant preoccupations over such matters as 'the right rate of entry' and raised concerns about the economic case for entering EMU that had never been addressed by the Government of Whitehall. The commitment was to join EMU on the right conditions, but at no time in opposition was there a serious attempt to identify the economic and political conditions that were necessary to make EMU work and the implication that these might have on the decision itself. In government, of course, it was too late in the sense that the policy had already been decided, and the economic tests announced in October 1997 were a belated and incomplete attempt drawn up by Gordon Brown to cover up a previous omission.

Not surprisingly, most civil servants see their job as providing support for the Government's declared policy, not challenging its very basis, although some individuals had doubts they would occasionally share in private. One of the Prime Minister's closest advisers said, 'Of course, you're right, there is no economic case, but the Prime Minister will not budge.' Tony Blair recognised that he needed a reasonable economic background to make the case for entry otherwise any campaign to adopt the euro would be dead before it started, but the case he wanted to make was not about economics. The Prime Minister was absolutely convinced of the political case for entering EMU and felt more at ease with this than with economics. All his major speeches on Europe reflected this priority, very few contained any economics beyond a mantra-like adherence to a form of words endorsing entry provided 'the economic conditions were right'. Economic advice was normally surplus to Tony's requirements on these occasions and I made a conscious decision to refrain from trying to qualify the political case he presented. In the main, this was because I thought this would make it less likely that the Prime Minister would register the economic ones, but it was also because after a few failed attempts to clarify some of the assertions made in the political sections of his speeches on Europe, I gave it up as a waste of time.

The prevailing consensus in Whitehall never really sought to challenge or probe the economic assumptions behind the Government's policy on EMU and provided little resistance to the Prime Minister's political rhetoric about Europe. There were a few shining individual exceptions but, as an institution, the Foreign Office was pretty well economically illiterate about EMU. Beyond economics, there was a less stereotyped attitude towards Europe among some younger officials in the Foreign Office, but the prevailing mood was one of worldly weariness with anyone who couldn't accept that, as with all other aspects of Europe, it was 'inevitable' that Britain would join in the end. This was an unresponsive background for me to work in. Leonard Shapiro wrote, 'The true object of propaganda is neither to convince nor even to persuade, but to produce a uniform pattern of public utterance in which the first trace of unorthodox thought reveals itself as a jarring dissonance.' I was a dissonant voice. A couple of times a year, Britain's EU ambassadors gather together at the Foreign Office for a pow-wow. Towards the end of October 1999, I was asked to talk to them one afternoon in the Map Room of the Foreign Office about the Government's attitude towards EMU. It was like being part of a Bateman cartoon: 'The man who told the truth about EMU'. They stared at me blankly. I was simply informed in a world-weary way, before they all broke for tea, that it was all very well but entry was inevitable, Britain always joins in the end.

The Prime Minister's key adviser on Europe was Sir Stephen Wall, who occupied a room looking out on Downing Street itself, which had previously been Alastair Campbell's before he moved with his expanded staff to No. 12 Downing Street. Stephen had worked in the private office of David Owen, Geoffrey Howe and John Major when they had been at the Foreign Office, and moved to join Major when he went to No. 10. There he had a key role in the Prime Minister's negotiations over the Maastricht Treaty and apparently played an important part in dissuading him from resignation after 'Black Wednesday' and the debacle of the ERM. Stephen has also held other important posts including being the head of the UK delegation to the EU. Stephen was a class act but he hadn't much grasp of economics and generally kept off the subject. When the Convention on the Future of Europe met, Tony was to put a lot of emphasis on getting its agreement to a stronger chairman or president for the European Council, some thought this an odd priority, but the attitude was if that's what the Prime Minister wanted that's what he must get. In a sense, this approach reflected the very best qualities of the civil service, but it did mean that there was very little scrutiny or questioning of the Prime Minister's objectives or strategy.

Nor did it get much scrutiny from any of the political appointments in No. 10. Alastair Campbell appeared instinctively opposed to EMU, but it didn't go beyond that and there was no evidence that either Sally Morgan or Peter Hyman, who were both close to Tony, saw their function as other than doing what Tony wanted. Tony's policy on EMU and Europe certainly didn't get critical scrutiny from Roger Liddle, another political appointment and someone whom I had known for over twenty years, and an enthusiastic believer in the euro as well as in more political and economic integration in Europe. In fact, Roger seemed to work for Peter Mandelson more than for Tony, and anyone who drafts a note on Europe for the Prime Minister stuck in Downing Street at the end of a miserable December in 1999, beginning with the words, 'On a weekend break in Marrakesh…' will not always be taken seriously. Roger's enthusiasm for Europe would often cloud his judgement, and sometimes with comic effect. In September 1999, there was a meeting of the policy unit in a small attic room of No. 10, and Roger expounded on the significance of the Blair-Schroeder letter. This was a joint letter designed to show that the so-called 'Third Way' had a common relevance to the economic prospects of both countries. I had drafted an initial economic core that was substantially watered down by Mandelson and Liddle, who both devoted a lot of time composing the letter and meeting the requirements of Schroeder's office. Despite the dilution, Schroeder received considerable flak in Germany when the text was published, since it was still regarded as too Anglo-Saxon, and not much was heard of the letter again. Nonetheless, Roger felt that the letter was the most significant event in German politics for thirty years. This put German unification in an interesting perspective and to be fair to Roger he joined in the general laughter that this absurd, but rather typical, remark provoked.

Potentially, Treasury ministers might have been an important source of support in my efforts to get the Prime Minister to engage in the economic and political implications of EMU. However, Gordon's team was even more reclusive about EMU than about other aspects of economic policy and in any case, the five tests, as noted in Chapter 11, were really only answers to second-order questions.

Gordon himself had been one the key figures, along with John Smith and Neil Kinnock, in committing Labour to support membership of the ERM, in part as a means of shaking off the notion that Labour was the party of devaluation. Even after the ERM broke up, Gordon did not apparently think this episode had any other wider lessons for attempts to prevent currencies moving up and down, writing that 'Labour rejects the notion that a free-market approach to currency markets will bring lasting benefits to the British economy' and that Labour continued to believe that 'a managed and stable exchange rate is essential for sustainable growth.'[9] However, Brown had been bruised by the collapse of the ERM and it was around this time that he took on Ed Balls, a journalist on the *Financial Times*, as his economic adviser. Ed had written a pamphlet for the Fabian Society that was very critical of the ERM, dismissing the notion that it provided a stable or workable economic framework, but the lessons for EMU that he and Gordon drew from the ERM experience were limited. 'ERM membership cannot provide, but instead requires, a credible, flexible and transparent macroeconomic policy framework and a medium term strategy for industrial regeneration.' In opposition, Ed and Gordon put together such a framework for implementing in government. In the current context there is no need to go into the details of this, but it was based on two 'rules' for fiscal policy and placed a great deal of emphasis on 'stability', a theme Gordon stressed time and time again as Chancellor. However, this was not seen as incompatible with eventual membership of EMU. In essence, the argument of Ed and Gordon was that the economy has to be in the right shape before joining, but, as should be clear to those who have followed the economic arguments of this book, that apparently sensible position doesn't hold water. On the contrary, in a dynamic economy, which Gordon and Ed said they wanted to promote, it is the freedom of the exchange rate to appreciate and depreciate that provides the best chance of ensuring overall economic stability. Even if the economy were stable or in the right shape before it entered EMU, it would become less so inside because monetary policy would inevitably be less appropriate than that set by the Bank of England.

One consistent feature of Tony Blair in government was his determination to keep control of the timing of any possible referendum campaign to join EMU. He described this to me as being like lighting a firework: only when you are ready do you light the blue touch paper and thereafter its all go, there is no turning back. What you can't do is light it and then put it out. It is simply incredible to launch a huge campaign for entry but then say, 'Oh by the way although it's absolutely essential we join, we can't do so at the moment because the economics are not right.'

This is why, in government, Tony was irritated from time to time by those who encouraged speculation that the campaign to enter the single currency was speeding up. Peter Mandelson and Robin Cook both did this in the first term. So too did others and, on one occasion in late January 2000, Stephen Byers phoned up No. 10 disclaiming any responsibility for the morning's headlines urging a more positive approach to EMU, and the Prime Minister was inclined to believe him, putting it down instead to the pro-EMU organisation 'Britain in Europe'. Occasionally, Tony also went further in public than he intended. Appearing on television in July 2000, he said, 'I believe we will be able to make a recommendation early in the next Parliament':[10] a recommendation rather than an assessment. The following day in No. 10 he admitted this had been a slip, though it was close to what he was saying to European leaders in private.

This desire to have as much control as possible over the timing of any referendum was understandable, but it led to some disappointment among euro-enthusiasts. The press, too, periodically missed the point and was often far too imaginative in its interpretations about the timing of making any decision to join the single currency. In the autumn of 2002, articles referred to decisions to postpone the assessment of the five tests from the autumn of 2002 until 2003, when there had never been any such intention in the first place. The newspapers examined speeches and articles for nuances and indications of shifting tactics. It was like reading wall posters in China's cultural revolution, but in the case of Britain the readers were often looking for messages that did not exist. And nowhere did they look more closely than at party conference.

At the 2001 annual conference in Brighton, the Prime Minister stressed the fundamental importance of the five tests. 'But if they are met, we should join, and if met in this Parliament, we should have the courage of our argument, to ask the British people for their consent in this Parliament.' The use of the word 'courage' was seen by some euro-enthusiasts as a rallying cry to arms, but there was probably a more mundane explanation. The perception had grown up that the emphasis on public services had pushed EMU into the long grass. The attack on the World Trade Center and the aftermath of '9/11' reinforced the impression that the single currency was being downgraded as a priority. But this was not the Prime Minister's intention and indeed was at odds with what Tony Blair and senior officials were telling other EU states: they all implied that early entry was still being pursued as an objective. (This process continued after the assessment in 2003. German officials were surprised in June of that year to be told by the Prime Minister's chief of staff, Jonathan Powell, that a referendum might be fought in 2004.) The speech at the 2001 annual conference put the single currency back where the Prime Minister thought it belonged, but it did not accelerate the process at all.

However, Tony's speech was interpreted as an indication that he was keen to get on with making the case for the euro and some of Gordon's team resented the implicit pressure. A little while later they felt they had redeemed their authority. The Prime Minister was due to speak on the Monday of the CBI conference, the day after Gordon Brown. The text of Brown's speech was only sent to No. 10 on the Saturday. We were told that there would be no story, though it was clearly the most detailed statement on EMU by the Chancellor since October 1997 and briefing heavily for the Monday papers inevitably distracted from the Prime Minister's own address to the country's businessmen.

Despite all this political manoeuvring, at this stage there was in fact little to separate Blair and Brown on EMU. When they came into office, both saw political advantages in joining, but both were worried about the economics. Over the next few years in government, both probably retained this general position, but whereas Blair continued to worry about the economics, he became more convinced about the political advantages; while Brown still appeared to accept the potential political advantages, he became more and more concerned about the economics of entry. This may have been no more than a reflection of the different perspectives and preoccupations of Prime Minister and Chancellor, as well as mirroring other tensions between the two. As noted in Chapter 1, No. 10 found it very difficult to get the willing cooperation of Gordon Brown on many areas of economic policy and this meant that Tony Blair and Gordon Brown rarely discussed the single currency once the five tests had been given to the Treasury to assess. Gordon took a very proprietary attitude towards them and the handling of this important issue became absurd through the latter part of 2002 and into 2003 when the Prime Minister, not unreasonably, wanted to know how the process of the assessment was getting along.

At a meeting between the two men in the middle of October 2002, less than nine months before the deadline for making the assessment on the tests, the Prime Minister said they needed to discuss the issue. The Chancellor replied that he thought it would be quite improper to pre-empt the Treasury's assessment of the tests, an absurdly prickly response to the man who was after all Prime Minister. At the beginning of 2003, Tony raised the issue again and was fobbed off by Gordon on the grounds that he had not yet discussed the assessment with Treasury officials, including his economic adviser and closest political and economic confidant, Ed Balls. This was an unlikely proposition given how closely they worked together and this nonsense continued with one meeting arranged to discuss the euro shifting into a rambling discourse on the merits or otherwise of Britain bidding to host the Olympic Games. But time was getting very short and a series of seminars was arranged through

January, February and March. The Prime Minister determined that I took no part in any of these discussions, which was a pity but came as no surprise since my views challenged the very basis of the economic case for entry rather than tinkering around the edges. Roger Liddle was also excluded, but for rather different reasons. The seminars[11] were attended by Sir Stephen Wall, Jeremy Heywood and Jonathan Powell from No. 10, and Ed Balls, with Gus O'Donnell, the permanent secretary, and other relevant officials from the Treasury.

The first papers on the assessment, which were particularly dry economic texts, arrived at No. 10 in late February 2003, but the formal presentation came much later, appropriately enough given all the shenanigans of the past months, on 1 April. By this time, of course, the Prime Minister was fully occupied with the Iraq war, but the budget was looming on 9 April. Having not deigned to discuss the matter for nine months, Gordon Brown tried to bounce the Prime Minister into an announcement in the budget statement, but Tony Blair was not having this. The result was the much briefed 'agreement' that there would be no assessment in the budget, though such was the tension between the two neighbours that some in No. 10 said, only half in jest, that when Gordon Brown got to the dispatch box he might still make an ad lib announcement! He didn't, and after the budget serious negotiations got underway.

For more than a year, Gordon Brown had been taking an interest in European issues that went well beyond his responsibilities on Ecofin. He had also become worried about the course being taken by the Convention on the Future of Europe, and these concerns were reflected in his original presentation of the Treasury's assessment to No. 10, but the Prime Minister wanted a more positive stance. Tony had no plan to hold a referendum at a particular date, but he did not want to narrow his room for manoeuvre in the following couple of years when he thought critical decisions about the workings of EMU might be made. In a discussion I had with him in his office a few days after the 2003 budget, he implied that joining later, in five or six years, might be the worst of all worlds.

After the budget, there was an intense and very fraught period between the Prime Minister and Chancellor and for a time No. 10 felt that Gordon Brown had them over a barrel and might dictate the terms of the announcement to Tony. These discussions were about the politics and presentation of the assessment, not its economic content or validity. Many long sessions were held between the two principal protagonists alone, but at other times they were accompanied. The only people involved in the discussions on the Prime Minister's side were, as before, his very closest political confidants, with no economic expertise, together with Jeremy Heywood and Stephen Wall. The five economic tests served as the backdrop, but the drama was entirely about political calculations not economics and that was as true of Gordon Brown as anyone else. In a sense there was nothing new in all this, his earlier reluctance to discuss the tests with the Prime Minister until close to the deadline for publishing the assessment cannot have been based on economic calculations, as though a bit more time would settle the matter in a manner that was 'clear and unambiguous'. The decision to join EMU on a permanent basis would not be affected by six months more data or another economic study. Gordon Brown needed to show that he was in charge of the economic tests and he was determined to take it to the wire.

The press coverage that accompanied the final stages of the assessment was reminiscent of the spats in the autumn of 1997, with both Brown and Blair camps engaged in a very public, but largely non-attributable, war. On the one hand, Brown would resign if he didn't get his way on the terms for the assessment;[12] on the other hand, Blair was ready to sack his Chancellor.[13] Other stories suggested that Blair had offered to stand down if Brown supported a referendum.[14] 'Friends' of both were quoted and misquoted and, as might be expected, the out-of-sorts Mandelson saw the chance to regain the headlines, suggesting among other things that Gordon Brown was 'politically obsessed' and had 'outmanoeuvred' the Prime Minister. Things got so bad that the Prime Minister and Chancellor held a swiftly arranged joint press conference to show their unity of purpose that only served to demonstrate the opposite.

During the final stages of the assessment in 2003, the Cabinet was brought into the discussion, collectively and in smaller gatherings with the Prime Minister and Chancellor. Much was made of this in the press, but the involvement of other senior ministers was inevitable since it was inconceivable that such an important decision would not ultimately be a collective one, or at least one in which all members had had their say. But the exercise also served several other useful purposes: it tied in the whole Government to the assessment decision and allowed it to be accompanied by much more pro-EMU rhetoric than would otherwise have been the case. It avoided the obvious pitfall of a joint decision by the Prime Minister and Chancellor when commentators would inevitably have highlighted differences between the two principals rather than any common ground. The discussions in Cabinet brought the Government together since they were pretty good-natured and Gordon Brown was more forthcoming than usual. Extending the decision to the whole Cabinet could be presented as reining in the Chancellor and thus broadening the basis for any subsequent decision. However, taking the decision to Cabinet also had the effect of reinforcing Gordon Brown's own reputation as the man who was still preoccupied with maintaining the integrity of the economic tests. Everyone was apparently happy.

Gordon Brown was, and is, concerned not to repeat what he sees as the mistakes of John Major, who as Chancellor took Britain into the ERM, only to have his own Government destroyed by the economic debacle that ensued. To that extent his economic preoccupation with EMU is focused on the two or three years after entry (when he hopes to be Prime Minister). His closest adviser, Ed Balls, set out the problem as seen from the Brown camp in a speech at the end of 2002,[15] which sought to contrast the thorough nature of the economic assessment by Gordon with previous decisions such as those to return to the Gold Standard in 1925 or enter the ERM in 1990. On the latter he concluded that, 'With hindsight, once more a British government underestimated the short-term transitional costs of their decision.' Of course, the costs of entering a fixed exchange rate regime or a single currency are far from 'transitional', but Gordon seems to believe that, if these difficulties can be contained, the longer-term adjustments will sort themselves out. As his adviser explained in the same speech: 'In a monetary union, convergence will, in the end, be realised. In principle, countries can choose whether they converge from the inside or before they join based on assessing the balance of benefits, costs and risks of the options.' In principle this may be true, but in the past such convergence has only taken place within a monetary union if preceded by political union; without that, if a single currency is to work it needs far greater economic convergence than that envisaged in the five tests. In fact, with the degree of economic convergence required, currencies would be stable anyway (see Chapter 11). In practice, without political union, the economic strains in producing convergence become intolerable, as the countries that have adopted the euro are just beginning to discover.

Nonetheless, the perception that the economic problems associated with entry to EMU were ones of 'transition' helps to explain why, following the assessment in June 2003, the Treasury began to examine issues that Gordon Brown thought necessary to address to help Britain 'foster convergence'. These included possible proposals to 'produce greater stability in the housing market', measures to improve 'flexibility' in labour markets (including a greater local and regional 'dimension' in public-sector pay), the possible outline for a more active fiscal policy and a modified fiscal framework should Britain enter EMU. Of course, some of these objectives may be desirable anyway, though others, like a more active fiscal policy, are not, and attempts to force economic convergence would do more harm than good, but politics was dictating the search for a short-term 'fix'.

On 9 June 2003, the Government announced its conclusions to the EMU assessment: there had been progress, but the five tests had not been met and the situation would be reviewed later. Relations between Tony Blair and Gordon Brown were very tense when they emerged from their negotiations on the assessment, as was obvious to any casual observer at the joint press conference afterwards. They sat next to each other in No. 10, but looked completely uninterested in what each other said, Tony fiddling with a pencil when Gordon spoke and Gordon gazing into the middle distance when the Prime Minister was answering a question. During the following few months, relations between the two men deteriorated further, on occasions barely speaking for days, but towards the end of the year things had improved. Perhaps they both realised that the very public differences between the two of them were harming both them and the Government. Under Michael Howard, the Conservatives were looking more credible as an alternative government and the next general election was perhaps only eighteen months away. Maybe a 'deal' had been done between the two of them (Granita II). Whatever the reasons, and although there were ups and downs, by the early months of 2004 Blair and Brown were generally on better terms than anyone had seen since the days of opposition.

In the 2004 budget, Gordon Brown kept his grip on any EMU decision: no new assessment was made, but the position was to be reviewed the following year, though most people, in Whitehall and outside, assumed that that nothing would happen until after another election, and quite possibly not for a long time after.

At some stage, all prime ministers become concerned with their place in history and there is little doubt that for Tony Blair this involves fulfilling his vision of Britain's position in Europe. Yet, although conscious of the judgement of history, Tony remained surprisingly unaware of the political history of Europe or the failings of earlier attempts at monetary integration, both of which are critical to understanding the EU and EMU and Britain's position in either. Tony Blair's desire to join EMU was clearly motivated by politics but he was unconcerned about the single currency's political implications and remained disinclined to recognise EMU's economic flaws. Of course, if the economic case were especially weak at a particular moment, the political judgement would come down against the tests being fulfilled, but that is a very different matter. That was essentially the position in 2003. All manner of economic obstacles were there for anyone to see, including the parlous state of many economies in Euroland and, in the wake of the Iraq crisis, relations with France were fraught. It did not take political genius to see that this was not the best moment for Tony Blair to tell a largely hostile public, 'Now is the time to join France and Germany in the euro.' However, the political objective remained in place and at that stage Tony Blair was still set on not leaving Downing Street without at least making the attempt to take Britain into EMU.

After six years in government, the relationship between Blair and Brown was very different to their most collaborative period in opposition. The terms, conditions and immediate objectives had altered but no one should underestimate their determination and effectiveness when working together in pursuit of their separate but dependent political objectives. In the right conditions they would make a powerful team if they decided it was time to enter EMU. The electorate would be softened up and any opponents of EMU branded as opponents of Europe or even anti-British. The 'patriotic case', a popular theme of both Tony Blair and Gordon Brown, would be to the fore. It would not be easy, but in the right circumstances it could work. Gordon would continue to protect his flank in speeches and articles that drew attention to the failings in Euroland: 'The economic challenge for Europe is to be flexible, competitive, reforming and open.'[16] However, at some stage along the road when economic conditions were temporarily more propitious, Gordon Brown might be prepared to jump off the fence in pursuit of his own political ambitions and the hope for proponents of entry would be that his vaunted 'prudence' and perceived scepticism in the past would carry disproportionate weight as the Government tried to take Britain in.

After another triumph in a general election, at some stage Tony Blair might be prepared to take a calculated gamble on EMU in pursuit of his place in history, and he would need to receive Gordon Brown's active support in return for the subsequent succession. If events and opinion conspired to make entry to EMU impossible, Gordon Brown's 'integrity' would be intact, and he would have delivered his side of the bargain and hope still to be in a position to succeed to No. 10. Of course, by then, politics being politics, there could be other claimants for Tony's crown, and Brown's reputation for handling the economy may be tarnished too.

However, by 2004, any earlier calculations about EMU had been further complicated by the implications of events elsewhere. The conduct of the Iraq war had undermined the public's trust in Tony Blair; whether this was justified or not, it had happened. The Government faced difficulties on a number of other fronts too, and Tony Blair was unpopular with large numbers of his own party, inside and outside Parliament. Blair had always argued that Margaret Thatcher went on too long and given all the speculation about the succession, even his close allies were concerned that any general election campaign with Tony Blair as leader would raise questions about the length of his intended tenure in Downing Street. Some commentators speculated that Tony Blair might use a decade as leader, or some other appropriate anniversary, as the opportunity to announce he was stepping down; Gordon Brown would be elected leader and he would then seek a new mandate, with the added bonus that emerging problems with the public finances would not be apparent until the new tenant was tucked up in No. 10. Tony Blair's reputation would be secure: not only two huge election victories in 1997 and 2001, he would also have further secured the transition to someone steeped in Labour's traditional values, establishing himself in Labour's pantheon, as well as a national leader and international figure.

When I left Downing Street, Tony Blair showed no sign of wanting to leave, but the pressures are intense and politics is unpredictable. However, whether Blair or Brown is in No. 10 Downing Street is probably less important for EMU than most other areas of policy. In 2003, some commentators took the view that Gordon Brown had become convinced that it was not in Britain's long-term interests to join EMU. He might even be a closet sceptic! It is true that if that had been the case Gordon Brown would have had to adopt a policy similar to the one he did adopt: procrastination and postponement. But that was not his position at all. There was no evidence that Gordon Brown thought that membership of EMU was undesirable and no reason to doubt that, if he (or any other likely successor) were to become Labour's next Prime Minister, he would want, like Tony Blair, to take Britain in, though his strategy and tactics might be different.

The euro has been kicked into touch but the game is still on. Whatever the current perceptions, EMU is not going to go away as an issue in British politics and it is now inextricably entangled with a wider one: the possibility of a new constitution for the EU.

CHAPTER SIXTEEN

An Untied Nation

Britain's Influence
in the EU and Beyond

> Britain needs its voice strong in Europe and bluntly Europe needs a
> strong Britain, rock solid in our alliance with the USA, yet determined to
> play its full part in shaping Europe's destiny.[1]

Robert Kagan, a popular American foreign policy intellectual, believes the
USA is increasingly willing to use raw political and military power to tackle
perceived global threats to its security. In contrast, he says, Europeans now
instinctively prefer a rule-based system of international law where military
action is legitimised only by multinational institutions, perhaps reflecting
the way that relationships between the countries of Europe have themselves
evolved since the end of the Second World War. People will have their own
views about this, but there are issues that go beyond security to consider. The
entire global economy relies on a defined system of rules, established through
institutions such as the World Trade Organisation, the International Monetary
Fund and the like. And this is an international system of order on which the US
economy also depends.

The world is changing, and Europe does have an important role helping to
shape the future. If Europe is to fulfil its potential, however, it has to put its
own house in order. Faced with the shifting scene in Europe and beyond, some
argue that the only way Britain will influence the course of events is by joining
EMU, only then will it be a full member of the club and be taken seriously.

However, this chapter will argue that the contrary is probably nearer the mark: it is only by remaining outside EMU that Britain's full potential to influence Europe and its relationship with the USA can be brought to bear.

The EU is faced with huge challenges to the way it runs itself and in its relationship and influence with the rest of the world. Plans for a new constitution were apparently set back in December 2003, but were revived in March 2004. The political evolution of the EU and its economic and political standing in the rest of the world will affect and will be affected by any decision that Britain takes in the future on the single currency.

The economic flaws of the single currency are fundamental ones. Any rational economic framework would reinforce sensible economic policies, but EMU does the opposite. Within the single currency, a government that embarks upon economic or other reforms and raises the rate of return on investment, a necessary accompaniment to raising productivity and real incomes, is ultimately penalised. Capital flows in and boom is followed by bust. This is because monetary policy has been handed over to an institution, the European Central Bank, which is not primarily focused on the needs of any individual economy. Of course, policy-makers will periodically make mistakes and a rational economic framework would help remedy these errors, or at least offer a viable framework for putting them right when they occur. But EMU does the opposite: an economy that gets into trouble, as it inevitably will do in EMU, is much more difficult to put straight if it does not retain the freedom to set interest rates to meet its own needs. Most countries in Euroland require fiscal consolidation, but this is not possible, or is at least much more difficult and more costly in terms of output and jobs, unless monetary policy can be set appropriately.

The loss of economic sovereignty in Euroland is one of substance not shadow and, as a result, membership of EMU is likely to further erode people's confidence and trust in politicians. Economic policy is not made in a vacuum, political pressures change and politicians have to respond to the views of the electorate as well as providing it with leadership. Politicians themselves may have different conceptions as to what constitute sensible economic policies. Electorates from time to time, perhaps for reasons totally unrelated to economics, may vote in a government that pursues economic policies that are not sensible. It has happened, and probably will again, in or out of EMU, but outside there is a way to put things right: because monetary policy can be set to meet British requirements enabling corrective measures to be introduced and budget deficits to be brought under control.

That is why people from all shades of the political spectrum can agree that Britain should stay out of the single currency. This is part of the democratic case against EMU. Outside the single currency, if the British electorate decides to vote into power a party that then pursues successful economic policies, the people will benefit too, in higher incomes and jobs. If, on the other hand, the policies fail, the electorate can 'turn the rascals out' and can be reassured that the new lot will be able to pursue alternative policies that have a chance of success. In EMU, successful policies are penalised and, when things go wrong, the old rascals can still be chucked out of power – but their replacements will be stuck in a straitjacket that precludes an effective response. The voters will vote, but nothing will change and this will simply increase the electorate's cynicism about the democratic process. As is already the case in some countries of Euroland, the merry-go-round continues and the same old faces reappear.

The ten new entrant countries have all expressed a wish to join the single currency. The economies of these countries are different from each other, but all have the opportunity to catch up with the productivity and income levels of the wealthier economies of the EU. Of course, this is only a potential, there is nothing inevitable about it and the dangers of them not catching up are obvious: the new entrants would find themselves, like the former East Germany, with a significant segment of the country dependent on welfare. In Germany, political tensions have been contained so far, because there is at least a common German identity and solidarity. If the new entrants to the EU end up in similar conditions to East Germany, there will be no flow of funds to help them out to match those going from West to East Germany, and no similar cultural constraints, no European identity, to curb political and social unrest.

However, catching up with the wealthier members of their new European club has its perils for the new entrants too, though perhaps less immediately obvious ones than the dangers of not doing so. Higher inflation is seen as part of the natural process of poorer countries catching up with richer ones. In economics, this is known as the Balassa-Samuelson effect and its rationale was set out in Chapter 8 but, as noted there, the thesis misses the point. In a fixed exchange rate regime, like EMU, in which monetary policy in any one country is not geared to the needs of the domestic economy, it is not possible to align real interest rates with a rise in the rate of return on investment, bringing the risk of asset price bubbles, overinvestment and unwise lending: the road to boom and bust. This danger threatens any country embarking on economic reform (see Chapter 8), but this is particularly pronounced in catch-up countries since there is potential for more dramatic increases in rates of return than is the case in already developed economies embarking on reform. The result is that any new entrant country joining EMU and pursuing policies to catch up with the more developed member states would find its economic and financial stability threatened. They would be subject to boom-busts, and the busts would lead to social and political, as well as economic and financial, distress.

This danger is not well appreciated and this was brought home to me in a meeting I had with the then Deputy Prime Minister and Finance Minister of Poland in February 2003. Mr Grzegorz Kolodko hoped that Poland could be in EMU within five years, but I was less interested in his thoughts about the timing of entry than about the more generic problems outlined above and elsewhere in this book. I believe Mr Kolodko had an economic training in the USA, but his reply went on for twenty minutes and didn't answer my question about the implications for Poland if it entered EMU and pursued economic policies to catch up with the wealthier countries of the EU. After our discussion, he was given a brief tour of No. 10 and while he was doing this one of his aides, who had clearly been itching to say something at the meeting, came up to me and said, 'The Minister didn't really answer your question, did he?' He was right, so I asked him what the answer was. 'Oh, lots of inflation.' Didn't he think this was a mistake? 'Of course; it's a real problem'.

There are at least two obvious implications for Britain in all this. First, Britain can only watch as the existing members of EMU struggle with the economic structure they have imposed upon themselves. But there is still time to convince the new entrants that it is against their economic and political interest to join – it would put their economic and financial – and ultimately political – stability at risk. Under the terms of accession, the new entrants have no opt-out from the single currency, but in practice it would be impossible to force a country to enter if its people refused to do so. A successful Britain inside the EU but outside EMU offers an alternative and more viable economic model for the new entrants to follow. The second implication for Britain is that if the new entrants do decide to enter the single currency, it will only add further instability to the whole enterprise, economically, financially and politically, further strengthening the case for retaining the ability to manage our own economic affairs. Proponents of the single currency suggest that this will leave Britain 'isolated', but such isolation can better be seen as the basis for maintaining economic and perhaps even political independence. However, for the moment, Britain is not isolated and shares with the most recent new entrants a common political and economic interest in creating a Europe that allows individual countries more control over their own affairs. When the countries of the former Soviet bloc expressed their support for America over Iraq, President Chirac made it clear what he thought of their temerity:

> These countries are very rude and rather reckless of the danger of aligning too quickly with the Americans. If they wanted to diminish their chances of joining the EU, they couldn't have chosen a better way... it is not well brought up behaviour... they missed an opportunity to shut up.[2]

But these new entrants to the EU haven't escaped the Soviet Empire to be engulfed in another, and they will be heard as the Poles made clear when the draft constitution was discussed at the 2003 intergovernmental conference in Brussels.

The recent expansion in membership was the ideal time to examine where the EU was heading, but an important opportunity was missed. Discussions on the EU constitution were moulded by the past not the future. The EU should be a useful framework for cooperation, helping buttress friendly relations among European countries, and as such it should be a method of organising relations between nations rather than a programme for further integration. The important thing is to decide what activities are best carried out at a European level and which best left to the member states. It then becomes much easier and more practical to devise means of holding the relevant source of decisions to scrutiny and account.

Clearly there are some policies that bring greater benefits to member states, individually and collectively, if they are carried out as a union than if implemented separately. In principle, these areas of mutual benefit might be quite wide, including aspects of economics, politics, social policy, law and order, security, defence or foreign affairs. But within these broad categories there is a much narrower group of specific issues that in practice deliver better results from being carried out in common or coordinated rather than being left to the differing inclinations of member states. The practical issue is less about precluding broad areas of activities from cooperation than it is about being selective within them as to those aspects best dealt with by a common policy at the European level.

In economics there is a concept known as 'Pareto improvement'. In simple terms this refers to a condition when a policy makes nobody worse off, but some gain. There are some winners and no losers. Europe would work better if a similar justification were used before countries of the EU considered adopting a common approach or embracing the 'Community method'. For example, in the field of economics, free trade and a genuinely single market bring clear benefits to those participating by raising economic growth and living standards. It could be helpful to agree on a timetable and process for ensuring market access and establishing the conditions that allow competitive markets to function properly. But relatively few require a common policy or harmonisation. Over time, competition will tend to produce more similar conditions across countries, but the introduction of common levels of tax, employment regulations or social legislation will actually prevent competitive markets working efficiently and thus reduce the mutual benefits to be gained from free trade and a single market. All or most of these should be returned to national governments and national parliaments to determine.

Of course, the EU is about more than economics and identifying the areas where a coordinated or even a common policy really is necessary to bring mutual benefits is not confined to economics either, but applies across the board. For example, there are clearly some areas of cross-border crime that benefit from a common approach, but there is no reason for the massive extension of the European judicial system or the consolidation of Justice and Home Affairs as a Community competence. There are clear advantages from increased cooperation on defence and foreign affairs, but it is not necessary or desirable to have a common foreign or defence policy, as opposed to cooperating as much as possible in these important fields with other countries of the EU.

These are only illustrative examples, but within the EU it is the accrual of competence to the centre that needs to be justified, not the other way around. Many activities should be retained or handed back to the member states. And the term 'handed back' is important since one of the factors holding Europe back from achieving its potential is the suffocating nature of the *acquis communitaire*, encompassing the entire body of laws, policies and practices of the EU, including not only the decisions of the Council of Ministers and the Commission, but also all the rulings of the European Court of Justice.

In principle, EU legislation can be repealed or amended, just like British or German law, but it is a much more difficult and cumbersome process at the European level. In practice, the present scope of the *acquis* is not reconcilable with the professed objective of 'subsidiarity': the notion that decisions in the EU should always be taken at the lowest feasible level. Competence acquired by the EU is never returned to the member states and the Maastricht Treaty actually declared an objective of the EU to 'maintain the *acquis communitaire* and build on it'. The result of all this is that disputes about the extent of subsidiarity only really arise in those areas of competence not yet acquired by the EU but these have been much reduced and many are effectively under siege.[3] The *acquis*, much of it created in different times and in different circumstances, never shrinks but only expands. It is an obstacle in the way of the reallocation of competence that is necessary if politicians and bureaucrats are to be held accountable effectively. Unfortunately, with a few exceptions, there is no inclination among the political and bureaucratic elite to redefine and clarify the functions of Europe in the light of the economic and political realities that apply today. In the modern world, as long as markets are open, the size of a country becomes less and less important as a determinant of prosperity and as the EU continues to expand, deeper political union becomes less and less appropriate. Yet there is still a preoccupation with creating not only a larger political and economic edifice, but one that is more integrated too – as with every previous enlargement, the accession of ten more countries was seen as an opportunity to deepen as well as broaden the EU. No one in their right mind is opposed to more cooperation between the countries of the EU. But there is a world of difference between that unexceptional objective and the kind of political and economic integration or the adoption of common policies that currently forms part of the mantra of the EU. Rather than looking forward to fulfilling its potential, the EU is stuck in a time warp and nowhere was this clearer than in the Convention on the Future of Europe and the draft constitution it produced for governments to consider in December 2003.

The Convention, under the chairmanship of Valéry Giscard d'Estaing, was set up after the Laeken summit in December 2001. The Laeken Declaration set out a broad agenda for the Convention and was drawn up by a so-called committee of 'wise men' under the chairmanship of Jean-Luc Dehaene, a long-standing federalist. It suggested that, 'European institutions must be brought closer to its citizens', but a genuinely decentralised, let alone democratically accountable, Europe was never on the agenda. The Declaration stated: 'The important thing is to clarify, simplify and adjust the division of competence between the Union and the member states in the light of the new challenges facing the Union.' However, these 'challenges' could only lead to more accretion of power at the centre because although the Convention was asked to consider whether there needed to be any reorganisation of competence, this was to be done 'while respecting the *acquis communitaire*'. This meant that there could be no successful attempt to remove competences from the Union and the only 'reorganisation' that could take place would be for the Union to take on even more authority and power. Nowhere in the Convention was there serious effort to restore power and authority to member states or make the EU more accountable to their parliaments.[4]

It was quite clear from the start where the Laeken Declaration was going to lead: all the previous European treaties – Rome, Maastricht, Amsterdam and Nice – were to be replaced by a comprehensive blueprint. Within a few months of starting work, the inner group of the Convention, the Presidium, unveiled its 'Preliminary Draft Constitutional Treaty', no more than a skeleton with outline articles and little detail, but an indication of things to come. The draft constitution that eventually emerged from this body was a bigger and glossier version of an old model, not one that looked to the future. The line taken by the British Government was predictable to anyone familiar with the dissembling of Macmillan and Heath: Peter Hain, the British Government's representative on the Convention, said that, 'three quarters of it [the constitution] is tidying up' and only later admitted that, even if that were the case, the remaining quarter 'was creating a new constitutional order for a new united Europe'.

All British governments had hitherto opposed a written constitution for Europe. Only two years earlier, the idea got short shrift from Tony Blair in a speech in Warsaw in October 2000. Yet once the Convention had been set up the Government actually put forward its own draft, albeit under the by-line of a Cambridge academic. Professor Alan Dashwood's constitution was sidelined, being regarded as too tame by other members of the EU, but a line had been crossed.

Stephen Wall, Tony Blair's adviser on Europe, wrote a draft article for *The Economist* setting out the case for a written constitution to appear under the name of the Foreign Secretary. This text proved to be insufficiently political for Jack Straw and a new version appeared just before the Presidium's own constitutional outline was published. Jack Straw's two pages in *The Economist* purred with reassurances, stressing the potential for clarity and brevity in any new constitution and he anticipated charges that a constitution would lead to a 'super-state' with absurd comparisons, first aired the previous August, with golf clubs and political parties. 'Political parties and golf clubs have constitutions and are not states.' But not many golf clubs or political parties make rules for other golf clubs or political parties, or have rules running to 80,000 pages, the length of the accumulated *acquis* today.

It was argued that a written constitution would define the limits of Community competence in ways that prevent the further erosion of national sovereignty, but this was not only a naive view of what happens with constitutions, it was at odds with how most of the elite in Europe saw things. The notion that a constitution would set limits for the further erosion of national sovereignty also failed to address the fact that those competences already allocated to the EU were regarded as beyond recall. Any remaining allocations to be distributed only concerned those that were still within the competence of member states or shared with the Union.

Of course, when the new constitution was discussed at the Convention and later at the Inter-Governmental Conference (IGC), there were some areas where the British Government dug its heels in. These were the so-called 'red lines', such as maintaining the national veto on tax, social security, foreign affairs and defence. They were important, but were by no means the only things to worry about given the nature of the political process in the EU and the objectives of other countries. In essence, the Government's response was tactical rather than strategic. The strategic issues were as much about proposals, sometimes apparently innocuous and reasonable in tone, providing openings for future integration that would only become apparent later, as they were from frontal attacks on Britain's defensive lines. At times, Tony Blair appeared unaware of the most basic history of the EU, the long-term objectives of other countries and the methods they use to achieve them. For example, Tony said that:

> To achieve a unified European foreign policy, we need to decide what
> we are unifying around. In matters of defence and security, they are so
> fundamental to a nation's sense of itself, that there is no institutional fix
> that can overcome a genuine difference of view.[5]

This was a very British, not to say rational, view of how things should happen: decide what is to be done and set up the institution to carry it out. But that is not the way the EU generally operates: the institutions are set up first and integration comes later, going well beyond that which could initially be agreed between member states, if necessary, in response to crisis. As noted in Chapter 13, there was an historic divide over EMU between those termed the 'economists' and the so-called 'monetarists', with the former the dominant tradition in Germany, seeing currency union as the final step after other aspects of economic integration had been completed. The 'monetarists', mainly from France, while accepting a minimum degree of convergence, regarded EMU as an agent for change and any periodic crisis an opportunity for forcing through changes that had previously not been agreed. And, after German unification, that was how EMU got underway: the 'monetarists' won. But the tendency to set up an institution before full agreement is established as to what it should do is not confined to EMU; it applies to other fields too, including justice and home affairs, health and social security and even defence and foreign affairs. In some areas, of course, the gaps between countries are very wide indeed and this is obviously the case with defence, where national competence remains broadly intact, at least for the moment. In these circumstances the institutional vice may initially only narrow the gap slightly. But once set up, institutional frameworks are used to promote more integration and a common policy and over time this process has in practice been difficult for Britain to counter.

The surprising thing was that at the Convention and the IGC, Tony Blair was preoccupied with ending the six-monthly rotating presidency of the Council, replacing it with a single person, elected by the Council for an extended period of time. The purpose was to provide the Council with more continuity and stronger leadership and reinforce the intergovernmental component in the EU. This emphasis surprised officials in the Foreign Office and Cabinet Office, who feared that concessions would inevitably be made in other areas to achieve the Prime Minister's chosen goal. Tony's purpose was to demonstrate that sovereign nation states, represented on the Council, were in control of the EU. He wanted to confirm and strengthen the intergovernmental method by enhancing the power of the institution representing member states compared to other institutions of the Union, not by actually strengthening the relative position of member states within the Union. It remained the case that only the Commission had the right to initiate new legislation and, because many areas of policy had already passed from national to Community competence, the Council itself is not accountable to electorates or parliaments in any meaningful way. The EU is not brought closer to its various peoples by the intergovernmental method any more than it is by the Community method. It is the unique combination of both that makes the EU so peculiarly undemocratic and unaccountable. Tony had an understandable concern to keep the word 'federal' out of any new constitution, since this would have made all too explicit the long-term aims of some others in the EU and played very badly in Britain. But its removal only serves to divert the electorate's attention from the real issues at stake. In Britain, both sides of the debate on Europe can become too obsessed with the federal nature, or otherwise, of the EU. Of course this is important and there remain many advocates for a federal Europe on the continent and in this country too, but for the moment this is not the most pressing issue – that is the consolidation of an undemocratic and unaccountable Europe, and the 'intergovernmental method' is as much a part of this as the 'community method.'

Whatever the disclaimers about the significance of the constitution, the emerging political structure proposed for the EU did in fact have many of the attributes of a state. A state has its own judicial system, its own laws and court, it can prosecute and it has a legal personality and power to enter treaties with third parties. Most states have facilities for border control and many have a charter of rights. A state has its own economic policies, its own tax and policies for industry and commerce, policies for health and social security and much else besides. A modern state will have a directly elected parliament and a central bank. A state will have an army and will have its own defence and foreign policy, a constitution and, of course, it will have its own currency. The EU has all of some of these and some of all of them, and it even has its own flag and anthem. It would pass the 'duck test': if it quacks and looks like a duck, it probably is a duck. If it looks like a state with the powers, attributes and institutions of a state, it probably is a state. The EU is not a federal state and certainly not a unitary one, but a state of some sort nonetheless, or at least more like a state than one of Jack Straw's golf clubs.

Of all the characteristics of a state that can be attributed to the EU, the single currency is the most significant. Not because others, such as defence or tax, are not important, they clearly are and should remain in British hands too; but a decision to exchange the pound for the single currency is irreversible in a way that is not the case with other common policies, even including defence since the process in this field is at least likely to be more gradual than adopting the euro. A government may agree to extend Community power, either knowingly and openly, or inadvertently or through the back door. For example, it is perfectly possible in the years ahead that the 'single market' will be used to bring the health service and pensions within the competence of the EU. And there can be no certainty that tax and defence will not also be slowly drawn into the net, whatever today's 'red lines'. Europe is full of instances where proposals that have initially been rebuffed end up later, sometimes years later, as part of the Treaty. There have been many occasions when 'never' turned out to mean 'not now, but later'.

Perhaps these pressures will be resisted. Let us hope so, but the point is that if a British government at some stage were to surrender British sovereignty in other areas – it would be termed 'pooling' – in most instances it could be recovered later if the British people were determined to do so. It would not be easy, but probably it could be done. Once a country ceases to have its own currency, things are very different. It is to all intents and purposes irreversible unless the area covered by such a currency is itself engulfed in a terminal political crisis, as was the case with the collapse of the USSR or Yugoslavia. Once Britain adopted the euro it would not only have lost the freedom and ability to manage its own economy, it would have surrendered its political independence too. Once inside EMU it would be much more difficult for Britain to resist even deeper political integration even if it wanted to.

The constitution put forward in 2003 and 2004 offered one route for the EU to follow, but it is not the only one. Over the next quarter of a century the structure of the EU could in principle take the shape of variations around three central themes.

The first path is broadly that outlined in the constitution, representing a further consolidation of the existing political structure that is based on a combination of the intergovernmental and the Community method: centralised, bureaucratic, undemocratic and unaccountable. This EU is run in the interest of a political elite, not reaching down to people in the street. It is a bureaucratic political structure that in many respects fits most easily with the economic requirements of EMU. The single currency is incompatible with economic dynamism and its political associate, vibrant democracy. On the other hand, the fact that the euro makes it impossible for Euroland to create and sustain economic dynamism that is necessary to raise living standards means that this model of the EU has within itself the possible cause of its own destruction. This will not happen soon, not least since the present generation of leaders on the continent has too much political capital tied up in the existing arrangements and its peoples have yet to experience the full economic cost of EMU. No bureaucracy ever favoured changes that reduce its influence and reason to exist, and in the short term at least the response to a political and economic crisis – slow growth and deteriorating public finance – would be more Europe not less.

However, Europe could go down another route, and one that is more internally consistent than the one now being followed. In continental Europe, it is widely accepted that economic and monetary union requires political union for it to work. The only choice is whether the political union is to be democratic or otherwise. So far the latter has predominated, but it is just possible that the EU could evolve into a political format that is genuinely accountable by adopting an overtly federal structure that could in principle make it democratic. Larry Siedentop has observed that 'behind the fig leaf provided by the rhetoric of economic and political integration is to be found a major development, the rapid accumulation of power in Brussels.'[6] He believed, with some others, that federalism is the right goal for Europe, but that Europe is not ready for federalism. However, in the EU, federalism is unlikely to come in a big bang, but gradually, following the example of Jean Monnet. In his support for the intergovernmental method, Tony Blair would do well to recall the assessment Monnet made at Chequers in 1972, when he explained to Edward Heath that the Council of Ministers had to be regarded as a 'transitional' stage to supranational government. An overtly federal and democratic Europe may not be the most likely immediate outcome since it would also challenge the bureaucratic and political elite and be difficult to accommodate the strong sense of national identities that still characterises Europe, but it was the dream of the founding fathers of Europe and remains so for many.

There is a third route that the EU could in principle choose to follow. It is possible that the accession of more countries could lead eventually to the EU being more decentralised, with defined and narrower functions allocated to Community competence but with power to deliver: more than EFTA but less than the EU. A Europe that really did focus on the benefits to be gained from cooperation of sovereign states rather than the architecture of political and economic integration or common policies would have clear advantages. It would fit in with the inclinations of the British people and be in tune with the economic prerequisites of Europe too. Much of the *acquis* would be returned to member states and their parliaments, reversing much of the ethos that has dominated Europe since the 1950s, bringing it up to date. Getting this outcome is in the long-term interest of both Europe and Britain, but at the moment is on few people's agenda on the continent and in some circles this is an argument carrying along the present integrationist road instead. But the tides may be turning, at least among the peoples of Europe, even if not yet the governments, and either Britain has the potential to influence the future of the EU or it doesn't. If influence amounts to no more than periodically getting small concessions to policies and objectives that are against the country's interests it doesn't amount to a row of beans. However, any hope of achieving this objective will be stymied by entering the single currency and indeed, looking ahead, all the possible political and likely economic frameworks for the EU argue for Britain staying out of EMU.

If the EU were to continue on its present course, consolidating an undemocratic and unaccountable directorate, founded on a mixture of the intergovernmental and community method, ultimately dominated by France and Germany, the less additional entanglement for Britain the better. Should Britain join EMU, it would not only be much more difficult to prevent EU taking this route, but it would be almost impossible for Britain to avoid being suffocated by the prevailing economic and political culture of Euroland. In September 2003, Tony Blair returned from his summit with Chirac and Schroeder convinced that he had made a breakthrough in his relationship with them and that Germany and France would agree that their three countries would together 'run Europe'. Of course this has been heard before and remains very unlikely, but the more important point is that it is not in Britain's longer-term interests that the EU is 'run' by anyone as part of some directorate, and it is deeply unhistorical to suggest that Britain should be part of it. As long as Britain remains outside the single currency, it can retain some control over its economy, offering an alternative model for those countries in the EU that have not yet adopted the euro. A federal Europe – the threat that dare not speak its name in

Britain – has at least the merit of honestly accommodating the need for EMU
to be accompanied by political union with the desire to make it recognisably
democratic in form. But the majority of the British people do not want to be
part of a federal Europe. As long as Britain did not adopt the single currency
it could remain friendly with but separate from such a political configuration,
should it eventually emerge. A more decentralised and flexible EU may in the
end turn out to be an unattainable objective, though Gordon Brown has made a
number of speeches and interventions arguing for a more flexible Europe. But
the only hope of ultimately bringing it about is to start from a position in which
Britain and the new entrants remain out of EMU. If such an outcome were to
be achieved, it would vindicate the decision to keep the pound; if not, Britain
would retain a base for maintaining its economic and political independence.

Outside EMU, a successful economy gives Britain a more powerful voice
as the EU enters the next stage of its development. At the end of 2002, the
Prime Minister of Portugal, Jose Barroso, said that Britain would be sidelined
if it did not join the euro. He said that 'if the UK does not share the duties of
membership in the euro, [it] cannot have the right to lead in defence, where
traditionally Britain has a very important profile, or the institutional debate.'
The impact of this was somewhat reduced by the fact that Portugal was in
the middle of a general strike brought about by the country's dire economic
state, created to a significant extent by its membership of EMU. But it was an
absurd proposition anyway. In or out of EMU, any credible defence or security
initiative for the EU has to include Britain. And going beyond this issue it is
laughable to imagine that, simply because Britain was in EMU, other countries,
including France and Germany, would agree any more than they do now with
Britain's position on the single market or the Common Agricultural Policy, let
alone Iraq and a host of other issues where disagreements exist. (People have
varying views on the course taken on Iraq by the British Government in 2003,
but that is a very different issue from whether or not being in EMU would have
increased Britain's persuasive powers.) Rightly or wrongly, countries disagree
because they have different perspectives and will defend their national interests
and that remains the case in or out of EMU. What is clear from the history of
the EU and beyond is that a country with a successful economy does have more
influence and weight than one that is hobbled.

Nobody can seriously believe that Britain will have more influence in Europe
if it is inside the single currency and its economy is weak than outside with an
economy that is strong. Even within systems such as the ERM or EMU, relative
economic performance matters. One of the important factors that put Germany
in the driving seat of the Franco-German partnership in the 1970s and early
1980s was the relative weakness of the French economy. One of the reasons
that France was more self-confident at the turn of the century was the poor
state of the German economy, brought about in part by the single currency and

certainly more difficult to remedy within the EMU framework. Outside EMU, the British economy has demonstrated the potential to outperform those inside the single currency, both relatively and absolutely.

In recent years, Britain has probably been more effective in Europe and it has certainly been listened to for more than a little while. Tony Blair can take some credit for that, but his voice only carried weight because for the past decade the British economy has been one of the most successful in Europe, outperforming both France and Germany by a significant margin. Whether this recent economic success continues depends in part on the policies pursued by the Government, and Chapter 1 drew attention to some potential dangers on this front. The outlook for the international economy also became more unpredictable in the early part of the twenty-first century. Nonetheless, as long as Britain retains the freedom to set monetary policy to meet the needs of its own economy, any mistakes are not beyond recall and retaining this freedom also gives Britain a better chance of riding out any bad weather in the world economy. The British economy can be stronger outside EMU than it can possibly be inside and in twenty-five years or so it has the potential to become the biggest in Europe. With a successful British economy a Prime Minister will not lack influence in the EU, if he or she wants to use it.

Staying out of EMU offers the best chance of challenging the predominant, if fluctuating, position of the Franco-German partnership within the EU, not by trying to drive a wedge between them or hoping in vain to separate one from the other, but by approaching the issue from a different angle. Enthusiasts for EMU say that it is only by ditching the pound that Britain can become a full member of the club, and it is only in this way that this country can bring its full weight to bear within the EU. This view simply fails to understand the nature and dynamics of the EU and in fact the opposite is a more accurate statement of the true position. The Franco-German alliance is based on geography and perceived mutual self-interest that makes the relationship 'special' despite differences on specific issues, and both countries continue to see it that way. On the anniversary of the Elysée Treaty, President Chirac declared, 'For forty years each decisive step was taken in Europe thanks to the motor that Germany and France represent... Experience shows that when Berlin and Paris agree, Europe can move forward; if there is disagreement, Europe marks time.'[7]

Inside EMU, Britain's potential economic strength would be stifled and its peripheral geographic position confirmed in other ways too. Outside the single currency, providing sensible economic policies are pursued, the geographical aspect of Britain's membership can be counterbalanced and outweighed by a superior economic performance. This gives Britain the best chance of influencing the future structure of and political settlement in Europe.

This is not the way Tony Blair sees things. Most prime ministers at some stage find it difficult to distinguish their own desires from British interests but, whatever the reason, there is no doubt that Tony Blair has convinced himself of the political case for joining and its own importance for establishing his own role in history. The political case is said to be 'overwhelming', but apparently not so overwhelming that if the economic case falls even a little short of being 'clear and unambiguous', Britain should enter the single currency. But nowhere is this 'overwhelming' political case spelt out other than by caricaturing the views of his opponents: it is merely asserted. 'It's our destiny'.

Well, in pursuit of this 'destiny', whether EMU or the EU constitution, the electorate needs to be alert to Tony Blair's methods of persuasion, which were outlined in the previous chapter. He is clearly an accomplished political strategist who starts by positioning himself where he wants to end up and as part of the process opponents are pushed into corners that are travesties of their true positions.

However, when and if it starts, any referendum campaign on EMU will test the political style favoured by Tony Blair for most of his political life. He does not like confrontation, preferring the 'big tent' politics in which as many people and groups as possible are brought within his political tepee. In pursuit of this, he attempts to reconcile the irreconcilable and the hard edges of policies are blurred. The same strategy will be used on the euro. But if Tony Blair were to come out for the euro in a referendum campaign he would be met with hostility from a large part of the electorate: it would not be possible to be on both sides at once and the other side would have conviction.

Of course, Tony Blair has also shown, over Iraq in particular, that he is prepared to take a lead in the face of hostility if he believes sufficiently strongly that the cause is right. True believers are ready to risk everything and the electorate senses their personal commitment, but it also smells the half-believer's lack of real conviction. On Iraq, Tony Blair believed passionately in the course he took, I admired him for his courage, and he was impressive in his resolve to get rid of a foul tyrant. The trouble with Europe is that true 'believers' like Edward Heath and most politicians on the continent, know that monetary union must in the end embrace or be embraced by political union, but this is something that Tony Blair wants to deny.

The British Government has been unique within the EU in purporting to judge the case for entry to the single currency on economic grounds. However, the British electorate rightly feels in its bones that politicians who want to scrap the pound and adopt the euro are too dismissive of its concerns that Britain will lose control over its own affairs. This has happened before, but EMU has much more significant and substantive implications for economic and political sovereignty than any previous step along the European road in the past half-century.

Paradoxically, given the reputation for being reluctant Europeans, Britain is the only country to have had an application to join Europe vetoed twice and one interesting result of the first attempt to enter the Common Market in 1961 was the creation of a new orthodoxy in establishment opinion in Britain. At the time this was a revolution: in a few years, entry into the Market moved from impossibility to imperative.

The establishment's commitment to Europe has lasted for over forty years and is shared by Tony Blair. The claustrophobic orthodoxy towards Europe has never been as pervasive as on the continent, even among the political class, but where it exists the tactics are the same: ridicule and caricature of those taking a contrary view. Myths are perpetuated, distortions encouraged and straw men built up to knock down. If Britain were to get close to making a decision on the single currency, whether under Tony Blair's leadership or someone else, there would be a great deal of this from those trying, in every sense of the term, 'to take Britain in'.

Those opposed to entering the single currency would be branded as insular, or latter-day imperialists, or both, since the proponents of entry cannot make up their minds whether their opponents exaggerate or demean the influence of Britain. Anyone questioning the desirability of joining EMU is said to be supporting 'isolation' or 'disengagement' from Europe as though for a thousand years Britain had been other than involved in Europe or given its geographical position that it could in future be other than a European nation or engaged in Europe. The question as ever is how and on what terms. For euro-enthusiasts, Britain has to step aboard the latest institutional train for fear of being left behind. It is 'inevitable' or, as Tony Blair declared in Blackpool in 2002 to the Labour Party's annual conference, 'EMU is not just about our economy but our destiny.' But Britain is not 'destined' to join EMU. Britain has a choice.

The same techniques of misrepresentation seen over the single currency have been used against those who oppose or have qualms about the EU constitution. In the spring of 2004, Tony Blair declared that, 'It is important above all, that we debate according to reality not according to myth,'[8] but his own tactics of persuasion on the EU constitution were based on creating his own myths: that his opponents wanted to 'disengage' from Europe, or that the new constitution was necessary for enlargement so that anyone opposed to it was preventing new members joining the EU, or that there were no alternatives to the constitutional text agreed by governments except withdrawal from the EU.

When the IGC broke up in December 2003, it looked as though there would be time to reconsider the contents of the EU constitution, and the British Government appeared to want to take advantage of the opportunity to reflect. However, after the change of government in Spain in March 2004, following the bombing of Madrid railway station, the EU constitution was brought back on the agenda and the British Government changed tack: a speedy settlement became essential, and this reawakened arguments for a referendum that had been gaining strength the previous year.

Within a few months, the Government had caved into the pressure, completely reversing its earlier stance. Previously the case for a referendum had been dismissed on the grounds that the constitution did not change the way Britain was governed or, more prosaically, in the words of the British Government's representative on the Convention, Peter Hain, it was just a matter of tidying up existing treaties, although, as noted earlier, he was then forced to acknowledge that twenty-five per cent was actually new. And even if the new treaty had simply spelled out matters previously agreed in earlier treaties it was probably the first time that the majority of people had become aware of what has been agreed in their name. As a Cabinet minister at the time, Ken Clarke took pride in not reading the Treaty of Maastricht, so why should the bulk of the electorate be assumed to know what had been agreed there or at Rome, Nice or Amsterdam or in the Single European Act? The Foreign Office recognised that the Treaty of Rome had huge implications for Britain's ability to retain control of its own affairs (see Chapter 14), and this shift in authority has been reinforced in all subsequent treaties. Opinions will differ as to whether overall effect of this has been good or bad for Britain, but no one can seriously deny that it has happened.

Towards the end of the Convention on the Future of Europe, several key advisers told Tony Blair that it would not be possible to hold the line against a referendum on the EU constitution. During the latter part of 2003, public opinion across the political spectrum, including some of those in favour of the constitution, came to favour a referendum, but Tony Blair seemed determined to defy it. The argument he used inside No. 10 at the time was that he had spent more than twelve months preoccupied with the war in Iraq and the last thing he wanted was to spend the best part of another year campaigning for an EU constitution, but the position of France was seen as a critical in holding the line. Germany's own constitution disallowed referendums (a reaction to Hitler's use of the plebiscite in the 1930s) but France faced no such prohibition. In the autumn of 2003, France's Prime Minister, Jean-Pierre Raffarin, was quoted as being in favour of holding a referendum in France on the proposed EU constitution, but this may have stemmed from an unguarded comment to a journalist on a plane during a visit to Russia, and shortly afterwards Raffarin retreated, saying any decision on a referendum was a matter for the President. Nonetheless, the British Government was nervous about being able to resist demands for a referendum if the French went ahead and Tony Blair and Jack Straw did all they could to stiffen their resolve. In November 2003, the No. 10 Policy Directorate had one of its regular meetings with their opposite numbers in Matignon, the French Prime Minister's office. I usually attended these gatherings and in the course of discussions it became clear that the French were not at all confident that a referendum on the EU constitution would be won. Several on our side stressed the importance Tony Blair attached to the French holding the line. I said nothing at the time, but what struck me was the total absence of any consideration of the merits or otherwise of a referendum: it was a decision made entirely on grounds of political expediency. The collapse, in December 2003, of the Brussels IGC meant that the need for further discussion on the process for ratification could be postponed. But when discussions on the constitution were revived under the Irish presidency in March 2004, Tony Blair reaffirmed his opposition to a referendum, though some Cabinet ministers and advisers again had their doubts whether this was a tenable position, and the Prime Minister was forced to examine ways out of his difficulties.

Among some enthusiastic supporters of EMU, for example Lord Haskins,[9] the Prime Minister's predicament over the EU constitution revived interest in a long-standing strategy for the single currency: they recognised the British people might never swallow the euro, but, despite the furore about the draft constitution, the majority of the electorate had usually been more reticent about the prospects of outright withdrawal from the EU. Why not put the British people into a position where they have to choose between entering EMU and withdrawing from the EU? Tony Blair himself had always been more comfortable talking about the broader sweep of Europe than the narrower one of the single currency, perhaps he could be tempted to offer a loaded choice in pursuit of his political objectives, and combining the two issues would change the nature of the question: in his own words, 'It is as it has always been, a matter of in or out'.

Such a ploy would have flown in the face of the spirit, if not precisely the letter, of all Tony Blair's (and Gordon Brown's) previous commitments about a referendum on the single currency, but the EU constitution was another matter. Here, there were options that Tony Blair could consider if his favoured strategy were no longer tenable. In the spring of 2004, Tony's preference was still for a quickly agreed constitutional treaty that would be speedily passed through Parliament. The trouble was that this could not be guaranteed. The Liberal Democrats, the most consistently pro-European party in Britain, had come out in favour of a referendum and, together with the Tories' stance, this would present problems in the House of Lords. The passage of any treaty through the Commons would not be without its problems either since a significant minority of Labour MPs were likely to join Conservatives and Liberals Democrats in calling for a referendum. It could all have got very messy with a general election not too far away.

In essence, by the late spring of 2004, Tony Blair had three alternatives. First, he could try to bludgeon the EU constitution through the Commons and Lords; or he could use a general election as a mandate for endorsing the constitution – the Labour manifesto could include a commitment to the new constitution so a Labour victory would give a mandate that would preclude the need for referendum; finally, Tony Blair could concede the case for a referendum (in principle a referendum bill could be introduced before or after a general election) but seek to change the nature of the question: it would be a matter of 'in or out'.

In March and early April, Tony Blair tried to convince people that there was no alternative to the constitution and this was reflected in briefings to friendly newspapers: 'The notion that Britain could decline the constitution but somehow remain in the part of the EU for all useful purposes is pie in the sky.'[10] This was nonsense: other countries that decided or were obliged to hold a referendum would not be confronted with such an artificial choice. They would vote simply for or against the new constitution and, if it were not ratified, all the commitments made under previous treaties would remain in place, but Tony Blair continued to peddle the notion that the only alternative to the agreed text was to leave the EU. Some people opposed to the constitution did want to get out, but the idea that that was true for everyone or that there were no alternative models was absurd. The broad outlines of possible alternative future paths for the EU were set out earlier in the chapter and there are many other variations. In 2004, the Liberal Democrats put forward one possible alternative model, including the suggestion that social policy be repatriated to nation states.[11] Does anyone think the Liberal Democrats want to take Britain out of the EU?

In the end, Tony Blair was forced to agree to a referendum on the constitution as a mater of political expediency. If he had not done so, the issue would have dragged and continued resistance only reinforced the perception, fostered by the Iraq war, that he was out of touch with, or unprepared to listen to, the electorate. This would have provided valuable ammunition for the Conservatives during the pending European elections and beyond. The decision on a referendum and its announcement on 20 April 2004 were badly handled, with half the Cabinet kept in the dark, but it was hoped that any short-term costs would be outweighed by longer-term benefits: above all, Europe might be neutralised as an issue in any forthcoming general election. Like EMU, the issue of ratification had been kicked into touch and in any case might never have to be faced: when the decision was made it was still possible that governments might not be able to agree on the text for a constitution, but if they did some other country might vote it down in their own referendum long before the British people had to vote on it.

If a referendum were to take place, some politicians may believe that the British people would be frightened into submission over the EU constitution if they thought the alternative was to leave the EU. In the same vein, they might even eventually be bullied into accepting the single currency, and the implications of the constitution would make resistance more difficult. However, such tactics could backfire and in any case is an unnecessary choice to present to the British people so long as our political leaders stand ready to use the veto to protect Britain's interests in any political settlement proposed for the EU.

Of course, if politicians are not ready to do that, then that is another matter, but such politicians would have declared themselves unready and unworthy to defend British interests, in or out of the single currency.

Notes

Introduction

1. *The Times* 9 September 2003.
2. For example, *This Blessed Plot*, an assessment of the relationship between Britain and Europe from Churchill to Blair, by the late Hugo Young makes no reference to either the Fouchet Plan or the Werner Report, both of which are important to the story of contemporary Europe. Young, *This Blessed Plot: Britain and Europe from Churchill to Blair* (Macmillan, 1998).

Chapter 1: Neighbours in Downing Street

1. Gordon Brown at a joint press conference with Tony Blair, 17 June 2003.
2. William Keegan, *The Prudence of Mr Gordon Brown* (John Wiley, 2003).
3. Nick Brown: MP for Newcastle upon Tyne and Wallsend since 1997 and for Newcastle upon Tyne East, 1983–1997; Chief Whip, 1997–1998; Minister for Agriculture, Fisheries and Food, 1998–2001; and Minister of State at the Department of Work and Pensions, 2001–2003.
4. Peter Mandelson: MP for Hartlepool, 1997–2004. Labour Party Director of Campaigns and Communications, 1985–1990; Minister without Portfolio, Cabinet Office, 1997–1998; Secretary of State for Trade and Industry, 1998; Secretary of State for Northern Ireland, 1999–2001.
5. Social Democratic Party, launched in 1981, came close to Labour in the popular vote in 1983, but after the 1987 election the majority of members decided to merge with the Liberals.
6. Michael Meacher: MP for Oldham West and Royton since 1997 and for Oldham West, 1970–1997; Minister of State at the Department of the Environment, Transport and

the Regions (DETR), 1997–2001 and at the Department of the Environment, Food and Rural Affairs (DEFRA), 2001–2003.

7. Anji Hunter: research assistant to Tony Blair, 1986–1990 and head of his office, 1990–1997; Special Assistant to the Prime Minister, 1997–2001; and Director of Government Relations, the Prime Minister's Office, 2001–2002.

8. Robin Cook: MP for Livingstone since 1983 and for Edinburgh Central, 1974–1983; Secretary of State for Foreign and Commonwealth Affairs, 1997–2001; Leader of the House of Commons, 2001–2003.

9. John Prescott: MP for Kingston upon Hull East since 1997, for Hull East, 1983–1997 and for Kinston upon Hull (East), 1970–1983; Deputy Prime Minister since 1997 and First Secretary of State from 2001; Secretary of State for Environment, Transport and the Regions (DETR), 1997–2001.

10. Sally Morgan: since 2001, Baroness Morgan of Huyton in the County of Merseyside; Director of Political and Government Relations, the Prime Minister's Office from 2001; Minister of State, Cabinet Office, 2001; Political Secretary to the Prime Minister, 1997–2001.

11. Peter Hyman: member of Tony Blair's staff in opposition and at No. 10 an influential and energetic part of the Communications team, 1997–2003.

12. Mais Lecture: annual lectures at the City University, established in 1973 at the initiative of the Lord Mayor of the City of London, Lord Mais.

13. Geoffrey Robinson, *The Unconventional Minister* (Michael Joseph, 2000).

14. Will Hutton: Economics Editor, *The Guardian*, 1990–1995; Assistant Editor, *The Guardian*, 1995–1996; Editor, *The Observer*, 1996–1998; Editor in Chief, *The Observer*, 1998–1999; Chief Executive, the Work Foundation since 1999.

15. Tom McNally: since 1985, Baron McNally of Blackpool in the County of Lancashire; Political Adviser to the Foreign and Commonwealth Secretary, 1974–1976 and to the Prime Minister, 1976–1979; MP for Stockport South, 1979–1981 (Labour) and 1981–1983 (SDP).

16. *The Guardian*, 6 June 2003.

17. *The Times*, 22 September 1997.

18. Alan Milburn: MP for Darlington since 1992; Minister of State, Department of Health, 1997–1998; Chief Secretary to the Treasury, 1998–2000; Secretary of State, Department of Health, 1999–2003.

19. Ian McCartney: MP for Makerfield since 1987; Minister without Portfolio, 2003; Minister of State at the Department of Trade and Industry, 1997–1999; Minister of State at the Cabinet Office, 1999–2001; Minister of Pensions, 2001–2003.

20. Richard Lambert: Member of the Bank of England's Monetary Policy Committee (MPC) since 2003; Editor of the *Financial Times*, 1991–2001.

21. Keegan, *The Prudence of Mr Gordon Brown*.

22. Robinson, *The Unconventional Minister*.

23. Adair Turner: Director General of the CBI, 1995–1999; Chairman of the Low Pay Commission, 2002.

24. Jonathan Powell: Chief of Staff in the Prime Minister's Office since 1997 and in the Office of the Leader of the Opposition, 1995–1997. He had joined the Foreign and Commonwealth Office in 1979 and his final posting before joining Tony Blair was in the British Embassy in Washington.

25. David Miliband: MP for South Shields since 2001; Minister of State in the Department of Education and Skills since 2002; Head of Policy in the Office of the Leader of the Opposition, 1995–1997; Director of Policy in Downing Street,, 1997 and Head of Policy, the Prime Minister's Policy Unit, 1998–2001.

Chapter 2: In for a Pound

1. Romano Prodi: Prime Minister of Italy, 1996–1998; President of the EU Commission, 1999–2004, quote in the *Daily Telegraph*, 26 June 2003.

Chapter 3: A Vision Takes Shape

1. 24 March 1998.
2. Jean Monnet (1888–1979): French economist and public official. He drafted a plan for French economic revival, the Monnet Plan (1947) and also the Schuman Plan that established the European Coal and Steel Community (ECSC), of which Monnet was the first president (1952–1955).
3. Robert Schuman (1886–1963): French politician; Finance Minister of France, 1946, 1947; Prime Minister, 1947–1948; Foreign Minister, 1948–1953, from which position he launched the Schuman Plan for the ECSC.
4. Jean Monnet, *Memoirs* (Collins, 1978).
5. Konrad Adenauer (1876–1967): the first Chancellor of West Germany, 1949–1963, he also served as his own foreign minister, 1951–1955; co-founder of the Christian Democratic Union (CDU); imprisoned twice by the Nazis (1933 and 1944). His political base was Cologne where he was first elected Mayor in 1917.
6. Alcide de Gasperi (1881–1954): Prime Minister of Italy, 1945–1953, when he led eight successive coalitions that were dominated by the Christian Democrats, which de Gasperi founded.
7. Aristide Briand (1862–1932): in the First World War, Briand headed two successive coalition cabinets (1915–1917) and made the decision to hold Verdun at any cost. After the war, he headed a cabinet in 1921 and re-emerged as advocate of international peace and cooperation. As Foreign Minister (1925–1932), he negotiated the Locarno Pact (1925) and the Kellogg-Briand Pact (1928) and shared the Nobel Peace Prize in 1926.
8. Paul-Henri Spaak (1899–1972): Prime Minister of Belgium, 1938–1939, 1947–1949 and 1961; President of the General Assembly of the European Coal and Steel Community, 1952–1953; Secretary-General of NATO, 1956–1961.
9. Rene Pleven (1901–1993): Prime Minister of France (1950–1951, 1951–1952) and held various other ministerial posts until 1958, but was kept out of office by Charles de Gaulle.
10. Christian Fouchet (1912–1974): French diplomat and Gaullist minister, he was one of the first Gaullists to arrive in London in 1940 and came to belong to de Gaulle's inner circle.

Chapter 4: The Birth of a Currency

1. House of Commons, 27 October 1997.
2. Press conference, 17 June 2003.
3. Bundesbank statement, 10 December 2003.

4. As noted earlier, an asymmetric shock is an event or series of events that affects real economic variables, growth and productivity, in one country more than in others.

Chapter 5: The Odd Man Out

1. Speech opening the European Research Institute at Birmingham University, 23 November 2001.
2. Ludwig Erhard (1897–1977): Minister of Economics, 1949–1963 and instigator of West Germany's *Wirtschaftswunder* (economic miracle); Chancellor of the Federal Republic of Germany, 1963–1966.
3. Noel Annan, *Changing Enemies: The Defeat and Regeneration of Germany* (HarperCollins, 1995).
4. Speech in Warsaw, 6 October 2000.
5. Jean Lacoutre, *De Gaulle*, 2 vols. (W.W. Norton, 1993).
6. Ibid.
7. Alain Peyrefitte, *C'était de Gaulle* (Editions de Fallois, 2000).
8. John Campbell, *Margaret Thatcher*, Vol. 1. (Jonathan Cape, 2000).
9. John Campbell, *Margaret Thatcher*, Vol. 2. (Jonathan Cape, 2003).
10. Ibid.
11. Ibid.
12. Ibid.
13. Margaret Thatcher, *The Downing Street Years* (HarperCollins, 1993).

Chapter 6: You Can Be Serious

1. James Forder and Christopher Huhne, *Both Sides of the Coin: The Arguments for the Euro and Monetary Union* (Profile Books, 1998).
2. Ibid.

Chapter 7: Back to the Future

1. See R.A. Mundell, 'A Theory of Optimum Currency Areas', *American Economic Review*, 1961.
2. Rudiger Dornbusch (1942–2002): Professor of Economics at MIT, 1984–2002; a prolific writer who helped define the study of international economics.
3. *Foreign Affairs*, September 1996.
4. Professor Willem Buiter: chief economist at the European Bank for Reconstruction and Development (EBRD) since 2000; member of the Bank of England Monetary Policy Committee (MPC), 1997–2000.

Chapter 8: Mind the Gap

1. In this chapter, data on GDP growth is from the OECD and comparative inflation rates for Europe use the Harmonised Index of Consumer Prices (HICP).
2. Autumn economic forecasts, 2003.
3. *Washington Post*, January 2001.

Chapter 10: Wrong Time, Wrong Rate

1. Nigel Lawson, *The View from No. 11* (Bantam Press, 1992).
2. Ibid.

Chapter 11: To Be or Not to Be

1. Article XIII, NATO Treaty, 1949.
2. HM Treasury, *The Exchange Rate and Macroeconomic Adjustment* (Stationery Office Books, 2003).
3. This point was made by Roger Bootle in *Britain's Trade with the EU and the Rest of the World: What Does Our Current Account Look Like?* (New Europe, 2001), and this section of the chapter has drawn on his work.
4. Patrick Minford, *Should Britain Join the Euro?* (Institute of Economic Affairs, 2002).
5. *Prices and Earnings Around the Globe: An International Comparison of Purchasing Power* (Union Bank of Switzerland, 2000).
6. HM Treasury, *EMU and Trade* (Stationery Office Books, 2003).
7. HM Treasury, *EMU and Business Sectors* (Stationery Office Books, 2003).
8. A.K. Rose, *One Money, One Market: Estimating the Effects of Common Currencies on Trade* (Centre for Economic Policy Research, 2000).
9. J. McCallum, *National Borders Matter: Canada-US Regional Trade Patterns* (Economic Review, 1995).
10. HM Treasury, *EMU and the Cost of Capital* (Stationery Office Books, 2003).
11. HM Treasury, *EMU and Business Sectors* (Stationery Office Books, 2003).
12. For example, Ernst & Young, 'European Investment Monitor: 2003 Report' and the 2003 Annual Report of UK Invest.
13. This section of the chapter draws on David Lascelles, *Confidence in the City Outside the Euro* (New Europe, 1999).
14. *Wall Street Journal*, 18 June 2003.
15. HM Treasury, *Fiscal Stabilisation and EMU* (Stationery Office Books, 2003).

Chapter 12: It's the Politics, Stupid

1. Professor Willem Buiter: Chief Economist at the European Bank for Reconstruction and Development (ERBD) since 2000; member of the Bank of England's Monetary Policy Committee (MPC), 1997–2000.
2. *Financial Times*, 14 June 1999.
3. This section of the chapter draws on Michael Bordo and Lars Jonung, *Lessons for EMU from the History of Monetary Unions* (Coronet Books, 2000).
4. *Wall Street Journal*, 25 March 1998.
5. H. Rockoff, 'How long did it take the United States to become an Optimal Currency Area?' (National Bureau of Economic Research [NBER], 2000) has been an invaluable source for this section of the chapter.

Chapter 13: Democracy or Directorate

1. Tommaso Padoa-Schioppa, *The Road to Monetary Union in Europe: The Emperor, the Kings and the Genies* (Oxford University Press, 2000).
2. Treaty of the European Union, Article 105.
3. B. Connolly and J. Whittaker, *What will happen to the Euro?* (IEA, 2003).
4. Speech, 1 August 1999.

Chapter 14: Deceivers and Dreamers

1. *Sunday Telegraph*, 14 June 2003.

2. Lionel Bell, *The Throw That Failed: Britain's 1961 Application to Join the Common Market* (New European Publications, 1995) has been an invaluable source for the key official papers on Macmillan's attempt to enter the EEC.
3. FCO 30/1048–1971.
4. *Sunday Telegraph*, 7 January 2001.
5. Young, *This Blessed Plot*.
6. Ibid.
7. BBC Radio 4, 3 February 2000.
8. Speech in Cardiff, 28 November 2002.
9. Speech in Birmingham, 23 November 2001.
10. Speech at Humboldt University, May 2000.
11. *Daily Mail*, 14 June 2003.
12. *Daily Telegraph*, 21 June 2003.
13. Speech in Athens, 16 April 2003.
14. Speech in Aachen, 13 May 1999.
15. Speech in Warsaw, 6 October 2000.

Chapter 15: The Art of Persuasion

1. Statement, 27 October 1997.
2. *Financial Times*, 11 January 2000.
3. *Financial Times*, 26 September 1997.
4. *Daily Mail*, 13 October 1997.
5. *The Independent*, 14 October 1997.
6. *The Times*, 18 October 1997.
7. Andrew Rawnsley, *Servants of the People* (Hamish Hamilton, 2000).
8. Speech, 30 April 1998.
9. William Keegan, *The Prudence of Mr Gordon Brown*.
10. *Question Time*, BBC1, 6 July 2000.
11. See *New Statesman*, 16 June 2003.
12. *Mail on Sunday*, 18 May 2003.
13. *The Sun*, 14 May 2003.
14. *The Independent*, 22 May 2003.
15. 'Why the five tests?', 4 December 2002.
16. *Wall Street Journal*, 16 October 2003.

Chapter 16: An Untied Nation

1. Tony Blair, speech to Labour Party Conference, 2001.
2. President Jacques Chirac, 17 February 2003.
3. The notion of subsidiarity does not apply to those areas where the Union, effectively the EU Commission, has 'exclusive competence' but only to areas of 'shared competence'. However, the latter is only 'shared' to the extent to which the Commission has not taken action: an extension of Commission's activities has to be agreed by member states, but the direction is only one way.
4. The only phrase in the 2003 draft constitution that could be interpreted as providing the basis for the theoretical return of competences was Article 11(2), which stated: 'The member states shall exercise their competence to the extent that the Union has

not exercised, *or has decided to cease exercising*, its competence.'

5. Speech in Cardiff, November 2002.
6. Larry Siedentop, *Democracy in Europe* (Penguin Books, 2001).
7. Speech, 21 January 2003.
8. *The Times*, 27 March 2004.
9. Christopher Haskins: created a Life Peer in 1998; Chairman, Northern Foods, 1986–2002; Chairman of the Better Regulation Task Force, 1997–2002; and member of the New Deal Task Force, 1997–2001.
10. Jackie Ashley, *The Guardian*, 8 April 2004.
11. Vincent Cable, Liberal Democrat treasury spokesman, *The Times*, 8 April 2004.

Index